McDougal, Littell

Wordskills

Gold Level

James E. Coomber
Concordia College
Moorhead, Minnesota

Howard D. Peet
North Dakota State University
Fargo, North Dakota

McDougal, Littell & Company
Evanston, Illinois
New York Dallas Sacramento Columbia, SC

ISBN: 0-395-97977-3

4 5 6 7 8 9 10–HWI–03 02 01

CONTENTS

To the Student xiv

Special Unit

Strategies for Unlocking Word Meaning

Part A Determining a Word's Meaning from Context 1

Definition and Restatement
Example
Comparison
Contrast
Cause and Effect
Inference from General Context

Part B Determining Meaning Through Word Analysis 7

Prefixes
Suffixes
Roots and Word Families

Unit 1

Part A Target Words and Their Meanings 14

Inferring Meaning from Context

Part B Target Words in Reading and Literature 16

"A Vanishing Breed"
by Howard Peet

Refining Your Understanding

Part C Ways to Make New Words Your Own 18

Using Language and Thinking Skills
- *True-False* • *Understanding Multiple Meanings*
- *Matching Ideas*

Practicing for Standardized Tests
- *Antonyms*

Spelling and Wordplay
- *Word Maze*

Word's Worth: *assault*

Part D Related Words 22
Understanding Related Words
• *Finding Examples*
Analyzing Word Parts
• *The Prefix* dis-
The Last Word 24

Unit 2

Part A Target Words and Their Meanings 25
Inferring Meaning from Context
Part B Target Words in Reading and Literature 27
"The Wolf in Sheep's Clothing"
by Aesop
Refining Your Understanding
Part C Ways to Make New Words Your Own 28
Using Language and Thinking Skills
• *Recognizing Shades of Meaning* • *Understanding Multiple Meanings*
Practicing for Standardized Tests
• *Synonyms* • *Antonyms*
Word's Worth: courteous
Spelling and Wordplay
• *Word Maze*
Part D Related Words 32
Understanding Related Words
• *Matching Examples*
Analyzing Word Parts
• *The Prefixes* un- *and* in-
The Last Word 34

Unit 3

Part A Target Words and Their Meanings 35
Inferring Meaning from Context
Part B Target Words in Reading and Literature 37
"The Missing Rinja"
by Howard Peet
Refining Your Understanding
Part C Ways to Make New Words Your Own 40
Using Language and Thinking Skills
• *Finding Examples* • *Understanding Multiple Meanings*

Word's Worth: fortune
Practicing for Standardized Tests
• *Antonyms* • *Synonyms*
Spelling and Wordplay
• *Crossword Puzzle*

Part D Related Words 44
Understanding Related Words
• *Synonym or Antonym?* • *True-False*
Analyzing Word Parts
• *The Suffixes* -er *and* -or

The Last Word 46

Unit 4 **Review of Units 1–3**
Part A Review Word List 47
Inferring Meaning from Context
Using Review Words in Context

Part B Review Word Reinforcement 50
Using Language and Thinking Skills
• *Sentence Writing* • *Matching Ideas*
Practicing for Standardized Tests
• *Antonyms* • *Synonyms*
Spelling and Wordplay
• *Fill-ins*

Part C Related Word Reinforcement 54
Using Related Words
• *True-False*
Reviewing Word Structures
• *Adding Word Parts*

Vocab Lab 1
Focus on: Maps and Travel 56
• *Sentence Completion*
Focus on: Analogies 58
• *Analogies*

Unit 5
Part A Target Words and Their Meanings 60
Inferring Meaning from Context

Part B Target Words in Reading and Literature 62
"Annie Dodge Wauneka"
by James Coomber
Refining Your Understanding

Part C Ways to Make New Words Your Own 64
Using Language and Thinking Skills
• *Understanding Multiple Meanings* • *True-False*
Practicing for Standardized Tests
• *Synonyms*
Spelling and Wordplay
• *Word Maze*
Word's Worth: claim

Part D Related Words 67
Understanding Related Words
• *Matching Examples*
Analyzing Word Parts
• *The Latin Root* socius • *The Latin Root* bene

The Last Word 69

Unit 6

Part A Target Words and Their Meanings 70
Inferring Meaning from Context

Part B Target Words in Reading and Literature 72
"Only You Can Prevent Forest Fires"
by James Coomber
Refining Your Understanding

Part C Ways to Make New Words Your Own 73
Using Language and Thinking Skills
• *Finding the Unrelated Word* • *Word Map*
Practicing for Standardized Tests
• *Analogies*
Word's Worth: slogan
Spelling and Wordplay
• *Word Maze*

Part D Related Words 76
Understanding Related Words
• *Finding Examples*
Analyzing Word Parts
• *The Latin Root* neg • *The Prefix* re-

The Last Word 79

Unit 7

Part A Target Words and Their Meanings 80
Inferring Meaning from Context

Part B Target Words in Reading and Literature 82
"How the Sun Came"
by James Coomber
Refining Your Understanding

Part C Ways to Make New Words Your Own 84
Using Language and Thinking Skills
• *Understanding Multiple Meanings* • *Finding Examples*
Practicing for Standardized Tests
• *Antonyms*
Spelling and Wordplay
• *Crossword Puzzle*
Word's Worth: plunge

Part D Related Words 87
Understanding Related Words
• *Synonyms-Antonyms*
Analyzing Word Parts
• *Word Endings* • *The Prefix* trans-

The Last Word 89

Unit 8

Review of Units 5–7

Part A Review Word List 90
Inferring Meaning from Context
Using Review Words in Context

Part B Review Word Reinforcement 93
Using Language and Thinking Skills
• *Writing Sentences* • *Sentence Completion*
Practicing for Standardized Tests
• *Analogies* • *Synonyms* • *Antonyms*
Spelling and Wordplay
• *Word Maze*

Part C Related Word Reinforcement 98
Using Related Words
• *True–False*
Reviewing Word Structures
• *Matching Definitions*

Vocab Lab 2

Focus on: Sports 100
- *Sentence Completion*

Focus on: The Language of Advertising 102
- *Identifying Advertising Techniques*
- *Writing Advertisements*

Special Unit

Taking Standardized Vocabulary Tests

Part A Synonyms 104

Part B Antonyms 105

Part C Sentence Completion 107

Part D General Strategies 109

Unit 9

Part A Target Words and Their Meanings 110

Inferring Meaning from Context

Part B Target Words in Reading and Literature 112

"The Black Hole"
by Howard Peet

Refining Your Understanding

Part C Ways to Make New Words Your Own 114

Using Language and Thinking Skills
- *Understanding Multiple Meanings*

Word's Worth: calculate

Practicing for Standardized Tests
- *Synonyms* • *Analogies*

Spelling and Wordplay
- *Word Maze*

Part D Related Words 117

Understanding Related Words
- *Sentence Completion*

Analyzing Word Parts
- *The Prefix* ex- • *The Latin Prefix* pro-

The Last Word 120

Unit 10

Part A Target Words and Their Meanings 121

Inferring Meaning from Context

Part B Target Words in Reading and Literature 123

"Hugh Glass and the Grizzly"
by James Coomber

Refining Your Understanding

Part C Ways to Make New Words Your Own 125
Using Language and Thinking Skills
• *True-False* • *Understanding Multiple Meanings*
Practicing for Standardized Tests
• *Synonyms*
Spelling and Wordplay
• *Crossword Puzzle*
Word's Worth: vicious

Part D Related Words 128
Understanding Related Words
• *Sentence Completion*
Analyzing Word Parts
• *The Prefix* pro-

The Last Word 130

Unit 11

Part A Target Words and Their Meanings 131
Inferring Meaning from Context

Part B Target Words in Reading and Literature 133
"Putting Geysers to Work for Us"
by James Coomber
Refining Your Understanding

Part C Ways to Make New Words Your Own 135
Using Language and Thinking Skills
• *True-False*
Practicing for Standardized Tests
• *Analogies*
Word's Worth: residence
Spelling and Wordplay
• *Word Maze*

Part D Related Words 137
Understanding Related Words
• *Finding Examples*
Analyzing Word Parts
• *The Suffix* -ful • *The Latin Root* duct

The Last Word 140

Unit 12

Review of Units 9–11
Part A Review Word List 141
Inferring Meaning from Context
Using Review Words in Context

Part B Review Word Reinforcement 144
Using Language and Thinking Skills
• *Sentence Completion* • *Finding the Unrelated Word*
Practicing for Standardized Tests
• *Analogies* • *Antonyms* • *Synonyms*
Spelling and Wordplay
• *Fill-ins*
Part C Related Word Reinforcement 148
Using Related Words
• *Matching Definitions*
Reviewing Word Structures
• *The Prefix* pro-

Vocab Lab 3
Focus on: Foreign Words and Phrases 150
• *Sentence Completion*
Focus on: How Words Enter Our Language 152
• *Word Origins* • *Word Sources*

Unit 13
Part A Target Words and Their Meanings 154
Inferring Meaning from Context
Part B Target Words in Reading and Literature 156
"The Dogholes"
by Howard Peet
Refining Your Understanding
Part C Ways to Make New Words Your Own 158
Using Language and Thinking Skills
• *Understanding Multiple Meanings* • *Finding Examples*
Practicing for Standardized Tests
• *Synonyms*
Spelling and Wordplay
• *Crossword Puzzle*
Part D Related Words 161
Understanding Related Words
• *Sentence Completion*
Analyzing Word Parts
• *The Greek Word* technē
Word's Worth: yarn
The Last Word 163

Unit 14

Part A Target Words and Their Meanings 164
Inferring Meaning from Context

Part B Target Words in Reading and Literature 166

"The Superstition Mountains"
by Howard Peet

Refining Your Understanding

Part C Ways to Make New Words Your Own 168
Using Language and Thinking Skills
- *True-False*

Practicing for Standardized Tests
- *Analogies*

Spelling and Wordplay
- *Word Maze*

Word's Worth: *mystery*

Part D Related Words 170
Understanding Related Words
- *Finding Examples*

Analyzing Word Parts
- *The Latin Root* migr • *The Prefix* fore-

The Last Word 173

Unit 15

Part A Target Words and Their Meanings 174
Inferring Meaning from Context

Part B Target Words in Reading and Literature 176

"The Nobel Prizes"
by Howard Peet

Refining Your Understanding

Part C Ways to Make New Words Your Own 178
Using Language and Thinking Skills
- *Finding Examples*

Practicing for Standardized Tests
- *Synonyms*

Spelling and Wordplay
- *Word Maze*

Word's Worth: *candidate*

Part D Related Words 181
Understanding Related Words
• *True-False* • *Matching Ideas*
Analyzing Word Parts
• *The Latin Root* plic
The Last Word 183

Unit 16 ***Review of Units 13–15***
Part A Review Word List 184
Inferring Meaning from Context
Using Review Words in Context
Part B Review Word Reinforcement 187
Using Language and Thinking Skills
• *Sentence Completion* • *Matching Ideas*
Practicing for Standardized Tests
• *Analogies* • *Antonyms* • *Synonyms*
Spelling and Wordplay
• *Fill-ins*
Part C Related Word Reinforcement 191
Using Related Words
• *Sentence Completion*
Reviewing Word Structures
• *The Word Parts* tech, migr, fore- *and* plic

Vocab Lab 4 **Focus on: Behavior** 194
• *Sentence Completion*
Focus on: Word Games 196
• *Words Within Words* • *Letter Additions*
• *Anagrams* • *Pyramids*

Standardized Vocabulary Test: Units 1–8 198
Synonyms
Sentence Completion
Antonyms
Analogies

Standardized Vocabulary Test: Units 9–16 203
Synonyms
Sentence Completion
Antonyms
Analogies

Spelling Handbook 208

Words with Prefixes 209
The Addition of Prefixes
The Prefix *ad-*
The Prefix *com-*
The Prefix *in-*
The Prefix *ex-*

Words with Suffixes 217
Words Ending in *y*
The Final Silent *e*
Doubling the Final Consonant
Words Ending in *-ize* or *-ise*
The Suffix *-ion*

Other Spelling Problems 225
Words with *ie* and *ei*
Words with the "Seed" sound
The Letter *c*
The Letter *g*

Spelling Review 230

Commonly Misspelled Words 233

Commonly Confused Words 234

Glossary 236
Pronunciation Key 243
Inventory Test 244
Pretest Strategies 246
Test Yourself 247
Acknowledgments 260
Personal Vocabulary Log 261

To the Student

Why study vocabulary? Increasing the number of words that you know helps you read, write, and speak better. You'll understand more of what you read with less reliance on the dictionary, and you'll be able to express yourself more accurately. This doesn't mean using twenty-dollar words to amaze others. It just means using the right words to say exactly what you mean.

How to Use This Book

You may notice something unusual about this vocabulary book. Definitions are not given with the word lists. Instead, you are given something more powerful—strategies for determining the meanings of words yourself. You'll find this information in a Special Unit starting on page 1. Then, in the following units, you will master new words using a five step process:

1. First you will infer the word's meaning through context clues.
2. Second you will refine your understanding by studying the word's use in a reading selection.
3. Then your understanding of the words will be reinforced through a variety of exercises.
4. Next you will relate the word to other words in the same family.
5. Finally you will use the word in writing and speaking.

The words in this book are ones you are likely to encounter in your reading. Some you may already know; others may be completely unfamiliar. As you study these words, try to move them into your "active vocabulary," the words you understand well enough to use in your speaking and writing.

A Personal Vocabulary-Building Program

You can apply the vocabulary skills in this book to learning any new words that you encounter. Here are several tips that will help you:

1. Keep a vocabulary notebook. Jot down the new words you encounter. Record the essential information for each word: correct spelling, part of speech, pronunciation, definition.
2. Review the words in your notebook. Take a few minutes each day to study them. Set a realistic goal of learning a certain number of new words per week.
3. Study the words actively. Active study means that you use as many senses as possible in studying the word. Listen to yourself say the word. See it in your mind's eye. Then use the word as soon as possible in speech or in writing. In general, if you use a word twice, it is yours.
4. Invent your own memory devices. Try to associate the word with other similar words you know. Create a mental image that relates to the word and helps you remember its meaning. One student remembered the meaning of the word *pretentious,* "showy, flaunting," by picturing a small boy playing make-believe, *pretending* to be a king.

There is one final reason for studying vocabulary, one that we hope you discover for yourself as you use this book: Words are fascinating! They are as surprising and alive and insightful as the people who use them.

Special Unit **Strategies for Unlocking Word Meaning**

What happens when you come across an unfamiliar word in your reading? If you have a dictionary at hand, you can look up the word. If you don't have a dictionary, you still have two excellent strategies that can help you make sense of the word: **context clues** and **word parts analysis.** You will be using these strategies in every unit of this book. With practice you can master these strategies and improve your reading skills.

Part A **Determining a Word's Meaning from Context**

Skilled readers often use context clues to figure out a word's meaning. **Context** refers to the words or sentences before or after a certain word that help explain what the word means. There are several types of context clues you can look for, including **definition and restatement, example, comparison, contrast,** and **cause and effect.**

Definition and Restatement

Sometimes a writer will directly define a word, especially if the word is a technical term that may be unfamiliar to readers. Here is an example:

> The settlers reached the *piedmont,* a gently rolling foothill area between a plain and mountains.

More often, a writer will restate the meaning of a word in a less precise form than a dictionary definition.

> The king's laws were often *arbitrary;* in other words, he made rules based on how he felt at the moment.

The meaning of *arbitrary*—"based on one's sudden desires or notions"—becomes clear from the restatement in the second part of the sentence. Definition and restatement are often signaled by punctuation (note the comma in the first example) and by certain key words and phrases.

Words Signaling Definition and Restatement

which is	or	also known as
that is	in other words	also called

Example

The context in which a word appears may include one or more **examples** that are clues to its meaning. Look at the following sentence.

Our science class is studying *crustaceans,* such as shrimps, crabs, and lobsters.

The phrase *such as* followed by a list of examples helps explain the meaning of *crustaceans*—"a group of water animals having a hard shell and jointed legs." The following words and phrases often signal an example.

Words Signaling an Example		
like	for example	other
including	for instance	this
such as	especially	these
		these include

Comparison

Another type of context clue is **comparison.** With this clue the writer compares the word in question with other, more familiar words. By noting the similarities between the things described, you can get an idea of the meaning of the unfamiliar word.

The *amethyst,* like other precious stones known for hardness, cannot be cut with a knife or scratched by glass.

The comparison context clue "like other precious stones known for hardness" clearly indicates that an *amethyst* is a type of precious stone. A comparison is often signaled by one of these key words or phrases.

Words Signaling a Comparison		
like	similar to	similarly
as	resembling	also
in the same way	likewise	identical
		related

Contrast

Context may also help reveal the meaning of a word through **contrast,** as in this example:

Lincoln's Gettysburg Address was *concise,* in sharp contrast to the long-winded, two-hour speech that preceded it.

In this sentence the phrase *in sharp contrast to* signals a contrast. Therefore, you can assume that a *concise* speech is the opposite of a *long-winded, two-hour speech.* A *concise* speech is a brief one. The following key words and phrases signal a contrast.

Words Signaling a Contrast		
but	on the other hand	instead
although	unlike	different
on the contrary	in contrast to	however

Cause and Effect

Another type of context clue is **cause and effect.** The cause of an action or event may be stated using an unfamiliar word. If, however, the effect is stated in familiar terms, it can help you understand the unfamiliar word. Consider the following example:

> Because the weeds in my garden are so *profuse,* I can no longer see the flowers.

In this sentence the cause—the profuse weeds—leads to the effect—not being able to see the flowers. Therefore, *profuse* must mean "a great quantity." Certain key words and phrases may signal cause and effect.

Words Signaling Cause and Effect		
because	consequently	so
since	therefore	as a result

Inference from General Context

Often the clues to the meaning of an unfamiliar word are not in the same sentence. In such cases you will need to look at the sentences that surround the word and **infer,** or draw a conclusion about, the word's meaning. A single piece of information several sentences away from the unfamiliar word may unlock the meaning. Study the following example:

> By the middle of the school year, Bob started to see the *fallacy* in his thinking. He had thought that because he was bright, he could get good grades in his classes without much work. Now he realized he had been mistaken. If he was going to get A's at this school, he would have to work very hard.

The clue to the meaning of *fallacy* is found later in the paragraph. The description *he had been mistaken* suggests that fallacy means "error."

Sometimes the supporting details in a paragraph must be examined together to help you infer the meaning of an unfamiliar word.

> The government was in a state of *chaos.* Nobody knew who was in charge. The president had not been seen for three days, and other officials were giving orders. Many citizens disobeyed the curfews. Army tanks moved into the capital city to control the crowds, but the soldiers disobeyed their commanders and refused to attack the people.

A series of descriptive details follows the unfamiliar word *chaos.* The details help you draw a conclusion about what *chaos* means—"disorder and extreme confusion."

Determining Meaning from Context Each of the following sentences and paragraphs contains an italicized word you may not know. Look for context clues to help you determine the meaning of the word. Write the definition in the blank.

1. A large portion of Brazil is a *savanna,* an area of grassland and scattered trees with year-round warm temperatures.

   Savanna- a area of grassland and trees with warm temperatures.

2. The twin toddlers, Timmy and Tammy, were as *frolicsome* as two kittens with a ball of yarn.

   Frolicsome - two kittens with a ball of yorn.

3. Although Erica had been speedy and energetic all week long in track practice, on the day of her race she felt *sluggish.*

   sluggish- tired stow.

4. Hercules faced a horrible *ordeal.* He had twelve tasks, or labors, that he had to perform. The first labor was to kill a lion that no weapons could harm. The second was to kill a creature with nine heads, called the Hydra. Perhaps the most dangerous task was to travel down to the underworld and bring back a terrible three-headed dog alive.

   X ordeal- prodlem bifficult

5. An examination showed that Phil was *myopic.* The doctor gave him eye glasses to help him see things at a distance better.

   X myopic- near sighted howing

6. My next door neighbor is an *eccentric.* He collects plastic pink flamingoes and has put dozens of them in his front yard. He has sprayed them with something that makes them glow at night and has given each of them a name.

   X eccentric - a peopls who collects strang something.

7. If they had a choice, most people would probably prefer a *democratic* society, one in which all citizens can vote and have a say in their government.

X equal what
democratic - people can do to do.
thay wont

8. Jerry is a peanut-butter-and-jelly-sandwich *gourmet.* He makes his own peanut butter, jams, and jellies. He also uses only the best kinds of bread. Every year at our town's summer fair, Jerry judges the peanut-butter-and-jelly-sandwich-making contest. a person like find goma.

X gourmet- uses the best stuff to make something.

9. The warm milk Helen drank in the evening acted as a *soporific.* Shortly after finishing the milk, Helen was asleep.

soporific - Something that puts you to sleep.

10. Manuella was very good at saving money, but her husband Diego was a *spendthrift.*

spendthrift - a person who likes to spend money

11. Dr. Krenshaw was an expert on *amphibians,* such as frogs, toads, and salamanders.

amphibians- like frogs and toads.

12. The planets in our solar system have an orbit that is an *ellipse,* a shape that looks like a flattened circle or an egg on its side.

ellipse- when the planets orbit each other

13. The tree nursery sold some evergreens, but it specialized in young *deciduous* trees, such as oaks, maples, and birches.

decidusus-sertain kinds of trees

14. The book I checked out was about Western gunslingers. Some were *notorious* outlaws, but others were people I had never heard of.

notorious- famouse

15. Karen was an *introvert,* unlike her outgoing, talkative sister Beth.

introvert- quiet.

Number correct _____ (total 15)

Understanding Context Clues Write a sentence for each of the words below. Each of your sentences should contain a different type of context clue—**definition and restatement, example, comparison, contrast,** or **cause and effect**. Then label each sentence according to the type of context clue used.

amiable　　depression　　optimist
carnivorous　　edelweiss

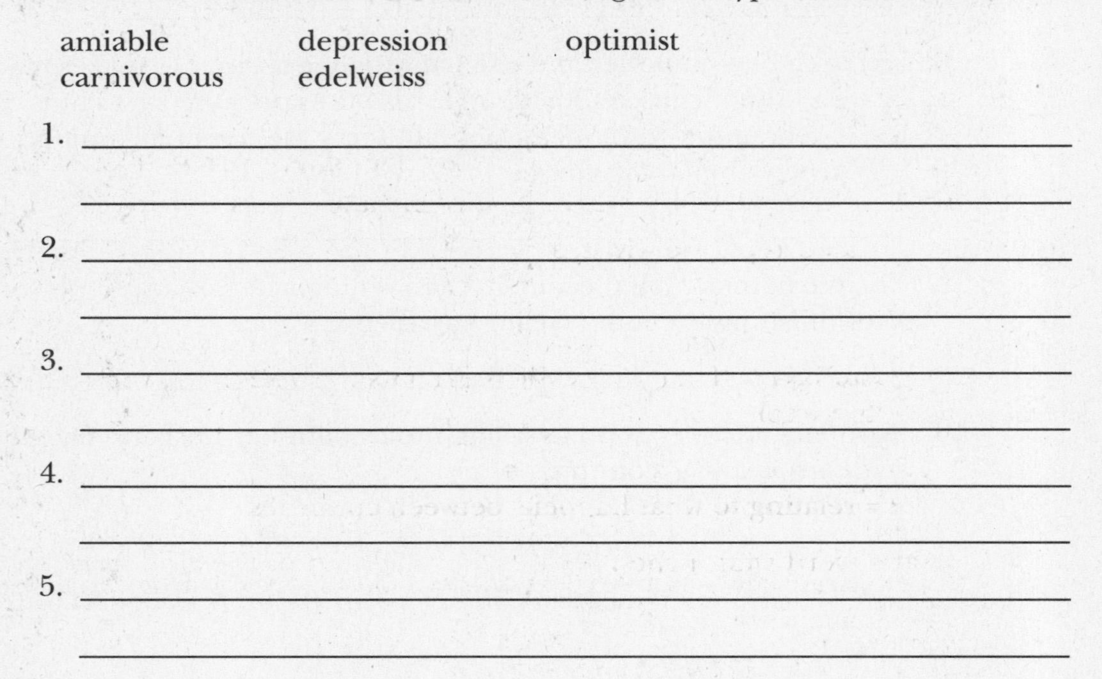

1. ______________________________

2. ______________________________

3. ______________________________

4. ______________________________

5. ______________________________

Number correct _____ (total 5)

Part B Determining Meaning Through Word Analysis

Words are made up of various combinations of the following parts: *prefix, suffix, base word,* and *root.* Analysis of these parts is another way to determine an unfamiliar word's meaning. The following terms are used in analyzing word parts.

Prefix a word part that is added to the beginning of another word or word part

Suffix a word part that is added to the end of another word or word part

Base word a complete word to which a prefix and/or a suffix may be added

Root a word part to which a prefix and/or a suffix must be added. A root cannot stand alone.

For example, the word *international* is made up of the prefix *inter-,* the base word *nation,* and the suffix *-al.* If you know the meanings of these parts, you can determine the meaning of the whole word.

inter- ("between") + *nation* ("country") + *-al* ("relating to")
international = relating to what happens between countries

Now look at a word with a root. *Inflexible* is made up of the prefix *in-* ("not"), the Latin root *flex* ("bend"), and the suffix *-ible* ("inclined to"). *Inflexible* means "not inclined to bend."

Prefixes

The following chart contains prefixes that have only one meaning.

Prefixes That Have a Single Meaning

Prefix	Meaning	Example
bene-	good	benefit
circum-	around	circumference
col-, com-, con-, cor-	with, together	collapse, compile construct, correspond
contra-	opposed	contradict
equi-	equal	equidistant
extra-	outside	extraordinary
hemi-	half	hemisphere
inter-	between, among	international
mal-	bad	maltreat, malignant
mid-	halfway	midday
mis-	wrong	misspell
non-	not	nonworking
post-	after in time or space	postpone
pre-	before	predawn
sub-	under, below	subzero

Some prefixes have more than one meaning. Study the common prefixes listed in the following chart.

Prefixes That Have More Than One Meaning

Prefix	**Meaning**	**Example**
a-, ab-	up, out	arise
	not	abnormal
	away	absent
anti-	against	antiaircraft
	prevents, cures	antidote
de-	away from, off	derail
	down	decline
	reverse action of	defrost
dis-	lack of	distrust
	not	dishonest
	away	disarm
em-, en-	to get into, on	embark
	to make, cause	enable
	in, into	enclose
il-, im-, in-, ir-	not	illegal
	in, into	investigate
pro-	in favor of	profamily
	forward, ahead	propel
re-	again	rethink
	back	repay
semi-	half	semicircle
	twice in a period	semiannual
	partly	semiconscious
super-	over and above	superhuman
	very large	supertanker
trans-	across	transcontinental
	beyond	transcend
un-	not	unhappy
	reverse of	unfasten

Suffixes

Like a prefix, a suffix has a meaning that can provide a strong clue to the definition of a whole word. Suffixes can also determine the part of speech. Certain suffixes make words nouns; others create adjectives, verbs, or adverbs.

Once you know suffixes and their meanings, you can form new words by attaching suffixes to base words or to roots. For instance, the suffix *-ity* can be added to the base word *sincere* to create the word *sincerity.* Notice that the spelling of a base word may change when a suffix is added. In the preceding example, the *e* from *sincere* was dropped when *-ity* was added. For information about spelling rules for adding suffixes, see the **Spelling Handbook,** pages 208–235.

Noun suffixes, when added to a base word or root, form nouns. Become familiar with the following common noun suffixes.

Noun Suffixes That Refer to Someone Who Does Something

Suffix	Examples
-ant	commandant, occupant
-eer	auctioneer
-er	manager
-ician	beautician, statistician
-ist	geologist
-or	counselor

Noun Suffixes That Make Abstract Words

Suffix	Examples
-ance, -ancy, -ence	vigilance, vacancy, independence
-ation, -ion, -ition	imagination, inspection, recognition
-cy	accuracy
-dom	freedom, kingdom
-hood	womanhood, brotherhood
-ice	cowardice, prejudice
-ism	realism, federalism
-ity, -ty	sincerity, frailty
-ment	encouragement, commitment
-ness	kindness, fondness
-ship	ownership, worship
-tude	gratitude, solitude

Adjective suffixes, when added to a base word or root, create adjectives—words that are used to modify nouns and pronouns.

Adjective Suffixes

Suffix	Meaning	Example
-able, -ible	able to be	readable, convertible
-al	relating to	musical
-ant	relating to	triumphant
-ar	relating to	polar
-ate	having, full of	passionate
-ful	full of	harmful
-ic	pertaining to, like	heroic
-ish	pertaining to, like	foolish
-ive	pertaining to	descriptive
-less	without	senseless
-like	like	lifelike
-ly	like	scholarly
-most	at the extreme	topmost
-ous	full of	furious

Verb suffixes change base words to verbs. The following chart lists four common verb suffixes.

Verb Suffixes

Suffix	Meaning	Example
-ate	to make	activate
-en	to become	strengthen
-fy	to make	simplify
-ise, -ize	to become	merchandise, computerize

Adverb suffixes change base words to adverbs—words that modify verbs, adjectives, and other adverbs. The following chart lists the most common adverb suffixes.

Adverb Suffixes

Suffix	Meaning	Example
-ily, -ly,	manner	happily, quickly
-ward	toward	skyward
-wise	like	clockwise

Roots and Word Families

A word root cannot stand alone but must be combined with other word parts. A great many roots used in our language come from Greek or Latin. A single root can generate many English words. A **word family** is a group of words with a common root. For example, all of the words in the following word family are derived from the Latin root *aud,* which means "hear."

audible	audiovisual	auditorium
audience	audition	auditory
audio	auditor	inaudible

Learning word roots will help you develop your vocabulary by enabling you to recognize roots in many related words. The following two charts show some common Greek and Latin roots.

Useful Greek Roots

Root	Meaning	Example
anthrop	human	anthropology
aster, astr	star	asterisk
auto	self, alone	autobiography
bibl, biblio	book	bibliography
bi, bio	life	biology
chron	time	chronology
cracy, crat	rule, government	democracy
dem	people	epidemic
gen	birth, race, kind	generation
geo	earth	geography
gram, graph	write, draw, describe	grammar, paragraph
hydr	water	hydrogen
log	word, reason, study	dialogue, logic, ecology
meter, metr	measure	barometer
neo	new	neoclassical
nom, nym	name, word, law	nominate, antonym
ortho	straight, correct	orthodontist, orthodox
pan	all, entire	panorama
phil	love	philosopher
phob	fear	claustrophobia
phon	sound	phonograph
psych	mind, soul, spirit	psychology
scope	see	telescope
soph	wise	sophisticated
tele	far, distant	television
theo	god	theology
therm	heat	thermometer

Useful Latin Roots

Root	Meaning	Example
capt, cept	take, have	capture, accept
cede, ceed, cess	go, yield, give way	secede, proceed, recess
cred	believe	credit, creed
dic, dict	speak, say, tell	dictate, dictionary
duc, duct	lead	introduce, conductor
fact, fect	do, make	factory, defect
fer	carry	transfer
ject	throw, hurl	eject, inject
junct	join	junction
miss, mit	send	dismiss, admit
mob, mot, mov	move	mobility, motion, movie
par, para	get ready	prepare, parachute
pon, pos, posit	place, put	opponent, deposit
port	carry	porter, portable
puls	throb, urge	pulsate, compulsory
scrib, script	write	prescribe, scripture
spec, spect, spic	look, see	speculate, spectacle, conspicuous
stat	stand, put in a place	statue, state
tain, ten, tent	hold	contain, tenant, attention
tract	pull, move	tractor, retract
ven, vent	come	convention, event
vers, vert	turn	versatile, invert
vid, vis	see	video, vista
voc, vok	voice, call	vocal, invoke
vol	wish	volunteer, malevolent
volv	roll	revolve, involve

Determining Word Meaning Through Prefixes and Suffixes Draw lines to separate each of the following words into three parts—prefix, base word, and suffix. Determine the meaning of the prefix and the suffix. Then, by adding the meanings of the prefix and the suffix to the base word, determine the meaning of the complete word and write the definition in the blank.

1. malformation: ______________________________
2. mismanagement: ______________________________
3. nonsensical: ______________________________
4. prehistoric: ______________________________
5. anticensorship: ______________________________
6. disrespectful: ______________________________
7. disagreeable: ______________________________

8. enlargement: ______________________________

9. semiprofessional: ______________________________

10. unhealthful: ______________________________

Number correct _____ (total 10)

Determining Word Meaning Through Prefixes, Suffixes, and Roots Each of the following words consists of a Greek or Latin root and a prefix or suffix. Use your knowledge of roots, prefixes, and suffixes to put together the meanings of the word parts and write a definition for each word. You may check your definitions with a dictionary.

1. compose: ______________________________

2. detract: ______________________________

3. invert: ______________________________

4. intervene: ______________________________

5. misanthrope: ______________________________

6. precede: ______________________________

7. hydrant: ______________________________

8. phobic: ______________________________

9. thermal: ______________________________

10. diction: ______________________________

Number correct _____ (total 10)

Number correct in unit _____ (total 40)

UNIT 1

Part A Target Words and Their Meanings

The fifteen words that follow will be the focus of this first unit. You will find them in the reading selection and in the exercises in this unit. For a guide to their pronunciations, refer to the **Pronunciation Key** on page 243.

1. assault (ə sôlt′) n., v.
2. collide (kə līd′) v.
3. completion (kəm plē′ shən) n.
4. demolish (di mäl′ ish) v.
5. disadvantage (dis′ əd van′ tij) n.
6. effective (ə fek′ tiv, i-) adj.
7. estimate (es′ tə mit′) n., (es′ tə māt′) v.
8. invader (in vād′ ər) n.
9. mishap (mis′ hap′) n.
10. mission (mish′ ən) n.
11. navigator (nav′ ə gāt′ ər) n.
12. realize (rē′ ə līz′) v.
13. severe (sə vir′) adj.
14. twilight (twī′ līt′) n., adj.
15. vicinity (və sin′ ə tē) n.

Inferring Meaning from Context

For each sentence write the letter of the word or phrase that is closest in meaning to the word or words in italics. Use context clues to help you choose the correct answer. (For information about how context helps you understand vocabulary, see pages 1–6.)

D 1. After he punched Officer Santos, Dan was jailed for *assault*.
a. robbery b. rudeness c. vandalism d. violent attack

B 2. A car crossed the center line of the highway and *collided with* another car, causing great damage.
a. narrowly missed b. crashed into c. scratched d. raced

B 3. The deadline for the *completion* of the building was only one month away, but many workers believed it would take at least six more months to finish it.
a. starting b. finishing c. painting d. destruction

C 4. Hurricane Molly *demolished* the coast, leaving houses, stores, and factories in ruins.
a. rained on b. chilled c. destroyed d. missed

_____ 5. One *disadvantage* of living on an island is the difficulty of getting to the mainland and back in stormy weather.

a. pleasure b. handicap c. accident d. convenience

_____ 6. Some doctors believe aspirin may be *an effective* treatment for heart disease, because it thins the blood so that the blood can flow better.

a. a useful b. a deadly c. an enjoyable d. a false

_____ 7. When an airline gives the arrival time of a flight, it is the airline's best *estimate* of how long the trip should take.

a. hope b. calculation c. rule d. decision

_____ 8. The people on the west coast of Europe feared the Viking *invaders,* who easily overpowered the defenders of the coastal towns.

a. traders b. spies c. poets d. attackers

_____ 9. Some people think that the Great Chicago Fire started with *a mishap* in Mrs. O'Leary's barn. O'Leary's cow kicked over a lantern, setting fire to the barn. The fire spread through much of the city.

a. a benefit b. an accident c. an adventure
d. a demonstration

_____ 10. Sergeant Collins's dangerous *mission* was to rescue miners trapped a mile underground.

a. flight b. prank c. party d. task

_____ 11. To go through a narrow, rocky channel in foggy weather, a ship needs a good *navigator.*

a. cabin boy b. recreation director c. helper on the shore
d. person who plots the course

_____ 12. You will *realize* the importance of a college education when you go looking for a job.

a. argue against b. hide c. forget d. understand

_____ 13. In seventeenth-century New England, laws were very *severe.* For example, children who disobeyed their parents could be publicly whipped.

a. harsh b. wise c. foolish d. fair

_____ 14. Since the cyclists did not have lights on their bicycles, they stopped riding at *twilight.*

a. noon b. midmorning c. sunset d. midnight

_____ 15. When we drove downtown, we stayed away from the *vicinity* of the stadium to avoid the heavy pregame traffic.

a. violence b. neighborhood c. distant area d. noise

Number correct _____ (total 15)

Part B **Target Words in Reading and Literature**

You should now have a general idea of the meaning of each target word. Sharpen your understanding by studying how these words are used in the following selection.

A Vanishing Breed

Howard Peet

A team of space explorers has had an accident on the planet Jupiter. You are about to join Commander Barry and Captain Sara on a rescue trip to outer space.

Commander Barry and Captain Sara were roasting marshmallows over a fire on the beach. Suddenly Sara's wrist telephone beeped. General Johnson's voice shouted, "There has been a **mishap** on Jupiter. Your **mission** is to fly there immediately and bring back the remaining members of the team stationed there."

In the **twilight** the flames from the fire seemed to push back the darkness. "I hate to leave, but I **realize** how much those people need us," Barry said.

They put out the fire, turned on their rocket backpacks and flew to the Houston launching pad. Their spaceship, the *Pegasus,* stood ready for takeoff. Barry and Sara scrambled aboard, and the ship blasted off.

Barry checked the instrument panel. The speedometer showed a speed of 20,000 miles per hour. Barry called the command center for an **estimate** of the time needed to fly to Jupiter. A reply came back at once: "Over two years at your pace. You have almost 400 million miles to go. Set the engines at full speed."

A few days later, Sara and Barry reached the **vicinity** of Jupiter. They marveled at the twelve moons orbiting the huge planet. Slowly the *Pegasus* settled onto Jupiter's surface. Near the landing site an American flag was waving over a group of silver tents.

Randy, the leader of the Jupiter team, greeted Sara and Barry. He told them about how the party had been on Jupiter for a whole year. One day, completely by surprise, their group was attacked by space pirates. A **disadvantage** for Randy's crew was that the **invaders'** laser rays were so **effective.** The enemy's laser-ray **assault** injured Randy's son and **demolished** the party's spaceship. At the **completion** of the attack, Randy and his party were left stranded on the huge planet.

Sara and Barry took Randy and his crew aboard the *Pegasus.* The spaceship roared away from Jupiter. Randy was nervously watching the large screen in the ship's control room when he saw something. "Here comes the enemy spaceship. I know it is the same ship by its name—*Rats*—printed on the side."

Sara tried to steer away from *Rats,* but the two spaceships **collided.** During the confusion following the crash, four strange creatures from the *Rats* ship entered the *Pegasus.* Each creature had a name printed on its spacesuit. The names were Pam, Tolip, Oidar, and Lareneg.

Lareneg called out an order to his followers: "Tie these people up and lock them in a cell on *Rats.*"

Barry calmly pointed his finger at the four creatures and shouted "Star!" With that, all four creatures vanished and so did the spaceship *Rats.*

Sara checked out the damage to the ship and reported that the damage was not very **severe.** "However, it's going to be a long, slow trip home," she said.

Randy looked at Barry and asked, "How did you know what to do?"

Barry grinned. "Do you remember hearing about a tribe of creatures who broke away from the Kingdom of Neptune to become space pirates? They settled near here back in the year 2000. They named themselves after their leader, Enog. Enog was powerful, but he had one weakness—his name. If someone said it backwards, he would vanish."

"When I saw those names on the spacesuits, I realized the names could be read backwards. 'Pam' is 'map,' and she was the **navigator.** 'Oidar' is 'radio,' and he was the radio operator. The other names were spelled backwards also. It crossed my mind that if I said the name of their spaceship backwards, they might all vanish, just like Enog did."

Refining Your Understanding

For each of the following items, consider how the target word is used in the selection. Write the letter of the word or phrase that best completes the sentence.

____ 1. A synonym of *mission* (line 4) is a. wish b. safety c. job.

____ 2. An automobile that is *demolished* (line 26) is damaged a. slightly b. so that it needs major repair c. beyond repair.

____ 3. An example of a *disadvantage* (line 23–24) would be a. living within walking distance of a shopping mall b. taking several major tests on the same day c. having several friends at school.

____ 4. When the spaceships hit each other, the damage was not very *severe* (line 42). Therefore the collision was probably a a. head-on collision b. near miss c. light hit.

____ 5. You might need a *navigator* (line 51) if you were a. umpiring a baseball game b. playing a video game c. traveling down the Mississippi River.

Number correct ______ (total 5)

Part C Ways to Make New Words Your Own

By now you are familiar with the target words and their meanings. This section presents activities that will help you make the words part of your permanent vocabulary.

Using Language and Thinking Skills

True-False Decide whether each statement is true **(T)** or false **(F).**

____ 1. A *disadvantage* for a *navigator* would be a broken radar system.

____ 2. A building always is *demolished* before its *completion.*

____ 3. It is likely that two friends living in the *vicinity* of one another rarely see each other.

____ 4. Someone with a *severe* illness probably will go to the hospital.

____ 5. An *assault* upon others is a way of lending them a helping hand.

____ 6. Two airplanes *colliding* is a *severe mishap.*

____ 7. *Twilight* is the most *effective* time for sunbathing.

____ 8. If you *realized* that a tornado was coming, you would go back to sleep.

____ 9. One way to guard against an *invader* is to station lookouts.

____ 10. Helping students read and write in an *effective* manner is an English teacher's *mission.*

Number correct ______ (total 10)

Understanding Multiple Meanings Many words have more than one meaning. For example, look at the word *star* in the following sentences.

My cousin Jesse is a basketball *star.*
People gazed at the bright *star* in the clear sky.

In the first sentence, *star* refers to a person who is outstanding. In the second sentence, *star* refers to a heavenly body shining in the night sky. Each of the following pairs of sentences uses the same target word. If this italicized target word has the same meaning in both sentences, write *same.* If the word has a different meaning, write *different.*

______________ 1. a. Corporal Jones's *mission* was to rescue ten children caught in a severe storm.
b. At the *mission* in St. Augustine, the priests have a long tradition of helping people.

______________ 2. a. Fortunately, the *navigator* of the smaller ship, Captain Holmes, kept the two ships from colliding.
b. Imagine the difficulties a *navigator* faced in sailing to North America in 1492!

______________ 3. a. Every evening at *twilight,* the bells at the mission ring.
b. Our grandparents have slowed down in their *twilight* years, but they still like to travel.

______________ 4. a. My brother never fully *realized* how much talent he had as a distance runner.
b. The company *realized* a profit of 10 million dollars last year.

______________ 5. a. Father studied the carpenter's *estimate* closely to see if all the costs were included.
b. Our *estimate* of the new coach was that he was demanding, but likable.

Number correct ______ (total 5)

Matching Ideas Write the word from the list below that is most clearly related to the situation described in the sentence.

assault estimate completion navigator twilight

________________ 1. Every airplane has an officer aboard who can tell the location of the plane by studying radar screens and charts.

________________ 2. A gentle kind of light comes just after sunset.

________________ 3. In 1869, work was finished on the first transcontinental railroad in America.

________________ 4. A person may be arrested for violently attacking someone.

________________ 5. Knowing the distance you must drive and how fast you are driving helps you figure out about how long it will take to get there.

Number correct ______ (total 5)

Practicing for Standardized Tests

Antonyms Write the letter of the word that is most nearly *opposite* in meaning to the capitalized word.

____ 1. EFFECTIVE: (A) evil (B) costly (C) powerless (D) useful (E) strong

____ 2. COLLIDE: (A) sell (B) clash (C) jolt (D) separate (E) crash

____ 3. COMPLETION: (A) ending (B) result (C) middle (D) beginning (E) accomplishment

____ 4. SEVERE: (A) harsh (B) mild (C) joined (D) difficult (E) demanding

____ 5. DEMOLISH: (A) destroy (B) solve (C) build (D) discuss (E) find

Number correct ______ (total 5)

Spelling and Wordplay

Word Maze All the words in the list below are hidden in the maze. The words are arranged forward, backward, up, down, and diagonally. Put a circle around each word as you find it, and cross the word off the list. Different words may overlap and use the same letter.

E S T I M A T E G B N D B
V F A K R J D M J S A I F
I L F X W M S I R E V S I
C S D E Q U T S E V I A N
I O E X C U A H A E G D V
N Y M F O T T A L R A V A
I A O P L W I P I E T A D
T S L Z L Y O V Z C O N E
Y S I N I E N C E H R T R
F A S V D L T P S X V A G
M U H A E O B I D Q U G K
T L U M I S S I O N P E N
E T W I L I G H T N D H C

assault
collide
completion
demolish
disadvantage
effective
estimate
invader
mishap
mission
navigator
realize
severe
twilight
vicinity

Word's Worth: assault

One fascinating aspect of word study is etymology, the history of words—where they came from and how their meanings have changed over the centuries. Tracing word meanings back to their sources helps us know those words even better.

For example, at one time the words *assault* and *insult* had similar meanings. *Assault* comes from the Latin *assilire,* meaning "to leap on." *Insult* comes from the Latin *insultare,* which also means "to leap on." People of ancient Rome probably used the words as synonyms. When these words came into the English language, before 1600, they still had similar meanings. How have they changed? What is the difference today between *assaulting* and *insulting* someone? In what ways might an *insult* be considered an *assault*—even today?

Part D **Related Words**

The words below are closely related to the target words. Use your knowledge of the target words and of word parts to determine the meaning of these words. (For information about word parts analysis, see pages 7–13.) Use your dictionary if necessary.

1. advantageous (ad′ vən tā′ jəs) adj.
2. collision (kə lizh′ ən) n.
3. demolition (dem′ ə lish′ ən) n.
4. disband (dis band′) v.
5. disorderly (dis ôr′ dər lē) adj.
6. dissolve (di zälv′, -zôlv′) v.
7. effect (ə fekt′, i-) n., v.
8. ineffective (in′ i fek′ tiv) adj.
9. invade (in vād′) v.
10. invasion (in vā′ zhən) n.
11. navigate (nav′ ə gāt′) v.
12. realization (rē′ ə lə zā′ shən) n.

Understanding Related Words

Finding Examples Write the letter of the situation that best shows the meaning of the boldfaced word.

Example

__b__ **hinder**

a. A crossing guard assists a child across a street.
b. A worker places a boulder in a roadway.
c. A fan watches a baseball game.

__A__ 1. **ineffective**

a. A player uses a hockey stick to hit a baseball.
b. A bus driver takes aspirin to cure a headache.
c. A student works hard to learn how to play a musical instrument.

__B__ 2. **navigate**

a. A bird sits on its nest.
b. An airline pilot plans the best course for a flight.
c. A ship's captain sleeps in his cabin.

__C__ 3. **invade**

a. A horse enters his stall.
b. Your best friend pays you a visit.
c. An army marches into an enemy country.

____ 4. **advantageous**

a. You set aside enough time to study for tests.
b. You tease a snarling dog.
c. You receive penalties in a hockey game.

____ 5. **demolition**

a. Workers tear down a building.
b. Architects draw plans for a house.
c. A train screeches to a halt.

Number correct ______ (total 5)

Turn to **The Addition of Prefixes** on pages 209-216 of the **Spelling Handbook.** Read the rules and complete the exercises provided.

Analyzing Word Parts

The Prefix *dis-* The common prefix *dis-* can mean "apart" *(dismiss),* "opposite of" *(disbelief),* or "refuse to" *(disassociate).* Refer to these three meanings as you answer the items below.

1. The teacher scolded the class for being *disorderly.*

   Disorderly means ______________________________

2. Temperatures over one hundred degrees cause people *discomfort.*

   Discomfort means ______________________________

3. After many arguments, the club decided to *disband,* never meet again.

   Disband means ______________________________

4. One warm, sunny winter day the snow *dissolved* into trickles of water.

   Dissolved means ______________________________

5. The two sisters wanted to get a pet boa constrictor, but the girls' parents *disapproved* of the idea.

   Disapproved means ______________________________

Number correct ______ (total 5)

Number correct in unit ______ (total 55)

The Last Word

Writing

One kind of *mission* is an important errand. Write about a mission that was important to you. Answer these questions in your paragraph:

a. Who was involved in the mission?
b. What was the goal of the mission?
c. Where did the mission send you?
d. Why was the mission important?
e. How did the mission turn out?

Speaking

What is the funniest *mishap* you have experienced or heard about? In a speech to the class, tell about this mishap. Use details to make the experience vivid for your audience.

Group Discussion

See how many famous *navigators* your class can name. Then, working with one partner, find out more about one of these navigators. Use an encyclopedia and other reference books for information. Share your findings with the class.

UNIT 2

Part A Target Words and Their Meanings

1. application (ap′ lə kā′ shən) n.
2. appreciate (ə prē′ shē āt′) v.
3. attention (ə ten′ shen) n.
4. career (kə rir′) n., adj.
5. common (käm′ ən) adj., n.
6. courteous (kur′ tē əs) adj.
7. deceive (di sēv′) v.
8. devour (di vour′) v.
9. direct (di rekt′, dī-) adj., v.
10. disguise (dis gīz′) v., n.
11. honorable (än′ ər ə b'l) adj.
12. landscape (land′ skāp′) n., v.
13. serious (sir′ ē əs) adj.
14. troubled (trub′ 'ld) adj.
15. victim (vik′ təm) n.

Inferring Meaning from Context

For each sentence write the letter of the word or phrase that is closest in meaning to the word or words in italics. Use context clues to help you choose the correct answer. (For information about how context helps you understand vocabulary, see pages 1–6.)

____ 1. The invention of the computer chip has led to practical *applications* in many machines—everything from digital watches to rocket engines.
a. examples b. uses c. ideas d. failures

____ 2. Ice cream lovers will *appreciate* the new restaurant's dessert menu, which includes ten kinds of sundaes.
a. think well of b. avoid c. create d. believe

____ 3. The colorful hot air balloon floating over the crowded baseball stadium must have caught the *attention* of nearly all the spectators.
a. notice b. excitement c. admiration d. sounds

____ 4. During his *career* as a park ranger, Sullivan was struck by lightning seven times.
a. retirement b. youth c. training d. work

____ 5. The number of horses in the world is estimated at 75 million, making the horse a very *common* animal.
a. familiar b. enjoyable c. trustworthy d. useful

____ 6. Mrs. Rollins taught her children to be *courteous.* They always said "please" and "thank you."

a. rude b. happy c. cooperative d. polite

____ 7. The employee *deceived* his boss for many months by stealing money a little at a time.

a. praised b. tricked c. attacked d. angered

____ 8. Within ten minutes after catching the zebra, the hungry lions had *devoured* it.

a. eaten b. shared c. tortured d. choked on

____ 9. The longest scheduled nonstop airline trip is a *direct* flight from San Francisco to Sydney, Australia.

a. first class b. yearly c. straight d. high altitude

____ 10. Because the children had *disguised* themselves with masks and costumes, I didn't recognize them at first.

a. enjoyed b. lost c. concealed d. found

____ 11. During the judge's long and *honorable* career, he had never strayed from his two goals—to uphold the law and to make fair decisions.

a. intelligent b. wealthy c. noble d. second-rate

____ 12. Glittering snow as far as the eye could see, icicles on the trees—the winter *landscape* was breathtaking.

a. sky b. disaster c. scenery d. season

____ 13. If you are *serious* about wanting that bicycle, then you must work hard to earn the money to pay for it.

a. not joking b. lying c. comical d. courageous

____ 14. The store manager was *troubled.* Business had been slow for weeks, and he was having a hard time paying bills.

a. lazy b. angry c. worried d. shy

____ 15. The jungle explorers met a terrible end. They were *victims of* crocodiles.

a. the keepers of b. searching for c. the killers of d. killed by

Number correct ______ (total 15)

Part B Target Words in Reading and Literature

You should now have a general idea of the meaning of each target word. Sharpen your understanding by studying how these words are used in the following selection.

The Wolf in Sheep's Clothing

Aesop

Aesop was a famous storyteller in ancient Greece. Most of Aesop's stories were fables. A fable often includes animal characters and is meant to teach a moral or lesson.

A clever wolf **disguised** himself one day. He had found the skin of a sheep, and he put it on. Then he walked in a **direct** line right into a flock of sheep. The wolf's disguise completely **deceived** the sheep. They thought he was just another **common, honorable** sheep. In fact, he seemed **courteous.** But at night, when the shepherd was asleep, the wolf would **devour** a sheep. 5

Naturally, the shepherd was **troubled** by this **serious** problem. He had lost several sheep. Nearly every morning the bones of a poor **victim** lay on the **landscape.** The shepherd was puzzled because he had never seen any wolves in his region. 10

But one day something caught the shepherd's **attention.** Looking over his flock, he suddenly realized that one sheep had a wolf's tail. The shepherd came closer to look. He could see now that under the fleece was a wolf. That was the end of the wolf's **career.** The shepherd threw a rope around the wolf's neck and hung the wolf from a tree limb. 15

The next day some other shepherds passed by. They saw what they thought was a dead sheep hanging from a tree.

"Why do you hang a sheep?" they asked the shepherd in the pasture.

"What sheep?" replied the shepherd. "I always hang wolves that devour my sheep." 20

Then the traveling shepherds saw their mistake. They **appreciated** their fellow shepherd discovering the clever wolf. They also understood that the lesson of the wolf in the sheepskin had a broad **application.**

Do not be deceived by appearances. Pay more attention to what is beneath the surface. 25

Refining Your Understanding

For each of the following items, consider how the target word is used in the passage. Write the letter of the word or phrase that best completes the sentence.

____ 1. When the wolf "*disguised* himself" (line 1), he a. went to sleep b. was thinking to himself c. made himself look different.

____ 2. A synonym of *deceived* (line 3) is a. pleased b. chased c. fooled.

____ 3. Since the wolf looked like a *common* sheep (line 4), he would probably not be a. believed b. noticed c. happy.

____ 4. Who would be most likely to *devour* (line 6) a meal? a. a very hungry animal b. a well-known chef c. someone at a formal dinner.

____ 5. "The lesson of the wolf . . . had a broad *application*" (line 23), means that the story a. was widely popular b. had a larger meaning for people c. had made the storyteller famous.

Number correct ______ (total 5)

Part C **Ways to Make New Words Your Own**

By now you are familiar with the target words and their meanings. This section presents activities that will help you make the words part of your permanent vocabulary.

Using Language and Thinking Skills

Recognizing Shades of Meaning In each of the five sets of words below, one word is marked **1.** Find that word's antonym, or opposite, and place a **4** beside it. Then put **2** beside the word that is close in meaning to word **1.** Finally, put **3** next to the word that is close in meaning to word **4.**

Example

1	excellent	1. ____	serious	2. ____	troubled
2	good	____	amusing	____	content
3	fair	____	tragic	____	joyful
4	poor	1	hilarious	1	miserable

3. ____	unusual	4. 1	refuse	5. ____	courteous
1	common	____	nibble	____	crude
____	rare	____	eat	____	impolite
____	once in a while	____	devour	1	knightly

Number correct ______ (total 15)

Understanding Multiple Meanings Many words have more than one meaning. In this exercise each target word appears in two sentences. Decide whether the target word has the same meaning or different meanings in the two sentences. Write *same* or *different* in the blank.

Example

___different___ **bank**

a. Rick and Jay fished from the north *bank* of the Clearwater River.
b. Ellen went to the *bank* to cash her check.

__________ 1. **direct**

a. While my brother went around to the bridge to cross the creek, I chose a more *direct* course.
b. Marilyn will *direct* the city orchestra.

__________ 2. **common**

a. The lodgepole pine is a *common* sight in Montana.
b. Our Fourth of July celebration is held on our village *common*.

__________ 3. **appreciate**

a. Teachers *appreciate* students who pay attention.
b. Did your mom *appreciate* your helping with the dishes?

__________ 4. **serious**

a. Cal suffered a *serious* injury in the collision.
b. Yoshi had a *serious* illness during the winter.

__________ 5. **application**

a. Jonas Salk's *application* of medical science to the problem of polio eventually resulted in his famous vaccine.
b. Kris completed an *application* form, hoping she would get the job at the gas station.

Number correct ______ (total 5)

Practicing for Standardized Tests

Synonyms Write the letter of the word that is closest in meaning to the capitalized word.

____ 1. CAREER: (A) mission (B) hobby (C) invasion (D) occupation (E) effect

____ 2. COMMON: (A) rare (B) usual (C) accidental (D) occasional (E) pure

____ 3. COURTEOUS: (A) decisive (B) disrespectful (C) old (D) athletic (E) polite

____ 4. DECEIVE: (A) trick (B) correct (C) inform (D) advise (E) acquaint

____ 5. TROUBLED: (A) demolished (B) unhealthy (C) carefree (D) serious (E) bothered

Number correct ______ (total 5)

Antonyms Write the letter of the word that is most nearly *opposite* in meaning to the capitalized word.

____ 1. ATTENTION: (A) calmness (B) compliment (C) understanding (D) concentration (E) forgetfulness

____ 2. DIRECT: (A) straight (B) useful (C) zigzag (D) common (E) unbroken

____ 3. DISGUISE: (A) uncover (B) dissolve (C) hide (D) love (E) mask

____ 4. HONORABLE: (A) courteous (B) upright (C) true (D) dishonest (E) troubled

____ 5. SERIOUS: (A) severe (B) unimportant (C) weighty (D) advantageous (E) disorderly

Number correct ______ (total 5)

Word's Worth: courteous

The word *courteous* comes from the Old French word *court.* In the Middle Ages (A.D. 500–1400), people who went to the court of a prince were expected to have good manners and to observe certain courtesies, such as bowing to the prince and showing respect to the ladies. Knights had to be warriors outside the castle. Inside the castle, however, they were known for their *courtly* (polite) behavior. One famous writer in the Middle Ages, Geoffrey Chaucer, describes a knight as a gentle man who never speaks in a rude way. A knight visiting our world today would probably find much of our behavior strange, but he would certainly understand the courtesies shown towards a host and the polite behavior seen at formal occasions.

Spelling and Wordplay

Word Maze All the words in the list below are hidden in the maze. The words are arranged forward, backward, up, down, and diagonally. Put a circle around each word as you find it, and cross the word off the list. Different words may overlap and use the same letter.

```
A P P R E C I A T E D A
T P L A N D S C A P E H
T D P H O N O R A B L E
E I D L E K Z I T S O M
N S E R I O U S P J R E
T G V C C C D I R E C T
I U O A Y G A X Q U O U
O I U R N Q U T K W M P
N S R E V I C T I M M I
D E C E I V E D X O O F
J E T R O U B L E D N B
C A Y C O U R T E O U S
```

application
appreciate
attention
career
common
courteous
deceive
devour
direct
disguise
honorable
landscape
serious
troubled
victim

Turn to **The Prefix *ad-*** on page 211 of the **Spelling Handbook.** Read the rule and complete the exercise provided.

Part D **Related Words**

The words below are closely related to the target words. Use your knowledge of the target words and of word parts to help you determine the meaning of these words. (For information about word parts analysis, see pages 7–13.)

1. applicable (ap′ li kə b′l) adj.
2. appreciative (ə prē′ shə tiv, -shē ə-) adj.
3. attentive (ə ten′ tiv) adj.
4. discourteous (dis kur′ tē əs) adj.
5. dishonorable (dis än′ ər ə b′l) adj.
6. inattentive (in′ ə ten′ tiv) adj.
7. indirect (in′ di rekt′, -dī-) adj.
8. indirectly (in′ di rekt′ lē, -dī-) adv.
9. unappreciative (un′ ə prē′ shə tiv, -shē ə-) adj.
10. uncommon (un käm′ ən) adj.
11. untroubled (un trub′ ′ld) adj.

Understanding Related Words

Matching Examples Write the word from the list above that is most clearly related to the situation described in the sentence.

_______________ 1. The Andersons moved to the mountains, believing they could lead simpler lives and have fewer worries.

_______________ 2. The football running back was most effective when he moved laterally, that is, in a sideways direction.

_______________ 3. Giving birth to quadruplets is a rare occurrence among humans. It happens only once in every 884,736 births.

_______________ 4. We were shocked when Edgar rudely began to criticize our host's cooking.

_______________ 5. I was so tired I could barely stay awake during class.

_______________ 6. Two soldiers were arrested after running from the battlefield.

_______________ 7. At the end of the season, the players thanked the coach by giving her a dozen roses.

_______________ 8. Erica was the first to notice the clue that solved the mystery—the muddy shoes near the basement door.

_______________ 9. Teresa's mother was upset about her children's lack of appreciation for all she had done.

_______________ 10. "The early bird catches the worm" is a saying that applies to many situations in life.

Number correct _____ (total 10)

Analyzing Word Parts

The Prefixes *un-* and *in-* mean "the opposite of." When you place *un-* or *in-* at the beginning of a word, the prefix gives the word an opposite meaning.

Examples *un-* + kind = unkind *in-* + correct = incorrect

In Unit One you studied the prefix *dis-*, which also means "the opposite of." In the related words list, *discourteous* and *dishonorable* show how *dis-* creates an antonym of the base word. Add the prefix *un-*, *in-*, or *dis-* to a word from the list below to complete each sentence. One word will be used twice.

applicable	attentive	courteous	directly	troubled
appreciative	common	direct	honorable	

______________ 1. Even though the quarterback's salary had doubled, he seemed __?__ and he grumbled about his contract.

______________ 2. The monarch butterfly takes a somewhat __?__ route. It travels from Canada to South America, not always moving in a straight line.

______________ 3. Andre ran into the street to get his ball. A car swerved to avoid hitting him and collided with another car. Andre had __?__ caused the accident.

______________ 4. Seeing a whooping crane is an __?__ experience—this bird is an endangered species and is rarely seen.

______________ 5. That judge is widely known as a crook; he has a __?__ reputation.

______________ 6. The children never said "thank you" for the presents. In fact, they even complained about some of them. They were certainly __?__ of their aunt's generosity.

______________ 7. One hour of TV per week is the rule in our family. However, this rule is __?__ when we watch certain important TV specials.

______________ 8. Not saying "please" when you ask someone to do something for you is considered __?__ behavior.

______________ 9. The student who is not listening and is __?__ in class will have a difficult time learning the material.

______________ 10. Although the players worried about their eight-game losing streak, the coach seemed __?__ and optimistic.

Number correct ______ (total 10)

Number correct in unit ______ (total 70)

The Last Word

Writing

Combine each of the following groups of sentences into one sentence as shown in the example. Experiment with various ways of combining the sentences.

Example The cat stretches.
The cat is black.
The cat is quiet.
<u>The black, quiet cat stretches.</u>

1. Kris enjoys her *career.*
   Her *career* is in medicine.

2. She works in a hospital emergency room.
   Her patients include *victims* of automobile accidents.

3. Some of her patients' injuries are *serious.*
   Some of her patients need immediate *attention.*

4. Most of Kris's patients are *appreciative* of her efforts.
   However, some patients can be *discourteous.*
   These patients are *troubled.*

5. Kris feels her work is *honorable.*
   She feels this way because she is helping people *directly* every day.

Group Discussion

In a small group, discuss one of the following topics:

- Are there times when the best solution to a problem is to *deceive* someone, or tell a lie? If so, describe such a situation.
- It once was considered *courteous* for a man to hold the door open for a woman and to allow the woman to enter first. Today some people consider this behavior unnecessary, and some even resent it. How do you feel—is this a courtesy that should be practiced or forgotten?
- You are given one million dollars to turn one empty block in the city into a beautiful *landscape.* Create the plans for this block.

UNIT 3

Part A Target Words and Their Meanings

1. deserve (di zʉrv′) v.
2. display (dis plā′) n., v.
3. especially (ə spesh′ əl ē, es pesh′-) adv.
4. financial (fə nan′ shəl, fī-) adj.
5. fortune (fôr′ chən) n.
6. information (in′ fər mā′ shən) n.
7. investigate (in ves′ tə gāt′) v.
8. observation (äb′ zər vā′ shən) n.
9. opportunity (äp′ ər to͞o′ nə tē, -tyo͞o′-) n.
10. position (pə zish′ ən) n., v.
11. private (prī′ vit) adj., n.
12. profit (praf′ it) v., n.
13. solution (sə lo͞o′ shən) n.
14. struggle (strug′ ′l) v., n.
15. temptation (temp tā′ shən) n.

Inferring Meaning from Context

For each sentence write the letter of the word or phrase that is closest in meaning to the word or words in italics. Use context clues to help you choose the correct answer. (For information about how context helps you understand vocabulary, see pages 1–6).

____ 1. The coach said that her players will *deserve* the championship if they play their hardest.
a. need b. not want c. earn d. refuse

____ 2. To amaze the crowd, Henrik lifted up the back end of the automobile. It was an incredible *display* of strength.
a. estimate b. trick c. mockery d. show

____ 3. The world has many vast deserts. One *especially* large desert is Africa's Sahara, which is almost as large as the United States.
a. seriously b. somewhat c. unusually d. not so

____ 4. In *financial* matters, Wilson was very smart. He invested his earnings wisely.
a. family b. religious c. educational d. money

____ 5. Early in his career, Milton Hershey made a *fortune* in the chocolate business. He earned over a million dollars by the time he was twenty-five.
a. mistake b. large amount of money c. correct prediction d. recipe

____ 6. You can find *information on* all fifty states in the encyclopedia, including their population, size, climate, and geographical features.

a. histories of b. beliefs about c. facts about d. maps for

____ 7. Scientists who *investigate* animal speeds have found that cheetahs can run seventy miles per hour.

a. study b. remember c. pay little attention to d. doubt

____ 8. A careful *observation of* the sky on a clear night is the key to seeing meteors. Your chances are best between midnight and dawn.

a. mapping of b. watching of c. flight through d. memory of

____ 9. Living in Germany for two years gave Tom the *opportunity* to learn the German language.

a. demand b. wisdom c. power d. chance

____ 10. Nancy's *position* as store manager gave her a great deal of responsibility.

a. job b. attitude c. carelessness d. opinion

____ 11. What a doctor learns about a patient's life is supposed to be a *private* matter. A doctor should not share this knowledge with anyone else.

a. secret b. severe c. common d. public

____ 12. Although the salaries of star baseball players are very high, one must understand that the team owners *profit from* having star players.

a. benefit from b. make plans for c. complain about
d. struggle against

____ 13. A dam on a river often is *a solution to* the problem of floods and water shortages. A dam is an excellent device for controlling the flow of water.

a. a mistake about b. the start of c. a completion of
d. an answer to

____ 14. It took some time and hard work for the rabbit to *struggle* out of the hunter's bag. When it finally got out, it scampered down the nearest hole.

a. fight its way b. hop c. sneak d. ease its way

____ 15. Michele said that she could not resist the *temptation* of the chocolate ice cream. She ate the entire quart.

a. attraction b. fun c. cost d. disadvantage

Number correct ______ (total 15)

Part B **Target Words in Reading and Literature**

You should now have a general idea of the meaning of each target word. Sharpen your understanding by studying how these words are used in the following selection.

The Missing Rinja

Howard Peet

The following story tells about "Sharp-eye" Jones, private detective. Jones is hired to find the famous Rinja diamond, which has been stolen from the Arden Hills Museum.

"Henry H. Jones, **Private** Investigations" was printed in black lettering on the window of the office door. To other detectives, Jones was known as Sharp-eye because no clue could escape his sharp **observation.** He noticed everything.

Mr. Harold Worthy, curator[1] of the Arden Hills Museum, tapped courteously on the glass. It had been two weeks since the great Rinja diamond had been stolen. Though the police had promised to **investigate** fully, no progress had been made. Officials from the museum's insurance company, knowing the company would lose a **fortune** if the diamond was not recovered, asked Mr. Worthy to hire the best detective in the city. That was why he came looking for Sharp-eye Jones.

To Mr. Worthy's amazement, a man wearing a gorilla mask opened the door. The mask was **especially** lifelike, with its large eyes, square jaw, and rough hair. "Come in, Mr. Worthy," boomed a deep voice from behind the mask.

Worthy was relieved when the mask was peeled off and a man's smiling face appeared. "I hope I didn't frighten you too much. I knew that you were coming to hire me to find the **solution** to the Rinja case. I estimated that you would arrive this morning so I thought I would try my new mask."

"But how did you know that I would be coming?" asked Mr. Worthy.

"I used my POW method," replied Sharp-eye. "POW stands for the three questions a good detective must ask. First, who will **profit** from the act? Second, who has the **opportunity** to do it? Third, who wants to do it the most? In this case, the insurance company will profit most by finding the Rinja. They have the opportunity to search for it, and they want it enough to hire the best—me. Simple deduction. That's how I figured out you would be coming to my office. You might as well tell me all the **information** you have about the Rinja case.

[1] curator: a person in charge of a museum

Mr. Worthy squirmed as he talked about the case. First he told Jones about his fear of losing his **position** as curator as a result of the theft. The deeply troubled Mr. Worthy said that the loss of the diamond would be a **financial** disaster for the insurance company. He complained that he did not **deserve** to have something like this happen during his first month on the job. 30

"No need to worry about that, now that I'm on the case," Jones said. "Tell me, who were the last people to be seen leaving the museum on the night of the theft?" 35

"Only three people were there that evening because the museum was closed to the public."

Mr. Worthy went on to tell what he knew about the three. Mike Purt, a **struggling** artist, was trying to sell his paintings to the museum so that he could buy an engagement ring for the woman he loved. He had come to the museum to set up an appointment with the curator. Mr. Worthy's secretary, Helen Sand, was there dealing with Mike. She loved the Rinja diamond and often told her boss how good it would look on her finger. But she had been far away from the Rinja diamond **display** all day. The third person present was the security guard, Vernon Pepper. He had been stationed next to the Rinja since its arrival at the museum. Two months ago Vernon had retired from the railroad with a full pension, and he was now working part-time for the museum. He bragged that he had all the money that he needed. He also showed little interest in the diamond. 40 45 50

"Say no more. I know who did it," said Sharp-eye. "I just applied my POW method and. . . . "

Do you know who did it?

Turn the page upside down to find out. 55

Sharp-eye explained his solution. "It couldn't have been you, Mr. Worthy. Although you had the opportunity, you didn't want the diamond; you wouldn't profit from it—indeed, you might lose your job. Helen Sand could profit from the theft, and she certainly wanted the diamond. But she had no opportunity to steal it. Vernon Pepper had the opportunity, but no great desire for the extra money it could bring. The thief has to be Mike Purt.

"Mike's paintings were not selling, yet he desperately wanted the money to buy a ring for his girlfriend. Being at the museum that day gave him the opportunity to steal it. That turned out to be too much of a **temptation.** Case closed."

As it turned out, the next day Mike Purt returned the Rinja on his own. He saved the museum from a serious scandal, and he saved himself from severe punishment.

Refining Your Understanding

For each of the following items, consider how the target word is used in the passage. Write the letter of the word or phrase that best completes the sentence.

____ 1. Mr. Jones is known as a *private* (line 1) investigator because a. he is independent and not connected to the police b. his job is not important c. he is tougher than the police.

____ 2. The loss of the diamond would be a *financial* (line 32) disaster for the insurance company because a. the insurance company owned the diamond b. the insurance company would have to pay the museum to make up for the museum's loss c. the museum would switch to a different insurance company.

____ 3. When Mr. Worthy shared his *information* (line 27) about the case, he a. told the facts that he knew b. gave donations to charity c. lied to protect himself.

____ 4. Another meaning of *position*, different from its meaning in line 30, is a. place b. organization c. job.

____ 5. Mike Purt is a *struggling* (line 41) artist. This means that a. he is in poor health b. he fights quite a bit c. he has trouble making money from his painting.

Number correct ______ (total 5)

Part C *Ways to Make New Words Your Own*

By now you are familiar with the target words and their meanings. This section presents activities that will help you make the words part of your permanent vocabulary.

Using Language and Thinking Skills

Finding Examples Write the letter of the situation that best shows the meaning of the boldfaced word.

Example

__c__ **fortune**

a. After hours of practice, Janet mastered the song.
b. Elsa's mother was recovering from a difficult illness.
c. Patricia won $1 million in the lottery.

____ 1. **opportunity**

a. Mr. Stinson explained to his son that there would be no money for college.
b. Mrs. Chin offered Ann a job in her store.
c. The factory workers were shocked at the news of the plant's closing.

____ 2. **display**

a. Chad liked to do his reading in his room.
b. The magician practiced her tricks by herself before the show.
c. Lisa showed her classmates a turtle she found by a lake.

____ 3. **investigate**

a. Sarah decided to try out for the softball team.
b. Matthew wondered what polar bears eat and decided to check out a book about bears.
c. Bob started a funny rumor at his school.

____ 4. **position**

a. Our swim in the lake was a fine activity for a hot day.
b. Mother placed the big chair in front of the television set.
c. Walking is a healthful sport with a low risk of injury.

____ 5. **solution**

a. Debbie figured out the answer to an arithmetic problem.
b. The police discovered a clue by the barn.
c. Ben forgot to bring his homework back to school.

Number correct ______ (total 5)

Understanding Multiple Meanings Each box in this exercise contains a boldfaced target word with its definitions. Read the definitions and then the sentences that use the word. Write the letter of the definition that applies to each sentence.

Example

bank
a. a business that deals in the lending and borrowing of money
b. a rising ridge of land along a stream

__b__ Rick and Jay fished from the north bank of the Clearwater River.

__a__ Ellen went to the bank to cash her check.

position
a. to put in a particular place (verb)
b. the way in which a person or thing is placed (noun)
c. a person's rank or job (noun)
d. a point of view or opinion (noun)

____ 1. Lying flat on the floor, face down, is the starting *position* for doing push-ups.

____ 2. Mrs. Murray holds the *position* of principal at Torrance Middle School.

____ 3. Congress debated the President's *position* on civil rights.

____ 4. From the window we could see the florist carefully *position* the cactus plant in the sunlight.

display
a. to put out or show (verb)
b. a presentation of something in open view (noun)

____ 5. The children happily watched the moving *display* in the store window.

____ 6. Every Saturday the baker would *display* the birthday cakes he made.

____ 7. Clarence would always *display* his skill during important moments in the game.

fortune
a. luck; success (noun)
b. wealth; riches (noun)
c. one's future (noun)

____ 8. I had the good *fortune* of finding a twenty-dollar bill on the sidewalk.

____ 9. The *fortune* teller told me my *fortune;* supposedly, I will become a scientist.

____ 10. Aunt Regina made a *fortune* in the oil business.

Number correct ______ (total 10)

Word's Worth: fortune

The word *fortune* can mean "wealth," "destiny," or "luck." All of these meanings can be traced back to the Roman goddess Fortuna. The Romans believed Fortuna controlled the events of people's lives. She decided who would be wealthy or poor. They imagined her turning a wheel to determine a person's fortune. In their artwork the Romans often pictured her holding a rudder—a symbol of how she steered people's lives. Sometimes the Romans showed Fortuna standing on a ball—a sign that the future is uncertain.

Practicing for Standardized Tests

Antonyms Write the letter of the word that is most nearly *opposite* in meaning to the capitalized word.

____ 1. DISPLAY: (A) reveal (B) observe (C) hide (D) attack (E) uncover

____ 2. INVESTIGATE: (A) evaluate (B) explore (C) escape (D) act (E) ignore

____ 3. FORTUNE: (A) wealth (B) honor (C) worth (D) poverty (E) courtesy

____ 4. PRIVATE: (A) uncertain (B) public (C) honorable (D) fast (E) secret

____ 5. STRUGGLE: (A) find (B) organize (C) surrender (D) battle (E) discuss

Number correct ______ (total 5)

Synonyms Write the letter of the word that is closest in meaning to the capitalized word.

____ 1. INFORMATION: (A) knowledge (B) ignorance (C) attention (D) advantage (E) topic

____ 2. OPPORTUNITY: (A) difficulty (B) fortune (C) mission (D) chance (E) disadvantage

____ 3. PROFIT: (A) loss (B) application (C) gain (D) fortune (E) business

____ 4. SOLUTION: (A) answer (B) problem (C) result (D) completion (E) question

____ 5. TEMPTATION: (A) destruction (B) unattractiveness (C) denial (D) mission (E) fascination

Number correct ______ (total 5)

Spelling and Wordplay

Crossword Puzzle Read the clues and print the correct answer to each in the proper squares. There are several target words in this puzzle.

ACROSS

1. A job or rank
7. Articles: a, __ __, & the
8. Once around a track
9. Abbr. extrasensory perception
13. To try hard
14. Shortened name of city in Brazil
15. A woman's name
17. A great deal of money
20. That thing
21. Not out
22. The doctor asks you to say __ __
24. It makes us want to do some wicked thing
28. Slang for hello
30. Abbr. American Automobile Association
33. Concerned with money matters (adv. form)
37. Soft and gentle
38. A toy, yo-__ __

DOWN

2. Abbr. street
3. A strong taste or smell
4. Not out
5. A chance
6. To be worthy of something
10. Abbr. saint
11. A gain
12. Jack climbed the __ __ __ __ stalk
14. Abbr. registered nurse
16. Clean and tidy
18. A single unit
19. A light knock
23. Same as 28 across
25. A man's title
26. To copy a picture by following its lines
27. An exclamation
29. __ __ __ as a fiddle
30. One __ __ __ two make three
31. What we breathe
32. A bird can __ __ __
34. Abbr. northeast
35. One
36. __ __ and behold

Part D **Related Words**

The words below are closely related to the target words. Use your knowledge of the target words and of word parts to help you determine the meaning of these words. (For information about word parts analysis, see pages 7–13.) Use your dictionary if necessary.

1. deserving (di zur′ viŋ) adj.
2. disregard (dis′ ri gärd′) v., n.
3. finance (fə nans′, fī′ nans) v., n.
4. fortunate (fôr′ chə nit) adj.
5. inform (in fôrm′) v.
6. informative (in fôr′ mə tiv) adj.
7. investigation (in ves′ tə gā′ shən) n.
8. observe (əb zurv′, ab-) v.
9. opportune (äp′ ər to͞on′, -tyo͞on′) adj.
10. pose (pōz) v., n.
11. privacy (prī′ və sē) n.
12. solve (sälv) v.
13. tempt (tempt) v.

Understanding Related Words

Synonym or Antonym? Each numbered word below is either a synonym or an antonym of the italicized word or words in the sentence. In the blank write **S** for synonym or **A** for antonym.

Because Hector had to drive many miles to work, he was *fortunate* to have a reliable car.

____ 1. luckless
____ 2. unlucky
____ 3. lucky

House prices are low right now, and it is *an opportune* time to buy.

____ 4. a profitable
____ 5. an unfortunate
____ 6. a favorable

Try to *disregard* the noise around you and finish writing.

____ 7. pay attention to
____ 8. ignore

The hard-working shortstop was *a deserving* winner of his team's Most Valuable Player award.

____ 9. an unqualified
____ 10. a worthy

Number correct ______ (total 10)

True-False Decide whether each statement is true (**T**) or false (**F**).

____ 1. The most effective way to *solve* personal problems is to pretend they do not exist.

____ 2. A sum of money missing from a village treasury would probably result in an *investigation.*

____ 3. The sight of a skunk usually *tempts* people to come closer to it.

____ 4. Actors normally *pose* as themselves in films.

____ 5. A banker is interested in *finance.*

____ 6. The *opportune* time to ask your parents for something is when they are angry at you.

____ 7. A telescope can help you *observe* distant objects.

____ 8. If you want *privacy,* you should go to a party.

____ 9. One of a newspaper reporter's goals is to *inform* the public.

____ 10. If you *disregard* good health habits, you may get sick.

Number correct ______ (total 10)

Analyzing Word Parts

The Suffixes *-er* and *-or* These suffixes make nouns out of the base words to which they are added. The suffixes give the meaning "one who does something." Since *-er* and *-or* are often pronounced the same way, it may be difficult to remember which spelling to use in words containing these suffixes. When in doubt, use your dictionary. Add the appropriate *-er* or *-or* suffix to the following words.

1. inform: ________________
2. investigate: ________________
3. observe: ________________
4. solve: ________________
5. tempt: ________________
6. conduct: ________________
7. bike: ________________
8. act: ________________
9. catch: ________________
10. direct: ________________

Number correct ______ (total 10)

Number correct in unit ______ (total 75)

Turn to **The Prefix *in-*** on page 213 of the **Spelling Handbook**. Read the rule and complete the exercises provided.

The Last Word

Writing

Write a sentence for each pair of target words below. Use both words in your sentence. Be sure you use the words correctly. (You may add endings to the target words.)

Example *struggle—information*

Jeremy *struggled* to find *information* about his great-grandparents who had lived in Russia.

1. display—position
2. investigate—information
3. temptation—profit
4. deserve—fortune
5. information—fortune
6. private—investigate
7. especially—display
8. observation—struggle
9. financial—solution
10. position—opportunity

Speaking

An extemporaneous speech is one that is given with little or no advance planning. Be ready to give a half-minute speech on any one of the following topics when called upon.

1. An *especially* memorable day
2. Unsung heroes who *deserve* more credit
3. One of the greatest *struggles* ever
4. A strong *temptation*
5. Summer jobs for fun and *profit*

Group Discussion

In small groups discuss one of the following topics:

1. "There is no more difficult art to acquire than the art of *observation.*" Sir William Osler
2. Who *deserves* to play on a sports team at a school? Should a school keep everyone who wants to play? Or should the team have only the best players? Should all players play an equal amount of time, or should the best players get more playing time?

UNIT 4: Review of Units 1–3

Part A Review Word List

Unit 1 Target Words

1. assault
2. collide
3. completion
4. demolish
5. disadvantage
6. effective
7. estimate
8. invader
9. mishap
10. mission
11. navigator
12. realize
13. severe
14. twilight
15. vicinity

Unit 1 Related Words

1. advantageous
2. collision
3. demolition
4. disband
5. disorderly
6. dissolve
7. effect
8. ineffective
9. invade
10. invasion
11. navigate
12. realization

Unit 2 Target Words

1. application
2. appreciate
3. attention
4. career
5. common
6. courteous
7. deceive
8. devour
9. direct
10. disguise
11. honorable
12. landscape
13. serious
14. troubled
15. victim

Unit 2 Related Words

1. applicable
2. appreciative
3. attentive
4. discourteous
5. dishonorable
6. inattentive
7. indirect
8. indirectly
9. unappreciative
10. uncommon
11. untroubled

Unit 3 Target Words

1. deserve
2. display
3. especially
4. financial
5. fortune
6. information
7. investigate
8. observation
9. opportunity
10. position
11. private
12. profit
13. solution
14. struggle
15. temptation

Unit 3 Related Words

1. deserving
2. disregard
3. finance
4. fortunate
5. inform
6. informative
7. investigation
8. observe
9. opportune
10. pose
11. privacy
12. solve
13. tempt

Inferring Meaning from Context

For each sentence write the letter of the word or phrase that is closest in meaning to the word or words in italics.

____ 1. A storm *demolished* the coast, uprooting trees and ripping roofs from houses.

a. cooled b. warmed c. destroyed d. blessed

____ 2. He *deserved* a spot on the football team because he had worked hard to build strength, speed, and stamina.

a. missed b. refused c. lost d. earned

____ 3. One *disadvantage* of rural life is that most rural areas are many miles away from the cultural attractions of large cities.

a. pleasure b. problem c. joy d. convenience

____ 4. Efficiency is *especially* noticeable in Hawaii's pineapple industry. One factory can process more than 3 million pineapples a day.

a. seldom b. always c. particularly d. never

____ 5. Wall Street in New York City is the *financial* center of the United States.

a. legal b. agricultural c. political d. money

____ 6. Mauna Loa, one of the largest active volcanoes on earth, is a major feature of the *landscape* of the island of Hawaii.

a. jungle b. city c. airspace d. natural scenery

____ 7. Several *mishaps* involving ships and planes have occurred in the Bermuda Triangle.

a. accidents b. happenings c. amusements d. raids

____ 8. On January 18, 1778, James Cook, the English explorer and *navigator,* landed in Hawaii.

a. person who plots the course b. first mate c. cook
d. cabin boy

____ 9. While serving in the air force, Terri had *an opportunity* to use her computer skills.

a. a chance b. an order c. a temptation d. an unwillingness

____ 10. Akeem finally gave in to the *temptation.* He stopped working on his homework and got one of his sister's freshly baked cookies.

a. attraction b. order c. dream d. request

Number correct ______ (total 10)

Using Review Words in Context

Using context clues, determine which word from the list below best fits in each blank. Write the word in the blank. Each word will be used only once.

appreciated	especially	observation	serious	troubled
completion	fortune	opportunity	solution	twilight
disguised	landscape	realized	struggled	vicinity

The Sun of Hawaii

Maui, a young god, and Hina, his mother, lived in the ________________ of Haleakala, a huge volcano overlooking the beautiful, green ________________ of the island, which was named after Maui.

One day Hina made an ________________ that ________________ and worried her. She saw that the sun loved to slide down the slopes of Haleakala. This caused a problem for people ________________ on laundry days. Because the sun came down so quickly, ________________ arrived before the clothes were dry. Although this was not a ________________ problem, not a life-and-death matter, putting on damp clothes was very uncomfortable.

Hina said to her son, "Maui, have you noticed how damp your clothes are when you put them on? It isn't that I have neglected to leave them in the sun. It is that the sun runs by so quickly that the clothes have no ________________ to dry."

Hina then made a request. "Maui, look for the ________________ to this problem. We are all tired of wearing wet clothes."

Maui thought and thought. Then one day he made ropes out of grass, tied the ropes to form lassos, and spread the lassos out along the eastern base of Haleakala. Upon the ________________ of this work, Maui ________________ the lassos so that they looked like plants.

The next morning when the first ray of the sun shone on the island, Maui pulled the first lasso tight and captured the ray. He did the same with the second, third, and fourth rays. The sun looked down at Maui and ________________ to get loose from the lassos. When the sun ________________ it could not get free, it asked Maui, "What do you want?"

Maui said, "I want you to walk across our sky slowly instead of sliding down Haleakala." After the sun agreed to Maui's request, Maui let the sun go. The people cheered as the sun limped over Haleakala very slowly.

All of the people on the island greatly ________________ Maui's solution to their problem. They realized their good _______________ every day as they watched the sun stroll across the sky. Often they called out, *"Maui no ka oi—mahalo nui loa,"* which means "Maui is the best—many thanks."

Number correct _____ (total 15)

Part B ***Review Word Reinforcement***

Using Language and Thinking Skills

Sentence Writing Write a sentence for each word listed below so that someone not familiar with the word can understand its meaning.

Example **rain**
Rain is water that falls from clouds.

1. position

____

____

2. attention

____

____

3. fortune

____

____

4. invader

____

____

5. deceive

____

____

Number correct _____ (total 5)

Matching Ideas In the blank write the word from the list that is most clearly related to the situation described in the sentence.

assault	deserve	information	mishap	vicinity
career	financial	investigate	twilight	victim

_______________ 1. We knew we were near the ballpark when we heard the fans shouting.

_______________ 2. Inspector Clouseau searched for clues relating to the robbery.

_______________ 3. Clearly the zebra was not going to be able to outrun the lion.

_______________ 4. The enemy attacked the outpost during the night.

_______________ 5. Yoko tripped on the electric cord, and the lamp fell off the table and broke.

_______________ 6. My favorite part of the day is the time just before darkness falls.

_______________ 7. Steve has chosen teaching as his profession.

_______________ 8. Bankers are skilled in money matters.

_______________ 9. Betty had worked hard in school, and she had certainly earned the honors she received.

_______________ 10. Reference books provide knowledge about a wide variety of subjects.

Number correct ______ (total 10)

Practicing for Standardized Tests

Antonyms Write the letter of the word that is most nearly *opposite* in meaning to the capitalized word.

____ 1. COLLIDE: (A) crash (B) meet (C) miss (D) discuss (E) mix

____ 2. COURTEOUS: (A) rude (B) indirect (C) friendly (D) polite (E) effective

____ 3. PROFIT: (A) advantage (B) fit (C) student (D) hint (E) loss

____ 4. DISGUISE: (A) delight (B) hide (C) investigate (D) miss (E) reveal

____ 5. DISADVANTAGE: (A) estimate (B) benefit (C) mishap (D) handicap (E) struggle

____ 6. DISPLAY: (A) show (B) hide (C) win (D) wish (E) accomplish

____ 7. EFFECTIVE: (A) useful (B) advantageous (C) powerful (D) informative (E) useless

____ 8. PRIVATE: (A) personal (B) special (C) serious (D) warlike (E) public

____ 9. COMMON: (A) fast (B) ordinary (C) unusual (D) complete (E) late

____ 10. SEVERE: (A) alike (B) mild (C) courageous (D) dumb (E) harsh

____ 11. HONORABLE: (A) noble (B) honest (C) rude (D) polite (E) dishonorable

____ 12. ASSAULT: (A) protect (B) deny (C) amuse (D) strike (E) annoy

____ 13. STRUGGLE: (A) fight (B) surrender (C) reach (D) call (E) insult

____ 14. COMPLETION: (A) disorder (B) conclusion (C) beginning (D) absence (E) ending

____ 15. TROUBLE: (A) stern (B) gentle (C) unhappy (D) upset (E) delighted

Number correct ______ (total 15)

Synonyms Write the letter of the word or phrase that is closest in meaning to the capitalized word.

____ 1. APPLICATION: (A) request (B) attack (C) illness (D) compliment (E) complaint

____ 2. SOLUTION: (A) answer (B) error (C) explosion (D) question (E) clue

____ 3. CAREER: (A) finance (B) hobby (C) entertainment (D) game (E) occupation

____ 4. DEVOUR: (A) ignore (B) swallow up (C) pass by (D) march (E) argue

____ 5. DIRECT: (A) foolish (B) silent (C) broken (D) straight (E) crooked

____ 6. ESTIMATE: (A) error (B) rule (C) hope (D) evaluation (E) decision

____ 7. DEMOLISH: (A) sell (B) ruin (C) build (D) pray (E) complete

____ 8. HONORABLE: (A) happy (B) wealthy (C) crooked (D) untroubled (E) respectable

____ 9. ASSAULT: (A) guess (B) movement (C) attack (D) invitation (E) scenery

____ 10. TWILIGHT: (A) noon (B) midnight (C) dusk (D) morning (E) sunrise

____ 11. MISHAP: (A) fortune (B) death (C) accident (D) blessing (E) correction

____ 12. DESERVE: (A) earn (B) find (C) take (D) waste (E) desire

____ 13. COMPLETION: (A) opening (B) polishing (C) filling (D) finishing (E) holding

____ 14. TROUBLED: (A) calm (B) worried (C) poor (D) diseased (E) comfortable

____ 15. MISSION: (A) escape (B) problem (C) job (D) religion (E) virtue

Number correct ______ (total 15)

Spelling and Wordplay

Fill-ins Spell the review word correctly in the blanks to the right of its definition.

1. to understand fully: r _ _ _ _ _ z e
2. useful: _ f f _ _ _ _ _ v e
3. gain: _ _ _ _ f _ t
4. a finishing: _ _ _ p _ e _ _ _ _ n
5. one who steers: n _ _ _ _ g _ t _ _
6. an attack: a s s _ _ _ _
7. to regard highly: _ p p _ _ c _ _ _ _ _
8. to examine: _ n v _ _ _ _ _ g a t _
9. to trick: _ _ c _ _ _ v e
10. an accident: _ _ s h _ _

Number correct ______ (total 10)

Part C *Related Word Reinforcement*

Using Related Words

True–False Decide whether each statement is true (T) or false (F).

____ 1. Smoking is *advantageous* to your health.

____ 2. An *attentive* student does not listen well.

____ 3. *Appreciative* people are likely to use the words "thank you."

____ 4. A *demolition* crew would be hired to rebuild a skyscraper.

____ 5. A city's *finance* department deals primarily with special events, parades, and festivals.

____ 6. The detour takes traffic on an *indirect* route.

____ 7. Part of a teacher's job is to *inform* his or her students.

____ 8. When there is a great sale on stereos at a department store, it is an *opportune* time to buy a stereo there.

____ 9. A *discourteous* person is always welcome at social gatherings.

____ 10. Sweets such as ice cream and candy rarely *tempt* dieters.

Number correct ______ (total 10)

Reviewing Word Structures

Adding Word Parts Add one of the word parts below to each related word. Write the new word you have formed and define it. Use your dictionary if necessary.

dis- un- in- -er

1. advantageous New word: ____________________

   Definition: ________________________________

2. applicable New word: ____________________

   Definition: ________________________________

3. deserving New word: ____________________

   Definition: ________________________________

4. observe New word: ____________________

   Definition: ________________________________

5. attentive New word: ____________________

Definition: ____

6. tempt New word: ____________________

Definition: ____

7. fortunate New word: ____________________

Definition: ____

8. appreciative New word: ____________________

Definition: ____

9. opportune New word: ____________________

Definition: ____

10. inform New word: ____________________

Definition: ____

Number correct _____ (total 10)

Number correct in unit _____ (total 100)

Vocab Lab 1

FOCUS ON: Maps and Travel

By now the words you learned in previous units should be part of your active vocabulary. You can expand your vocabulary even further by becoming familiar with the following words, which are useful to know when traveling.

atlas (at′ ləs) n. a book of maps. • As Uncle John started planning his next trip, he reached for the *atlas.*

brochure (brō shoor′) n. a pamphlet used to explain, promote, or advertise something, such as a tourist attraction. • Looking at the wonderful pictures in the *brochure,* we decided to vacation in Hawaii.

currency (kur′ ən sē) n. the money used in a country. • We exchanged our American dollars for the local *currency,* pesos, when we went to Mexico City.

detour (dē′ toor) n. a route used when the direct or regular way is closed off. • The *detour* took us out of our way and added an hour to our trip but gave us a good view of the countryside.

elevation (el′ ə vā′ shən) n. the height above sea level. • The map showed Fargo, North Dakota, to have an *elevation* of over 900 feet.

gallery (gal′ ə rē) n. a collection of paintings or statues; any of the display rooms of a museum. • The *gallery* had several paintings by Grandma Moses on display.

itinerary (ī tin′ ər rer′ ē) n. a detailed plan, showing routes and stopping places, for a proposed trip. • Our California *itinerary* included Disneyland for the kids, the Getty gallery for Mom, and a fishing cruise for Dad.

landmark n. any prominent feature of the landscape that serves to identify a particular place. • The Sears Tower is the tallest building in the world and a *landmark* in downtown Chicago.

legend n. a short description or key to the various markings on a map. • The map's *legend* indicated that the roads marked in red were the scenic routes.

national monument n. a natural area or historical site, such as a mountain or an old fort, preserved by the Federal government so that the public may visit it. • The site of the Battle of the Little Big Horn in southeastern Montana is now a *national monument.*

passport n. a government document indicating a person's identity and citizenship and granting that person the protection of his or her country when traveling abroad. • At the border between Germany and Poland, a guard checked our *passports.*

relief map n. a map that shows the different heights of landforms, such as hills and valleys, by using different colors. • By checking a *relief map,* we could easily find out where the low areas were in the country.

statute mile (stach′ oot) n. the standard length for one mile, which is 5,280 feet, or 1,609.35 meters. • The distance around the world at the equator is 24,902 *statute miles.*

terminal (tur′ mə n'l) n. a station—bus station, train depot, or airport at any important point of a transportation line. • O'Hare International Airport is said to be the busiest air *terminal* in the world.

topography (tə päg′ rə fē) n. features of an area, such as rivers, mountains, and lakes, that are drawn on certain maps. • The map indicated that the *topography* was hilly, with few roads.

Sentence Completion Complete each sentence below by writing the appropriate focus word.

_______________ 1. Mount Everest, the highest mountain in the world, has an ? of 29,028 feet.

_______________ 2. The Golden Gate Bridge is San Francisco's most famous ? .

_______________ 3. A United States ? generally contains maps of the fifty states and of the larger cities.

_______________ 4. The ? of our African trip included stops in Morocco, Egypt, Kenya, and Zaire.

_______________ 5. One ? had pictures of Mammoth Cave in central Kentucky and told about the 150 miles of passageways.

_______________ 6. The dark blue color on the ? indicated that parts of Lake Superior are more than 1,300 feet deep.

_______________ 7. The unit of ? used in Germany is the mark; in France it is the franc; and in Greece, the drachma.

_______________ 8. According to the ? on the map, the black lines were highways and the triangles, state parks.

_______________ 9. Denver is often called the Mile High City because its elevation is a ?, 5,280 feet.

_______________ 10. Castillo de San Marcos in Florida has been designated a ?. It is the oldest masonry fort in the United States.

_______________ 11. The U. S. Department of State issues a ? to any American citizen who plans to travel in a foreign country.

_______________ 12. At the airport's ?, passengers buy tickets, make reservations, deplane, or wait for flights.

_______________ 13. The museum had a ? that displayed a large collection of paintings.

_______________ 14. The bridge was closed so we were forced to take a ?.

_______________ 15. A skilled mapmaker can show the ? of an area in great detail.

Number correct ______ (total 15)

FOCUS ON: **Analogies**

Various activities—such as synonym, antonym, and sentence completion exercises—help build vocabulary skills. An analogy exercise is another way to enrich your understanding of words. An **analogy** shows a relationship between words. A typical **analogy** question might look like this:

Determine the relationship between the capitalized words. Then decide which other word pair expresses a similar relationship. Write the letter of this word pair.

____ 1. VIOLIN : INSTRUMENT :: (A) fish : water (B) bird : eagle (C) airplane : hangar (D) crow : bird (E) train : railroad

The analogy can also be stated this way:
"A *violin* is to an *instrument* as a __?__ is to a(n) __?__."

Use the following four steps to find the answer to an analogy question.

1. Determine the relationship between the first two words.
2. Make up a sentence using the two words: A *violin* is a type of *instrument.*
3. Decide which of the choices given has a similar type of relationship.
4. Test your choice by substituting the pair of words for the original pair in the sentence you made up.

It becomes obvious that (D) is the best answer to this question when you use the test: "A *crow* is a type of *bird.*"

Below are a few types of relationships used in analogies:

Type of Analogy	**Example**
part to whole	finger : hand :: spoke : wheel
object to purpose	car : transportation :: lamp : light
action to object	dribble : basketball :: fly : kite
word to synonym	nice : pleasant :: glad : happy
word to antonym	good : bad :: slow : fast
object to its material	shoe : leather :: tire : rubber
product to source	apple : tree :: milk : cow
worker and tool	musician : horn :: carpenter : hammer
time sequence	sunrise : sunset :: winter : spring
word and derived form	act : action :: image : imagine

Analogies Determine the relationship between the capitalized words. Then decide which other word pair expresses a similar relationship. Write the letter of this word.

____ 1. ASSAULT : ATTACK :: (A) deceive : reveal (B) walk : run (C) buy : purchase (D) yell : whisper (E) sleep : die

____ 2. FARMER : FARM :: (A) hammer : nail (B) joke : humor (C) ball : ballgame (D) teacher : school (E) sand : sandcastle

____ 3. SUNSET : SUNRISE :: (A) evening : twilight (B) opening : closing (C) winter : January (D) daybreak : noon (E) fall : autumn

____ 4. FORTUNATE : UNFORTUNATE :: (A) evil : dishonorable (B) rich : poor (C) rude : loud (D) polite : courteous (E) suggest : hint

____ 5. STEER : BICYCLE :: (A) work : worker (B) listen : ear (C) clean : dirt (D) coach : team (E) talk : school

____ 6. JOURNALISM : CAREER :: (A) dog : bird (B) plane : wings (C) earth : water (D) duck : duckling (E) baseball : game

____ 7. INVESTIGATOR : INVESTIGATE :: (A) addition : subtract (B) explorer : explore (C) runner : walk (D) food : buy (E) religion : pray

____ 8. EAT : DEVOUR :: (A) forget : remember (B) answer : solve (C) search : find (D) run : sprint (E) smell : hear

____ 9. TROUBLED : WORRIED :: (A) effective : useless (B) long : longest (C) appreciative : grateful (D) attentive : unaware (E) strong : healthy

____ 10. COMMON : RARE :: (A) honest : honorable (B) unfinished : complete (C) severe : serious (D) silly : humorous (E) pure : fresh

Number correct ______ (total 10)

Number correct in Vocab Lab ______ (total 25)

UNIT 5

Part A Target Words and Their Meanings

1. assure (ə shoor′) v.
2. benefit (ben′ ə fit) n., v.
3. claim (klām) v., n.
4. condition (kən dish′ ən) n., v.
5. contribution (kän′ trə byōō′ shən) n.
6. effort (ef′ ərt) n.
7. express (ik spres′) v., adj., adv., n.
8. immediate (i mē′ dē it) adj.
9. increase (in krēs′) v. (in′ krēs) n.
10. issue (ish′ ōō) n., v.
11. oppose (ə pōz′) v.
12. participate (pär tis′ ə pāt′) v.
13. prompt (prämpt) adj., v.
14. result (ri zult′) n., v.
15. society (sə sī′ ə tē) n.

Inferring Meaning from Context

For each sentence write the letter of the word or phrase that is closest in meaning to the word or words in italics. Use context clues to help you choose the correct answer. (For information about how context helps you understand vocabulary, see pages 1–6.)

____ 1. Vicky was afraid to go on the roller coaster, but her brother *assured* her that the ride was perfectly safe. She went on and enjoyed the ride.

a. convinced b. lied to c. refused to tell d. expressed doubts to

____ 2. Several top rock bands gave a concert for the *benefit* of the survivors of the earthquake. The concert raised money for food, clothing, and shelter.

a. release b. help c. memorial d. majority

____ 3. The grateful parrot owner *claimed* his lost bird after the bird told the finders its name and address.

a. collected b. scolded c. never found d. chained

____ 4. The doctor was shocked to see people living in such terrible *conditions.* The building was crumbling, there was no indoor plumbing, and dirt was everywhere.

a. confusion b. conflicts c. situations d. moods

____ 5. Jonas Salk made a major *contribution* to the field of medicine when he developed a vaccine for polio that helped millions of people.
a. misjudgment of b. comment about c. criticism of d. addition to

____ 6. With a great deal of *effort,* we finally scaled the 14,692-foot-high Matterhorn in the Swiss Alps. We were exhausted when we reached the top.
a. work b. talk c. luck d. equipment

____ 7. After hitting the home run, Ventura *expressed* his thanks to the crowd by tipping his hat.
a. denied b. took back c. communicated d. faked

____ 8. When the lightning hit our tree, the flash of light was accompanied by *an immediate* crack of thunder. It seemed as if the tree exploded.
a. an instant b. a distant c. a muffled d. a quiet

____ 9. Cucumbers can grow huge; one cucumber *increased* in size until it was over ten feet long.
a. expanded b. quickly decreased c. rotated d. gradually lessened

____ 10. Should all bicycle riders be required to wear a helmet? This *issue* was debated in the town meeting.
a. question b. tragedy c. installment d. joke

____ 11. The owl butterfly has few enemies to *oppose* it. It scares off attackers because its spots give it the appearance of a vicious owl.
a. defend b. pose for c. go against d. observe

____ 12. Will you *participate in* softball again, or will you sit out this season?
a. pass up b. observe c. quit d. take part in

____ 13. Because of the *prompt* medical attention the crash victims received, many of them survived.
a. severe b. tragic c. quick d. slow

____ 14. As *a result* of her brave deeds, Captain Ahern received the Medal of Honor.
a. a cause b. a condition c. an outcome d. an event

____ 15. Margaret Mead is famous for her study of Samoan *society.* She wrote extensively about the Samoans' social order and their way of life.
a. community b. war c. art d. club

Number correct ______ (total 15)

Part B Target Words in Reading and Literature

You should now have a general idea of the meaning of each target word. Sharpen your understanding by studying how these words are used in the following selection.

Annie Dodge Wauneka

James Coomber

It has been said that we are on this earth to serve others. That is exactly what Annie Dodge Wauneka, a Native American of Navaho descent, spent her life doing. This selection focuses on the way she met challenges on an Arizona reservation.

The Presidential Medal of Freedom, America's highest civilian honor, is an award of appreciation given to individuals who have made great **contributions** to **society.** In 1963, President Lyndon Johnson gave this award to an Arizona Navaho leader, Annie Dodge Wauneka.

When Annie was a teenager, her father, Chee Dodge, became head of (5) the Navaho Tribal Council. Annie often attended Council meetings with her father. At these meetings she heard many important tribal **issues** discussed. Annie, a shy girl, observed what was going on, but she did not say anything. Her father, noticing this shyness, **assured** her that she could **express** her opinions. He told her that being young was no reason (10) to avoid speaking up. Even teenagers had the right to **participate** in tribal meetings. And participate she did.

When she was in her twenties, Annie Dodge Wauneka was elected to the Navaho Tribal Council. For twenty- (15) eight years she was chairperson of the Council's Health and Welfare Committee. She used this position to begin her fight against a longtime enemy of the Navaho—tuberculosis. (20) This disease **claimed** many lives on the Navaho reservation every year.

Wauneka faced numerous obstacles in her **efforts** to fight this disease. Living **conditions** were a great prob- (25) lem. Impure drinking water helped spread the disease, and the dirt floors of many homes resulted in unsanitary conditions. In addition, Navaho

Wearing the Freedom Medal, 1964

medicine men often did not appreciate the benefits of modern medicine and **opposed** Annie's plans for treatment and prevention. The victims of the disease routinely refused hospital treatment. Those who did become hospitalized often tried to escape. 30

Wauneka worked tirelessly to solve these problems. She told her people that unclean conditions such as dirt floors cause disease, and she helped them get money for new homes. She went on the radio and for ten years gave information on tuberculosis to the people in their native language. She instructed people that with a disease like tuberculosis, **prompt** attention and **immediate** treatment are often a matter of life and death. She spent many hours assuring patients that the hospital was for their **benefit.** 35 40

Wauneka's struggles brought **results.** The reservation water systems were improved, and people could rely on having pure water. The number of Navahos who got medical help **increased** greatly. Even the medicine men started to work with the doctors rather than against them. Gradually, the Navaho began to realize that better living conditions result in healthier people. 45

Thanks to Annie Dodge Wauneka, tuberculosis is no longer a serious health problem for the Navaho.

Refining Your Understanding

For each of the following items, consider how the target word is used in the passage. Write the letter of the word or phrase that best completes the sentence.

____ 1. In line 3 *society* refers to a. all Americans b. the Navaho people c. all women in the Southwest.

____ 2. You would expect Annie to *express* (line 10) her opinions by a. talking fast b. sharing her ideas with other members of the tribe c. agreeing with her elders.

____ 3. The best synonym for *claimed* in line 21 is a. took b. influenced c. requested.

____ 4. When the medicine men *opposed* (line 31) Wauneka's efforts, it is likely that they a. helped her get her message out to the people b. visited the hospitals and doctors themselves c. warned their people against "white man's" medicine.

____ 5. People who want *prompt* (line 39) medical attention will a. wait until the symptoms worsen b. seek a doctor's help immediately c. write a note to remind themselves to schedule an appointment.

Number correct ______ (total 5)

Part C **Ways to Make New Words Your Own**

By now you are familiar with the target words and their meanings. This section presents activities that will help you make the words part of your permanent vocabulary.

Using Language and Thinking Skills

Understanding Multiple Meanings The target word in the box below is followed by its definitions. Read the definitions and then the sentences that use the word. Write the letter of the definition that applies to each sentence.

issue
a. publication of a magazine (noun)
b. to pass out, pour forth (verb)
c. a matter of disagreement, question (noun)

____ 1. Society members argued the *issue* of increasing their dues.

____ 2. Coach Medford *issued* shirts and towels to each team member.

____ 3. Mrs. Doyle *issued* a dictionary to each member of her class.

____ 4. The August *issue* of *National Geographic* featured an article about Greece.

____ 5. The principal assured the students that they could discuss any *issues* that concerned them.

Number correct ______ (total 5)

True-False Decide whether each statement is true (**T**) or false (**F**).

____ 1. A person sitting alone on a desert island is an example of a *society*.

____ 2. United States senators debate *issues* of national importance.

____ 3. By answering a question thoughtfully, you make a *contribution* to a class discussion.

____ 4. Regular exercise *benefits* your health.

____ 5. Airline passengers usually *participate* in piloting the airplane.

____ 6. You are *claiming* a lost item when you turn it in to the Lost and Found Department.

____ 7. When you *express* your feelings, you keep them hidden.

____ 8. A political candidate is not interested in the voting *results* on election night.

____ 9. Teachers appreciate students who are *prompt*.

____ 10. In the Revolutionary War, the British army *opposed* the American colonial army.

Number correct ______ (total 10)

Practicing for Standardized Tests

Synonyms Write the letter of the word that is closest in meaning to the capitalized word.

____ 1. ASSURE: (A) trouble (B) alarm (C) inform (D) give (E) guarantee

____ 2. BENEFIT: (A) disadvantage (B) harm (C) aid (D) temptation (E) disguise

____ 3. CLAIM: (A) take (B) devour (C) refuse (D) dig (E) deny

____ 4. CONTRIBUTION: (A) award (B) donation (C) claim (D) completion (E) theft

____ 5. EFFORT: (A) mishap (B) laziness (C) career (D) labor (E) realization

____ 6. CONDITION: (A) strength (B) climate (C) state (D) contribution (E) weakness

____ 7. IMMEDIATE: (A) important (B) instant (C) late (D) fortunate (E) secondhand

____ 8. INCREASE: (A) complete (B) enlarge (C) reduce (D) fold (E) shrink

____ 9. PARTICIPATE: (A) oppose (B) observe (C) decline (D) share (E) assure

____ 10. RESULT: (A) opportunity (B) source (C) mission (D) beginning (E) effect

Number correct ______ (total 10)

Spelling and Wordplay

Word Maze Find and circle each target word in this maze.

C	O	N	D	I	T	I	O	N	E	A	P
L	O	P	P	O	S	E	I	I	J	R	A
A	B	N	R	D	H	Q	S	M	E	M	R
I	S	E	T	O	Z	U	S	M	F	E	T
M	T	Y	N	R	M	X	U	E	F	X	I
Y	A	J	V	E	I	P	E	D	O	P	C
D	C	Q	M	U	F	B	T	I	R	R	I
P	L	T	K	A	W	I	U	A	T	E	P
R	E	S	U	L	T	L	T	T	N	S	A
G	I	N	C	R	E	A	S	E	I	S	T
C	L	A	S	S	U	R	E	V	K	O	E
S	O	C	I	E	T	Y	S	O	F	A	N

assure
benefit
claim
condition
contribution
effort
express
immediate
increase
issue
oppose
participate
prompt
result
society

Word's Worth: claim

A prospector files a *claim* for a rich new vein of gold, and he shouts in excitement. You *claim* an opponent has fouled you in a basketball game, and you yell about it. The notion of *claim* in these two examples is very close to the way the ancient Romans understood the word. *Claim* comes from the Latin word *clamo,* meaning "to cry out." When we claim something as our own, we are apt to express it in a loud voice. The word *clamor,* meaning "a loud noise," comes from the same Latin word. When you speak with great emotion or verbally attack someone, you *declaim*. The Romans coined this word by adding to *claim* the prefix *de-,* which means "thoroughly."

Part D **Related Words**

The words below are closely related to the target words. Use your knowledge of the target words and of word parts to determine the meaning of these words. (For information about word parts analysis, see pages 7–13.) Use your dictionary if necessary.

1. associate (ə sō′ shē āt′, -sē āt′) v.
   (ə sō′ shē it, -sē it′) n., adj.
2. assurance (ə shoor′ əns) n.
3. beneficial (ben′ ə fish′ əl) adj.
4. decrease (di krēs′, dē-′) v., (dē′ krēs) n.
5. effortless (ef′ ərt lis) adj.
6. expression (ik spresh′ ən) n.
7. opponent (ə pō′ nənt) n.
8. opposition (äp′ ə zish′ ən) n.
9. participation (pär tis′ ə pā′ shən) n.
10. sociable (sō′ shə b'l) adj.
11. socialize (sō′ shə līz′) v.
12. sociology (sō′ sē äl′ ə jē) n.

Understanding Related Words

Matching Examples Write the word from the list below that is most clearly related to the situation described in each sentence.

associate	beneficial	effortless	opponent	sociable
assurance	decrease	expression	participation	sociology

_______________ 1. Sports such as swimming and running have been found to be very helpful in maintaining good health.

_______________ 2. After only one month on his diet, Ted dropped from 205 pounds to 185.

_______________ 3. On Friday night we play our rivals in basketball, Garfield Junior High.

_______________ 4. Melissa loves to meet people, and she enjoys parties.

_______________ 5. Mr. Popovich was in such good shape that his exercising seemed easy and painless.

_______________ 6. Fiona gave me her promise that she would not tell my secret to anyone.

_______________ 7. The saying "to pull the wool over someone's eyes" comes from the days when men wore wigs; a person might trick the wearer of a wig if the person pulled the wig over the wearer's eyes.

_______________ 8. Mrs. Chesniak's business partner at the Maple Street Candy Company was her longtime friend, Alice Randall.

_______________ 9. Professor Biko was an expert in the study of the beliefs and values of various groups in society.

_______________ 10. Many students at Fox Middle School go out for after-school sports or clubs.

Number correct _____ (total 10)

Turn to **Words Ending in *-ize* or *-ise*** on page 223 in the **Spelling Handbook.** Read the rules and complete the exercise provided.

Analyzing Word Parts

The Latin Root *socius* *Socius* is a Latin word meaning "companion" or "sharing." In this unit, one target word and four related words contain the *socius* root and deal in some way with people or companions. Match each definition on the right with the appropriate word on the left. Write the letter of the correct definition in the blank.

____ 1. associate (n.)   a. acting in a friendly manner (adj.)

____ 2. society   b. a group of people with the same customs and beliefs (n.)

____ 3. sociable   c. the study of people in groups (n.)

____ 4. socialize   d. to take part in activities (v.)

____ 5. sociology   e. a friend or partner (n.)

Number correct _____ (total 5)

The Latin Root *bene* The target word *benefit* and the related word *beneficial* come from the Latin root *bene,* meaning "well." The following words also contain the root *bene: benefactor, beneficiary, beneficent.* Match each definition on the right with the appropriate word on the left. Write the letter of the correct definition in the blank. If needed, refer to the list of suffixes on pages 9 and 10 or to your dictionary.

____ 1. benefit (n.)   a. a person who receives help (n.)

____ 2. beneficial   b. showing kindness or doing good for others (adj.)

____ 3. beneficent   c. a person who gives help (n.)

____ 4. benefactor   d. a performance that raises money for a needy cause (n.)

____ 5. beneficiary   e. producing helpful effects (adj.)

Number correct _____ (total 5)

Number correct in unit _____ (total 65)

The Last Word

Writing

Answer each of the following questions in one to three sentences.

1. What is one *benefit* you gain from education?
   Sample starter: One *benefit* I gain from education is . . .
2. Explain one idea you can *claim* as your own.
3. What kind of training would you do to get into top physical *condition?*
4. What do you think is the most important scientific *contribution* of this century? Why?
5. Which of your school subjects takes the most *effort?* Explain.
6. What trend is *increasing* in your school or community?
7. What is an important *issue* in your town that people are currently discussing?
8. Name one idea you are *opposed to* and tell why.
9. In what sports or organizations do you like to *participate?*
10. Briefly describe a *society* in another part of the world or in another period of history.

Group Discussion

Do you think that the people who create television shows have made a genuine *effort* to understand young people such as you and your friends? Do they portray young adolescents accurately on television? Explain why or why not, using examples from television shows to support your opinion.

UNIT 6

Part A Target Words and Their Meanings

1. assume (ə so͞om′) v.
2. dense (dens) adj.
3. dependent (di pen′ dənt) adj., n.
4. dispose (dis pōz′) v.
5. extinguish (ik stiŋ′ gwish) v.
6. factor (fak′ tər) n.
7. judgment (juj′ mənt) n.
8. majority (mə jôr′ ə tē, mə jär′) n.
9. neglect (ni glekt′) v., n.
10. restore (ri stôr′) v.
11. slogan (slō′ gən) n.
12. surplus (sur′ plus) adj., n.
13. thorough (*th*ur′ ō) adj.
14. utter (ut′ ər) v., adj.
15. various (var′ ē əs) adj.

Inferring Meaning from Context

For each sentence write the letter of the word or phrase that is closest in meaning to the word or words in italics. Use context clues to help you choose the correct answer. (For information about how context helps you understand vocabulary, see pages 1–6.)

____ 1. Jasper had never set foot on a golf course; however, golf looked easy, and he *assumed* that it would be an easy game to learn.
a. forgot b. feared c. knew d. supposed

____ 2. The trees and the underbrush were so *dense* that the hikers' progress was slowed, and they soon lost their way.
a. thick b. thin c. beautiful d. bare

____ 3. Before the invention of trains and automobiles, most people *were dependent on* horses as a means of transportation.
a. relied on b. traded c. stayed away from
d. had forgotten about

____ 4. Today many people *dispose of* their newspapers, bottles, and cans by putting them in recycling bins.
a. increase b. keep c. sell d. get rid of

____ 5. After calling for more equipment, firefighters fought to *extinguish* a fire raging in a store near a school.
a. report b. feed c. start d. put out

____ 6. One important *factor* in the success of a basketball team is the winning attitude of the players.

a. surprise b. ingredient c. handicap d. problem

____ 7. The bystander used good *judgment* when she rescued a drowning child by throwing him an inner tube.

a. courage b. endurance c. sense d. communication

____ 8. In the election a *majority* of the students in our class voted for Vicki. Therefore, she became our class representative to the student council.

a. representative b. small number c. large number d. few

____ 9. Because Annette *neglected* to turn off the running water in the bathtub, she came home to a flooded bathroom.

a. tried b. remembered c. failed d. hoped

____ 10. A team of artists worked to *restore* a priceless painting that had been damaged in the flood.

a. repair b. steal c. destroy d. begin

____ 11. The *slogan* "Pike's Peak or Bust" was scrawled on many covered wagons that crossed the Great Plains in the nineteenth century.

a. cartoon b. saying c. insult d. poem

____ 12. A gardener who had *surplus* cucumbers gave the extras to friends and neighbors.

a. delicious b. huge c. leftover d. small

____ 13. His *thorough* knowledge of baseball helped him become the most successful manager in the league.

a. partial b. useless c. limited d. complete

____ 14. This is a secret; don't *utter* a word of this, even if people ask.

a. conceal b. sing c. speak d. hold back

____ 15. The Australian pitta bird has feathers of *various* colors, including blue, green, red, white, purple, and orange.

a. dull b. several c. unusual d. similar

Number correct ______ (total 15)

Part B **Target Words in Reading and Literature**

You should now have a general idea of the meaning of each target word. Sharpen your understanding by studying how these words are used in the following selection.

Only You Can Prevent Forest Fires

James Coomber

Since the dawn of civilization, forests have provided people with food, shelter, clothing, and fuel. Today, people are still **dependent** on forests for **various** products ranging from lumber and plywood to cellophane, paper, and adhesives. Consider the use of just one product, paper; Americans use an average of 640 pounds of it per person, per year.

Nearly one third of the land in the United States and Canada consists of **dense** forests. However, we cannot **assume** that this **surplus** of trees will last forever. We must make every effort to protect and maintain this great natural resource.

Fires are a major threat to our forests. Each year fire destroys about 3 million acres of timber in the United States. Some fires are caused by lightning. Little can be done to prevent these fires. However, a large **majority** of the fires—about 90%—are caused by human beings. Hunters and campers sometimes fail to use good **judgment**. They may **dispose** of lighted matches and cigarettes carelessly or may **neglect** to **extinguish** a campfire, which can smolder and feed on fallen leaves, twigs, and underbrush. Such thoughtlessness has led to tragic forest fires.

After a forest is destroyed, forestry experts may plant seedlings in the bare areas. However, it takes years before a forest is **restored** to its original condition.

A major **factor** in preventing forest fires is education. People need to have a **thorough** understanding of the importance of protecting trees. All those who enjoy camping, hiking, and hunting in our nation's forests must take to heart the **slogan uttered** by Smokey the Bear: "Only *you* can prevent forest fires."

Refining Your Understanding

For each of the following items, consider how the target word is used in the passage. Write the letter of the word or phrase that best completes each sentence.

____ 1. The phrase a "*surplus* of trees" (line 7) means a. a few trees b. enough trees c. more trees than we need.

____ 2. It takes years before a forest is *restored* (line 19) because a. it takes a long time for trees to grow b. forest fires keep occurring c. few people are willing to plant trees.

____ 3. An example of *neglect* (line 15) would be a. not putting out a campfire before leaving a campsite b. not camping in very dry regions c. cutting down a tree for lumber.

____ 4. A person can *extinguish* (line 15–16) a fire with a. matches b. binoculars c. water.

____ 5. An example of a *slogan* (line 27–28) is a. a legal description of a product b. an expression used to advertise a product c. a brand name for a product.

Number correct ______ (total 5)

Part C **Ways to Make New Words Your Own**

By now you are familiar with the target words and their meanings. This section presents reinforcement activities that will help you make the words part of your permanent vocabulary.

Using Language and Thinking Skills

Finding the Unrelated Word Write the letter of the word that is not related in meaning to the other words in the set.

____ 1. a. independent b. dependent c. free d. separate

____ 2. a. surplus b. shortage c. oversupply d. excess

____ 3. a. majority b. most c. more than half d. few

____ 4. a. single b. many c. several d. various

____ 5. a. thin b. dense c. thick d. crowded

____ 6. a. factor b. part c. aspect d. failure

____ 7. a. investigation b. judgment c. opinion d. belief

____ 8. a. transport b. guess c. suppose d. assume

____ 9. a. say b. utter c. hide d. state

____ 10. a. limited b. thorough c. incomplete d. partial

Number correct ______ (total 10)

Word Map Create a word map for *extinguish.* Include two synonyms and two antonyms of *extinguish.* Also use the word *extinguish* in a sentence of your own.

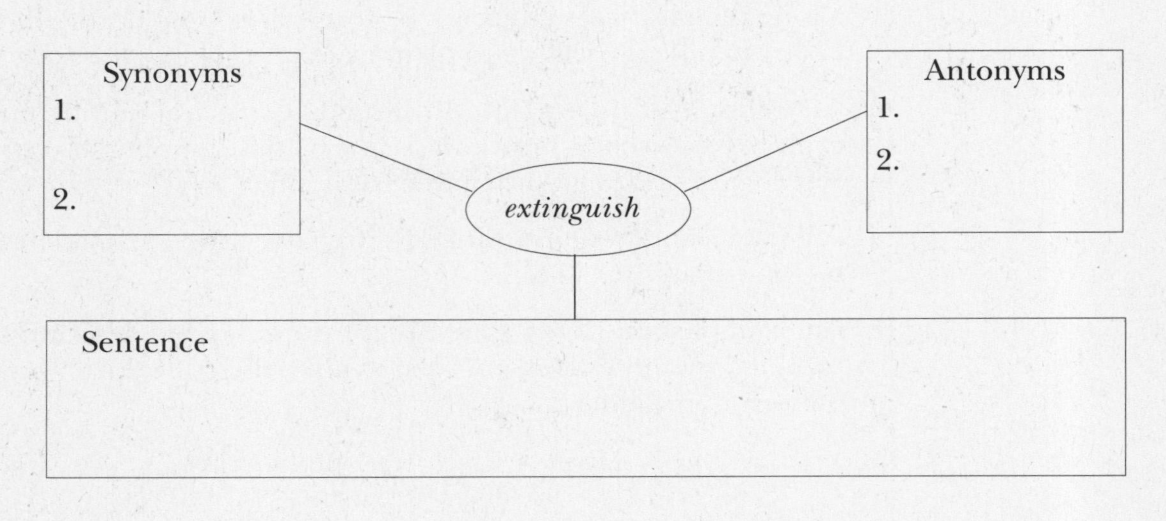

Number correct ______ (total 5)

Practicing for Standardized Tests

Analogies Determine the relationship between the pair of capitalized words. Then decide which word could be paired with the third word to express a relationship similar to the one between the pair of capitalized words. Write the letter of this word.

____ 1. "ONLY YOU CAN PREVENT FOREST FIRES" : SLOGAN :: "The early bird catches the worm" : ? (A) morning (B) answer (C) title (D) saying

____ 2. WATER : EXTINGUISH :: match : ? (A) pump (B) drive (C) douse (D) ignite

____ 3. DECEIT : HONESTY :: surplus : ? (A) shortage (B) solution (C) benefit (D) observation

____ 4. JUDGE : JUDGMENT :: state : ? (A) country (B) statement (C) government (D) document

____ 5. UTTER : SPEAK :: assume : ? (A) assign (B) prove (C) guess (D) deserve

Number correct ______ (total 5)

Word's Worth: slogan

Slogan is made up of two very old words. The Celtic tribe had the word *sluagh,* which meant "crowd." The Gaelic people had the word *gairm,* meaning "shout." The Scottish put the two together to make a word that meant "war cry." The Scottish war cry was a bugle call—or often simply a clan name. Later, *slogan* came to mean a phrase used by a family to stand for an attitude or a goal, similar to a *motto*.

Today's *slogans* are the war cries of advertisers and political campaigners: "We try harder!" "Quality is Job One" "Just Do It!" Like the original *sluagh-gairm,* today's slogans serve as bold announcements and labels for causes.

Spelling and Wordplay

Word Maze Find and circle each target word in this maze.

D	Q	C	H	A	P	R	O	D	A	M	S
I	E	C	U	T	T	E	R	J	C	N	L
S	X	P	U	J	Z	S	O	U	O	R	O
P	T	H	E	D	Q	T	V	D	M	U	G
O	I	T	A	N	A	O	U	G	P	T	A
S	N	G	Y	G	D	R	O	M	O	F	N
E	G	D	E	N	S	E	X	E	S	A	E
S	U	R	P	L	U	S	N	N	E	C	G
P	I	M	A	J	O	R	I	T	Y	T	L
A	S	S	U	M	E	W	O	S	C	O	E
T	H	O	R	O	U	G	H	V	Y	R	C
B	L	V	A	R	I	O	U	S	K	F	T

assume
dense
dependent
dispose
extinguish
factor
judgment
majority
neglect
restore
slogan
surplus
thorough
utter
various

Part D Related Words

The words below are closely related to the target words. Use your knowledge of the target words and of word parts to determine the meaning of these words. (For information about word parts analysis, see pages 7–13.) Use your dictionary if necessary.

1. assumption (ə sump′ shən) n.
2. density (den′ sə tē) n.
3. depend (di pend′) v.
4. dependence (di pen′ dəns) n.
5. extinct (ik stiŋkt′) adj.
6. extinguisher (ik stiŋ′ gwish ər)
7. independent (in′ di pen′ dənt) adj., n.
8. judge (juj) v., n.
9. judgmental (juj men′ t'l) adj.
10. negate (ni gāt′) v.
11. negative (neg′ ə tiv) adj., n.
12. negligent (neg′ li jənt) adj.
13. negligible (neg′ li jə b'l) adj.
14. vary (ver′ -e, var′ -) v.

Understanding Related Words

Finding Examples Write the letter of the situation that best shows the meaning of the boldfaced word.

____ 1. **assumption**
a. The world is round.
b. Two plus two equals four.
c. There is no life on other planets.

____ 2. **judgmental**
a. Uncle Willie took two days to repair the roof.
b. The coach criticized her team for the poor job she felt they did.
c. Lincoln is the capital of Nebraska.

____ 3. **vary**
a. Aunt Hortense thinks about nothing except money.
b. For two days Joachim has eaten only peanut butter.
c. When Rachel swims, she practices the backstroke, the sidestroke, and the crawl.

____ 4. **density**
a. The ice cream is an odd shade of purple.
b. The sky is black in outer space.
c. New York has more people per square mile than any other city in the United States.

____ 5. **negligent**
a. We hauled out the garbage as part of our daily chores.
b. Raul was leaning toward a career in detective work.
c. I didn't turn off the oven when I left the house this morning.

____ 6. **judge**

a. Craig looked at the three bikes and finally chose the best one.
b. Margaret kept a pet chameleon in her room.
c. A cheetah crept into our campsite on the first night.

____ 7. **depend**

a. The bear looked up at Sarah in a surprised way.
b. Diego was someone on whom you could always rely.
c. In football, a team has four tries to move the ball ten yards.

____ 8. **extinct**

a. The dinosaurs died out millions of years ago.
b. Kiki came to America in 1975 from Vietnam.
c. That food has the worst smell I have ever encountered.

____ 9. **dependence**

a. Roberto climbed onto the roof of the school to get his softball.
b. Until he found a job, Paul could not afford to move out of his parents' home.
c. The Fourth of July is my favorite holiday.

____ 10. **independent**

a. You may find your jacket in the school's "lost and found" box.
b. In 1991, Lithuania broke away from the Soviet Union.
c. When we are not home, our dog Goofy must stay in a cage.

Number correct ______ (total 10)

Turn to **The Final Silent *e*** on page 219 of the **Spelling Handbook.** Read the rule and complete the exercises provided.

Analyzing Word Parts

The Latin Root *neg* The root *neg,* which is in the target word *neglect,* means "not." Each sentence below contains an italicized word with the *neg* root. Following each sentence, write the italicized word's definition. Use your knowledge of *neg* and the context of the sentence to determine the meaning of the italicized word. Write your definition in the blank.

1. Dereck's response to our idea was *negative;* he refused to participate in our plans.

____

2. Anne was *negligent* in leaving the canary in the same room with the cat.

____

3. Jody *reneged* on her promise to pay me back.

____

4. Since the amount of rain that fell was *negligible,* no one needed an umbrella.

____

5. Our disastrous losses this year will *negate* the profits we made last year.

____

Number correct ______ (total 5)

The Prefix *re-* The common prefix *re-* means "again" and "back." It means "again" in such words as *rebuild, reconsider,* and *review.* It means "back" in such words as *react, repay,* and *restore.* Add the prefix *re-* to the following verbs taken from earlier units. Then use each newly formed verb in a sentence. Use your dictionary if necessary.

1. assure ____________________

____

2. claim ____________________

____

3. direct ____________________

____

4. issue ____________________

____

5. position ____________________

____

Number correct ______ (total 5)

Number correct in unit ______ (total 60)

The Last Word

Writing

Choose one or more items from each of the two columns below. Then write a story based on the items. Let your imagination wander.

Characters

- *various* animals in a zoo
- a leader with a *slogan*
- a child wanting to be more *independent*
- a *negligent* doctor
- a *judge* with a *negative* attitude
- an *extinct* creature that comes back to life

Incidents

- *extinguishing* a big fire
- making an *assumption* that leads to trouble
- *uttering* magic words
- trying to *dispose* of a bag of money
- *restoring* good *judgment* to the *majority* of people
- exploring a *dense* jungle

Speaking

Give a brief speech on the following topic: How do you *judge* a new song? What are the *factors* one should consider in judging a song?

Group Discussion

Create a *slogan* for a team or an organization. Explain:

- What the team or organization does.
- What that team or organization wants others to think of it.
- How your new *slogan* will help get the team's message out to others.

UNIT 7

Part A Target Words and Their Meanings

1. brilliant (bril′ yənt) adj.
2. conference (kän′ fər əns, -frəns) n.
3. destination (des′ tə nā′ shən) n.
4. discourage (dis kur′ ij) v.
5. indebted (in det′ id) adj.
6. jointly (joint′ lē) adv.
7. lack (lak) n., v.
8. opinion (ə -pin′ yən) n.
9. plunge (plunj) n., v.
10. possess (pə zes′) v.
11. prefer (pri fur′) v.
12. segment (seg′ mənt) n. (-ment) v.
13. suspect (sə spekt′) v. (sus′ pekt) n., adj.
14. transform (trans fôrm′) v.
15. urgent (ur′ jənt) adj.

Inferring Meaning from Context

For each sentence write the letter of the word or phrase that is closest in meaning to the word or words in italics. Use context clues to help you choose the correct answer. (For information about how context helps you understand vocabulary, see pages 1–6.)

____ 1. The *most brilliant* star in the heavens is Sirius, the Dog Star; its radiant shine makes it easy to pick out at night.
a. densest b. most easily overlooked c. nearest d. brightest

____ 2. An annual dental convention is held in Chicago in February. It is the largest *conference* for dentists in the United States.
a. problem b. trip c. meeting d. society

____ 3. Darren boarded a plane in Chicago. The plane's *destination* was San Francisco. Darren was going there to visit his brother.
a. name b. place of arrival c. place of departure d. navigator

____ 4. Mrs. Hargrave was *discouraged*. She had failed her automobile driving test thirty-nine times.
a. poor b. downhearted c. cheerful d. nearsighted

____ 5. Nineteen people in our town *are indebted to* Leroy Jones. These people have been rescued from drowning by Leroy during his job as lifeguard.
a. owe money to b. owe thanks to c. know d. are related to

____ 6. The first climb to the top of Mt. Everest was accomplished not by a single person but *jointly* by two people. One was Edmund Hillary of New Zealand and the other was Tensing Norkay of Nepal.

a. in one day b. fortunately c. together d. separately

____ 7. In much of the Arctic during the winter, the sun never appears in the sky. This *lack* of sunshine is difficult for newcomers to get used to.

a. amount b. increase c. absence d. memory

____ 8. I believe that wearing a bike helmet increases safety. It is my *opinion* that our town's law requiring people to wear a helmet while bicycling is a good one.

a. information b. judgment c. plan d. doubt

____ 9. Without a parachute, Lieutenant Chisov fell out of a plane at an altitude of nearly twenty-two thousand feet. Incredibly, he landed in a snow-filled ditch and survived his *plunge.*

a. task b. fall c. climb d. attempt

____ 10. To become an Olympic gymnast, one must *possess* the following qualities: strength, balance, a willingness to work hard, and a desire for perfection.

a. have b. observe c. appreciate d. lack

____ 11. My brother and I both love turkey. I *prefer* dark meat, but my brother favors light meat.

a. choose b. avoid c. plan for d. deserve

____ 12. The surgeon removed a small *segment* of the patient's intestine.

a. factor b. part c. whole d. result

____ 13. Before I finished the novel, I *suspected* that the hero would not catch the criminal. When I read the final chapter, I found that I was right—the villain got away.

a. discovered b. hoped c. doubted d. guessed

____ 14. Water was piped in to irrigate the desert, and soon the desert was *transformed into* green farmland.

a. destroying b. changed into c. a result of the d. moved to

____ 15. When the temperature dropped to –72°F, the polar explorers had *an urgent* need for warmer clothing.

a. a decreased b. a serious c. little d. a mild

Number correct ______ (total 15)

Part B Target Words in Reading and Literature

You should now have a general idea of the meaning of each target word. Sharpen your understanding by studying how these words are used in the following selection.

How the Sun Came

James Coomber

Myths are old, traditional stories that imaginatively explain why the world is the way it is. The following myth has been told by the Cherokee Indians to explain how sunlight came to their land.

Long ago, darkness covered the earth. Animals kept bumping into one another and complaining, "It is so dark. What we need is light." Finally the animals called a **conference** to explore the problem **jointly**.

The redheaded woodpecker began, "They say some people on the other side of the earth **possess** light. Maybe one of us could go there (5) and bring back some light. Who shall go?"

The opossum spoke up. "I can hide a piece of the sun in my bushy, furry tail. I will go." As the opossum traveled to the east, the sky became brighter and brighter. Because of the **brilliant** sun, the opossum had to squint to keep from being blinded. To this day the opossum's eyes are (10) tiny from this squinting, and opossums **prefer** darkness to daylight.

The opossum arrived at his **destination**, the sun. He snatched a small **segment** of the sun, and he put it in the fur of his tail. But the sun was so terribly hot that it scorched his fur. When he returned, his tail **lacked** fur (that is why opossums' tails are bare today), and he had no light. (15)

Next the buzzard volunteered to make the trip. In his **opinion** a tail was no place to hold the sun. "I am too smart to put the sun on my tail," he said. "I'll set it on my head." So the buzzard journeyed eastward until he came to the sun. From high in the sky he **plunged,** grabbed a piece of the sun, and set it on his head. But the hot sun burned off his head feath- (20) ers, which explains how the buzzard came to be bald. He too had failed to bring back the light.

The creatures now were very **discouraged.** They were tired of the darkness. The need for light seemed more **urgent.** Everyone agreed that the opossum and the buzzard had done their best. They wondered what (25) else they could do to get the light.

A small, soft voice spoke up. "This is Grandmother Spider speaking," said she. "I **suspect** it is up to me to bring you light. At least, I would really like to try." The others agreed to let her make the attempt.

Before she headed eastward, Grandmother Spider made a bowl of wet clay. With her bowl she approached the sun, spinning a thread behind her so she could find her way home. As quiet as she was, neither the sun nor the sun people noticed Grandmother Spider. Gently, she took only a tiny piece of the sun and put it in her bowl. Then westward she made her way, following the thread she had spun before. The sun's light spread before her as she went. You can observe today that a spider's web has a sun-shape in the middle with rays spreading out from it. 30 35

Everyone was **indebted** to Grandmother Spider and promised to remember her always. The world was **transformed** by the light.

Refining Your Understanding

For each of the following items, consider how the target word is used in the passage. Write the letter of the word or phrase that best completes the sentence.

____ 1. The opposite of doing things *jointly* (line 3) would be doing them a. with others b. carelessly c. alone.

____ 2. Today the opossum's tail *lacks* fur (line 14) because a. the light caused the fur to grow rapidly b. the sun god cast a curse upon the creature c. the hot sun burned off the fur.

____ 3. The creatures became *discouraged* (line 23) because a. the buzzard became bald b. no one seemed able to bring back the light c. they knew they were cowards.

____ 4. The people were *indebted* to Grandmother Spider (line 38) because she a. allowed the opossum and the buzzard to succeed in their task b. brought back the light to everyone c. failed to bring back enough of the sun to light their sky.

____ 5. One example of how the world might be *transformed* by light (line 39) is that a. everyone could see better and they could make and invent things b. the world was still dark and the animals remained weak and afraid c. the light resulted in forest fires and destruction.

Number correct ______ (total 5)

Part C *Ways to Make New Words Your Own*

By now you are familiar with the target words and their meanings. This section presents activities that will help you make the words part of your permanent vocabulary.

Using Language and Thinking Skills

Understanding Multiple Meanings The box in this exercise contains a boldfaced word with its definitions. Read the definitions and then the sentences that use the word. Write the letter of the definition that applies to each sentence.

suspect
a. a person who is considered guilty (n.)
b. to think it likely; guess (v.)
c. to believe to be guilty of something (v.)

____ 1. Police suspected Dirty Dan of participating in the burglary.

____ 2. I suspect Jodi will be very tired after running the ten-mile obstacle course.

____ 3. Who would have suspected that Mr. Jones would arrive early?

____ 4. For hours the police questioned the suspect.

____ 5. Mrs. Briggs suspected that Kelly was struggling with the assignment and needed help.

Number correct ______ (total 5)

Finding Examples Write the letter of the situation that best shows the meaning of the boldfaced word.

____ 1. **transform**
a. A boy had a pet rabbit named Scruffy.
b. People were walking to the train in the morning.
c. The caterpillar had changed into a beautiful butterfly.

____ 2. **conference**
a. A teacher and a student met to talk about the student's work.
b. Two new restaurants have opened in our town recently.
c. We took several great photos at the zoo.

____ 3. **indebted**
a. Derek finally paid off his loan at the bank.
b. A classmate borrowed money from you.
c. Through hard work, Teresa became a fine athlete.

____ 4. **segment**
   a. A snail makes its way slowly up Mt. Fuji.
   b. Wilson did not put down the novel until he had read the whole thing.
   c. Each of us ate a piece of the apple pie.

____ 5. **brilliant**
   a. The carpenter studied the chair he had built.
   b. The students had no answer for the teacher's strange question.
   c. The lake surface reflected the rays of the sun.

Number correct ______ (total 5)

Practicing for Standardized Tests

Antonyms Write the letter of the word that is most nearly *opposite* in meaning to the capitalized word.

____ 1. BRILLIANT: (A) angry (B) bright (C) dull (D) serious (E) cowardly

____ 2. DESTINATION: (A) beginning (B) solution (C) goal (D) position (E) fortune

____ 3. DISCOURAGE: (A) neglect (B) disapprove (C) deceive (D) depress (E) urge

____ 4. INDEBTED: (A) honorable (B) ungrateful (C) appreciative (D) thankful (E) effective

____ 5. LACK: (A) shortage (B) surplus (C) effect (D) emptiness (E) disadvantage

____ 6. OPINION: (A) belief (B) difficulty (C) judgment (D) freedom (E) fact

____ 7. POSSESS: (A) dispose (B) make (C) have (D) keep (E) assure

____ 8. PREFER: (A) choose (B) dislike (C) return (D) realize (E) elect

____ 9. SEGMENT: (A) part (B) factor (C) whole (D) issue (E) section

____ 10. URGENT: (A) serious (B) effective (C) strong (D) important (E) unnecessary

Number correct ______ (total 10)

Spelling and Wordplay

Crossword Puzzle Read the clues and print the correct answer to each in the proper squares. There are several target words in this puzzle.

ACROSS

1. A place at the end of a trip
8. 2,000 pounds
9. String tied together making a device to catch fish
10. Abbr. street
12. Abbr. Parent Teachers Association
14. Abbr. compact disc
15. A meeting
20. Beliefs
21. To perform an action
22. Abbr. United States of America
24. That girl
25. A rowboat's paddle
27. Abbr. American Medical Association
29. Immediately necessary
31. Football cheer
32. Fe, __ __, fo, fum
33. To think it likely
37. Stick out your tongue and say __ __.
39. A certain amount of space; region
40. A piece; section

DOWN

1. To cause to lose hope
2. Abbr. saint
3. In the direction of; toward
4. Not out
5. Changes
6. A single time
7. Man's name, rhymes with Ted
11. A cone-shaped toy, spun on its pointed end (plural)
12. Slang for a professional athlete
13. Comes after nine
16. __ __ __ gara Falls
17. Abbr. footnote
18. Comes after seventh
19. Shared with someone else; done together
23. Likes best
26. Abbr. agriculture
28. Made by artists
30. Pleasing; well-behaved
34. Father
35. A light knock
36. Objective case of "I"
37. Morning hours
38. That man

Word's Worth: plunge

Consider the sound of the word *plunge.* Isn't it a little bit like the sound of someone diving into water? *Plunge* has a sound that echoes its meaning. Several relatives of the word *plunge* do the same thing. The Latin word for lead is *plumbum,* the sound that a piece of lead makes when thrown into water. A *plumb,* a lead weight on a string, is a device used to measure the depth of water. *Plunk, kerplunk, plop,* and *thump* are other words that echo the sound of things dropping or hitting.

Part D **Related Words**

The words below are closely related to the target words. Use your knowledge of the target words and of word parts to determine the meanings of these words. (For information about word parts analysis, see pages 7–13.) Use your dictionary if necessary.

1. brilliance (bril′ yəns) n.
2. confer (kən fur′) v.
3. destiny (des′ tə nē) n.
4. discouragement (dis kur′ ij mənt) n.
5. dispossess (dis′ pə zes′) v.
6. encourage (in kur′ ij) v.
7. preference (pref′ ər əns, pref′ rəns) n.
8. suspicion (sə spish′ ən) n.
9. transfer (trans fûr′, trans′ fər) v., n.
10. transfusion (trans fyo͞o′ zhən) n.
11. transmit (trans mit′, tranz-) v.
12. transplant (trans plant′) v. (trans′ plant′) n.

Understanding Related Words

Synonyms-Antonyms Decide if the following pairs of words are synonyms or antonyms. In the blank write **S** for Synonym or **A** for Antonym.

____ 1. confer—discuss

____ 2. brilliance—dullness

____ 3. destiny—fate

____ 4. discouragement—hopefulness

____ 5. dispossess—take away

____ 6. encourage—criticize

____ 7. preference—dislike

____ 8. suspicion—distrust

____ 9. transfer—keep

____ 10. transmit—deliver

Number correct ______ (total 10)

Turn to **Doubling the Final Consonant** on page 222 of the **Spelling Handbook.** Read the rule and complete the exercise that follows.

Analyzing Word Parts

Word Endings Add *-ed* and *-ing* to each of the words below. Write the two new words on the lines provided. Use a dictionary if needed.

1. **confer**

____

____

2. **prefer**

____

____

3. **encourage**

____

____

4. **transfer**

____

____

5. **transmit**

____

____

Number correct _____ (total 10)

The Prefix *trans-* The Latin prefix *trans-* has three meanings: "across" (*transatlantic*), "beyond" (*transcend*), and "change completely" (*transform*). Use your understanding of *trans-* to define each of the words below in the blanks. Use your dictionary if necessary.

1. transfusion: ____
2. transoceanic: ____
3. transplant: ____
4. transpose: ____
5. transcribe: ____

Number correct ____ (total 5)

Number correct in unit ____ (total 65)

The Last Word

Writing

Write a sentence for each pair of target words. Use both words in the same sentence. Be sure your sentence makes sense.

1. discouraged—indebted
2. suspect—opinion
3. brilliant—transform
4. urgent—destination
5. prefer—plunge
6. lack—opinion
7. transform—indebted
8. jointly—possess
9. possess—brilliant
10. transform—segment

Speaking

Prepare a one-minute talk on one of the following topics.

My *opinion* of . . .
I am *indebted* to . . .
The quality I would most like to *possess* . . .
I once received an *urgent* message . . .
How I plan to win the *conference* championship . . .
A person I consider *brilliant* is . . .

Group Discussion

"To pretend to satisfy one's desires by
possessions is like using straw to put out a fire." — Chinese proverb

In a small group, discuss this proverb. Put the proverb into your own words. What does it mean? Discuss what the most important aspects of life are. To what extent are possessions important?

UNIT 8: Review of Units 5–7

Part A Review Word List

Unit 5 Target Words

1. assure
2. benefit
3. claim
4. condition
5. contribution
6. effort
7. express
8. immediate
9. increase
10. issue
11. oppose
12. participate
13. prompt
14. result
15. society

Unit 5 Related Words

1. associate
2. assurance
3. beneficial
4. decrease
5. effortless
6. expression
7. opponent
8. opposition
9. participation
10. sociable
11. socialize
12. sociology

Unit 6 Target Words

1. assume
2. dense
3. dependent
4. dispose
5. extinguish
6. factor
7. judgment
8. majority
9. neglect
10. restore
11. slogan
12. surplus
13. thorough
14. utter
15. various

Unit 6 Related Words

1. assumption
2. density
3. depend
4. dependence
5. extinct
6. extinguisher
7. independent
8. judge
9. judgmental
10. negate
11. negative
12. negligent
13. negligible
14. vary

Unit 7 Target Words

1. brilliant
2. conference
3. destination
4. discourage
5. indebted
6. jointly
7. lack
8. opinion
9. plunge
10. possess
11. prefer
12. segment
13. suspect
14. transform
15. urgent

Unit 7 Related Words

1. brilliance
2. confer
3. destiny
4. discouragement
5. dispossess
6. encourage
7. preference
8. suspicion
9. transfer
10. transfusion
11. transmit
12. transplant

Inferring Meaning from Context

For each sentence write the letter of the word or phrase that is closest in meaning to the word or words in italics.

____ 1. After taking the speech class, Philip found he could *express* his thoughts more clearly.

a. organize b. remember c. disguise d. communicate

____ 2. My father wants our family to go camping in the Rocky Mountains, but my sister is *opposed to* the idea.

a. against b. afraid of c. in favor of d. excited about

____ 3. Why did Helen break up with Tony? She said that one *factor* was his lack of a sense of humor.

a. problem b. possibility c. reason d. goal

____ 4. Holmes began to *suspect* that the butler was involved in the murder when he found one of the butler's gloves at the crime scene.

a. hope b. believe c. know d. deny

____ 5. The students brought in some of their old toys as their *contribution* to the Charity Fund.

a. answer b. donation c. response d. reward

____ 6. Blood was flowing from the wound; therefore, the cut required *immediate* attention.

a. instant b. careful c. delayed d. serious

____ 7. Because Kendra and Marjorie were interested in the same subject, they decided to work on their science project *jointly*.

a. reluctantly b. with pleasure c. quickly d. together

____ 8. Thanks to the *prompt* action of the firefighters, the family was rescued from the burning building.

a. courageous b. quick c. smart d. careful

____ 9. I *prefer to* read mysteries, but I sometimes enjoy biographies.

a. choose to b. have no desire to c. seldom like to d. plan to

____ 10. In just one season the new coach has *transformed* the basketball team. The team won the championship this year.

a. strengthened b. criticized c. helped d. changed

____ 11. Even though Peter did poorly on his math exam, he did not let it *discourage* him.

a. destroy b. amuse c. depress d. annoy

____ 12. Pouring baking soda on certain types of fires will *extinguish* the fires.

a. extend b. limit c. put out d. control

____ 13. In "Sleeping Beauty" the wicked witch caused a *dense* forest to grow up around the castle.

a. small b. thick c. dangerous d. huge

____ 14. Presidential candidates must have *opinions on* many national issues.

a. facts about b. experiences with c. advisers on d. views about

____ 15. Due to *neglect,* my plants are not growing very well.

a. lack of attention b. lack of knowledge c. mistakes d. care

Number correct ______ (total 15)

Using Review Words in Context

Using context clues, determine which word from the list below best fits in each blank. Write the word in the blank. Each word will be used only once.

benefits	effort	lack	restore	surplus
dependent	factor	possess	result	transform
dispose	increases	prompt	segment	various

The Blood of Life

Did you know that your life is completely ________________ on three to five quarts of blood? The body of a typical young adolescent has about a gallon, or four quarts, of blood. Blood is necessary for maintaining life and good health.

The human body derives many ________________ from blood. This fluid of life carries oxygen and nutrients to all parts of the body, and no ________________ of the body can live without it. Blood also serves as a cleaning system for the body. Waste products are carried by the blood to organs that ________________ of them or ________________ them into harmless substances. In addition, blood helps the body fight disease.

________________ factors influence the amount of blood produced by an individual's body. The most important ________________ is the weight of the individual. An infant of 9 pounds, for example, needs to ________________ only 10 ounces of blood in order to survive. A person who weighs 160 pounds needs about 5 quarts, while a person who weighs 80 pounds needs about half of that. The need for blood ________________ at higher altitudes. As a ________________ of this fact, people who live at high altitudes may need two additional quarts of blood. Without extra blood, these people would suffer from a ________________ of oxygen.

Your body carries a ________________ of blood so that a small loss will not hurt you. For instance, a healthy adult can donate as much as a pint of blood and experience no harmful effects. Without much ________________, the body can ________________ the lost blood, completely replacing it in a matter of weeks.

However, if blood is lost very quickly or if too great an amount is lost, ________________ medical attention is needed. Sometimes, even people who lose huge quantities of blood can survive, if given immediate care. Such people can be saved by a blood transfusion, which involves pumping another person's blood into the patient's body. Many people are alive today thanks to such "borrowed" blood. In an important sense, all of us owe our lives to the blood racing within our bodies, the blood of life.

Number correct ______ (total 15)

Part B ***Review Word Reinforcement***

Using Language and Thinking Skills

Writing Sentences In the blank write a sentence using each of the words below. Be sure the sentence shows you know the word's meaning.

Example **cold** The arctic winter was very cold.

1. judgment

   ____

2. majority

   ____

3. neglect

   ____

4. participate

   ____

5. society

   ____

Number correct ______ (total 5)

Sentence Completion Write the word from the list below that best completes the meaning of the sentence.

assume	effort	plunge
brilliance	increases	possesses
claimed	indebted	result
conditions	lack	urgent
dependent	opinion	various

________ 1. Plankton is the term given to the ? tiny plants and animals that live on or near the surface of oceans or lakes.

________ 2. It would take a great deal of ? to move some king crabs. They sometimes span five feet and can weigh as much as twenty-five pounds.

________ 3. The polyp is so small it can only be seen with a magnifying glass. However, the Great Barrier Reef, 1,250 miles long, is a ? of the skeletons left by these tiny animals.

________ 4. Some seashells are so rare that they are worth a small fortune. According to the ? of experts, the Glory-of-the-sea shell is worth up to $2,000.

________ 5. The giant killer clam weighs up to 500 pounds and has a shell nearly five feet wide. It has ? the lives of several swimmers by clamping down on an arm or leg, causing the victim to drown.

________ 6. Anyone who is stung by the poisonous wasp jellyfish needs ? medical attention. Its victims may die in a matter of minutes.

________ 7. Many people depend on the sea for their livelihood. These people are ? to the abundant sea life.

________ 8. Coral can be shined until it gains the ? that makes it suitable for jewelry.

________ 9. People should not ? that the four-inch spotted octopus is harmless. This octopus has enough poison to kill eight to ten people.

________ 10. Though the copepod is no larger than a pinhead, many fish are ? on it as a main source of food.

_______________ 11. The ocean's water pressure is one ton per square inch at a depth of 6,000 feet. The pressure __?__ to six tons at 35,640 feet.

_______________ 12. The underwater world __?__ beauty, mystery, and an incredible variety of life.

_______________ 13. The __?__ at the bottom of the ocean are extreme; the temperature there remains just slightly above the freezing point.

_______________ 14. A __?__ to the bottom of the Marianas Trench near Guam would take you down 35,800 feet. It is the deepest point of the oceans.

_______________ 15. There is no __?__ of salt in sea water. Each cubic yard contains about 730 ounces of salt.

Number correct ______ (total 15)

Practicing for Standardized Tests

Analogies Determine the relationship between the pair of capitalized words. Then decide which other word pair expresses a similar relationship. Write the letter of this word pair.

____ 1. ASSURE : ALARM : (A) sing : dance (B) exercise : swim (C) trust : believe (D) attack : defend (E) annoy : irritate

____ 2. CONFERENCE : MEETING : (A) play : work (B) jeans : denim (C) money : bank (D) autumn : fall (E) music : concert

____ 3. URGENT : UNIMPORTANT : (A) reliable : unreliable (B) honest : kind (C) thin : skinny (D) rude : loud (E) intelligent : bright

____ 4. DESTINATION : GOAL : (A) city : suburb (B) instrument : guitar (C) road : intersection (D) job : task (E) decrease : increase

____ 5. MINISTER : PREACH (A) deception : spy (B) government : govern (C) salesperson : buy (D) athlete : tire (E) boxer : fight

Number correct ______ (total 5)

Synonyms Write the letter of the word or phrase that is closest in meaning to the capitalized word.

____ 1. ASSUME: (A) appreciate (B) suppose (C) apply (D) deny (E) prefer

____ 2. CONFERENCE: (A) opportunity (B) benefit (C) disagreement (D) discussion (E) situation

____ 3. DENSE: (A) tense (B) serious (C) thin (D) thick (E) loose

____ 4. SLOGAN: (A) technique (B) motto (C) speed (D) lie (E) profit

____ 5. ISSUE: (A) discuss (B) argue (C) stop (D) flow (E) transform

____ 6. UTTER: (A) plan (B) milk (C) glide (D) decide (E) speak

____ 7. PARTICIPATE: (A) observe (B) join in (C) depend upon (D) retire from (E) encourage

____ 8. PLUNGE: (A) slip (B) devour (C) dive (D) slide (E) oppose

____ 9. THOROUGH: (A) incomplete (B) thoughtful (C) partial (D) profitable (E) complete

____ 10. SEGMENT: (A) part (B) dirt (C) whole (D) building (E) material

Number correct ______ (total 10)

Antonyms Write the letter of the word that is most nearly *opposite* in meaning to the capitalized word.

____ 1. ASSURE: (A) insure (B) lie (C) judge (D) relax (E) prefer

____ 2. BENEFIT: (A) advantage (B) solution (C) opportunity (D) preference (E) disadvantage

____ 3. BRILLIANT: (A) difficult (B) round (C) dull (D) sharp (E) intelligent

____ 4. DISCOURAGE: (A) trouble (B) encourage (C) dissolve (D) depress (E) deceive

____ 5. DISPOSE: (A) discard (B) suppose (C) keep (D) throw out (E) issue

____ 6. EFFORT: (A) struggle (B) shelter (C) attempt (D) rest (E) benefit

____ 7. OPPOSE: (A) worry (B) battle (C) operate (D) associate (E) support

____ 8. PROMPT: (A) timely (B) direct (C) late (D) fierce (E) opportune

____ 9. RESTORE: (A) reclaim (B) correct (C) save (D) sell (E) demolish

____ 10. URGENT: (A) unnecessary (B) tasty (C) essential (D) unreliable (E) grave

Number correct ______ (total 10)

Spelling and Wordplay

Word Maze Find and circle each listed review word in this maze.

C	A	D	Q	V	M	A	J	O	R	I	T	Y	J	K	N
O	B	V	X	I	I	Y	K	N	P	E	R	Q	A	P	G
N	F	Z	A	S	B	V	C	H	D	X	E	Z	J	V	W
D	N	L	S	X	O	Y	D	I	S	P	O	S	E	V	G
I	C	U	L	U	L	Z	F	E	H	R	E	T	T	U	I
T	E	G	Y	S	R	I	D	E	P	E	N	D	E	N	T
I	X	H	J	O	K	P	L	F	G	S	Y	U	M	A	B
O	X	T	T	K	D	V	L	P	O	S	S	E	S	S	M
N	W	C	T	H	O	R	O	U	G	H	N	S	M	W	O
W	A	R	E	H	O	Q	J	P	S	Q	U	P	N	Q	L
F	N	A	G	O	L	S	U	Q	R	M	D	W	S	I	C
T	O	X	V	J	U	D	G	M	E	N	T	P	Q	R	F

assume
claim
condition
dependent
dispose
express
factor
issue
judgment
majority
possess
slogan
surplus
thorough
utter

Part C Related Word Reinforcement

Using Related Words

True–False Decide whether each statement is true **(T)** or false **(F)**.

____ 1. *Associates* ordinarily avoid each other.

____ 2. The *density* of rock is greater than that of air.

____ 3. A zoo usually contains several *extinct* animals.

____ 4. A book reviewer is not supposed to be *judgmental.*

____ 5. In a crime the suspects are those people who are under *suspicion.*

____ 6. If you have a *preference* for chocolate, you usually avoid eating it.

____ 7. A fortune teller claims to be able to know things about your *destiny.*

____ 8. One of the best ways to get students to do better is to *encourage* them.

____ 9. A book of quotations contains famous *expressions.*

____ 10. The best way to start working on a new project is with a *negative* attitude.

Number correct ______ (total 10)

Reviewing Word Structures

Matching Definitions Before completing this exercise, review the following word parts from Units 5–7: *bene, socius, neg,* and *trans-* (pages 68, 77, and 88). Then match each word in the list below with its definition. Write the matching word in the blank.

beneficial	socialize
negate	sociology
negative	transfer
negligent	transfusion
sociable	transplant

______________ 1. careless

______________ 2. friendly

______________ 3. helpful

______________ 4. to send something from one place to another

______________ 5. to transfer an organ by surgery from one person to another

_______________ 6. to deny the truth of, make ineffective

_______________ 7. to take part in parties or other social activities

_______________ 8. opposite to what is positive

_______________ 9. a transferring of blood

_______________ 10. the study of the beliefs and values of groups in society

Number correct _____ (total 10)

Number correct in unit _____ (total 95)

Vocab Lab 2

FOCUS ON: **Sports**

Several words and expressions from sports terminology have become part of everyday speech. Perhaps you have heard someone who has made a mistake say, "I really dropped the ball on that one." The following words will give you an idea of the rich and colorful language of sports.

aerobic (er ō′ bik) adj. referring to any exercise that conditions the lungs and heart. • Ann's *aerobic* exercises improved her stamina quite a bit.

amateur (am′ ə chər) adj. playing a sport for pleasure rather than for pay. • The *amateur* boxer could not receive prize money for his bouts.

birdie (bur′ dē) n. in golf, a score of one below par for a hole. (*Par* means "the number of strokes considered a skillful score.") • Mike's three strokes gave him a *birdie* on the par-four hole.

blitz (blits) n. in football, a charge by a defensive player through the line in an effort to tackle the opposing quarterback. • The *blitz* was successful, and the quarterback was tackled for a ten-yard loss.

check (chek) n. in hockey, a bump or block to stop an opponent's play. • Wayne Gretzsky's *check* stopped the opposing player from reaching the puck.

decathlon (di kath′ län) n. an athletic contest in which contestants take part in ten events: 100-meter dash, 400-meter dash, long jump, shot put, high jump, 110-meter hurdles, discus throw, pole vault, javelin throw, and 1500-meter run. • In the final event, the British athlete scored enough points to win the *decathlon*.

equestrian (i kwes′ trē ən) adj. relating to horses or horseback riding. • The *equestrian* events in the Olympic Games test the ability of horses and riders.

field goal (fēld gōl) n. in basketball, a shot made from play scoring two or three points; in football, a place kick that sails over the goal post, scoring three points. • With two seconds left, Butler kicked a *field goal* to win the game.

free agent (frē ā′ jənt) n. a professional athlete not under contract and therefore free to sign with any team. • Bill went to the Minnesota Vikings' football camp as a *free agent* in hopes of signing with the team.

freestyle (frē′ stīl′) n. in swimming, a race in which swimmers may use any stroke. • The American swimmer excelled at *freestyle*.

marathon (mar′ ə thän′) n. a footrace of 26 miles, 385 yards (42 kilometers and 352 meters); any long-distance contest. • In the final mile of the *marathon*, Alicia's legs felt like rubber.

sacrifice fly (sak′ rə fīs′ flī) n. in baseball, a play in which a batter flies out and a runner scores from third base after the catch. • With a teammate on third base, Sandberg tried to hit a *sacrifice fly* to tie the game.

spare (sper) n. in bowling, knocking down all the pins with two consecutive rolls of the ball. • By making the final *spare*, Sally boosted her score to 140.

triathlon (trī ath′ län′) n. an athletic contest involving three consecutive events, usually swimming, bicycling, and running. • Dave was happy to get to the cycling phase of the *triathlon.*

varsity (vär′ sə tē) n. a school's main team in any given sport. • Christopher ran home to tell his parents that he had made the *varsity* basketball team.

Sentence Completion Complete each sentence below by writing the appropriate focus word.

_______________ 1. The horses in the _?_ competition were highly skilled.

_______________ 2. Some _?_ athletes eventually turn professional and play for money.

_______________ 3. To a quarterback, the _?_ can be terrifying, especially when a 300-pound tackler bursts through the line.

_______________ 4. Dawn was such a talented basketball player that she made the _?_ team as a freshman.

_______________ 5. The 50-meter _?_ is the fastest race in swimming.

_______________ 6. In hockey a solid _?_ can strip the puck from an opponent.

_______________ 7. In bowling it is difficult to make a _?_ when the remaining pins are split, or not close together.

_______________ 8. Swimming and running are considered _?_ activities because they make the heart and lungs work harder.

_______________ 9. The _?_ will begin at the lake, where all contestants will swim one mile. The biking and running will take place on the road circling the town.

_______________ 10. Terry's twenty-foot putt gave him a _?_.

_______________ 11. When the quarterback's contract ended with the Bears, he became a _?_. Later he was pleased when eight teams wanted to sign him.

_______________ 12. Racing well in a _?_ requires many miles of distance running practice, some faster training on a track, and a certain amount of good luck.

_______________ 13. The _?_ enabled the runner on third base to score.

_______________ 14. The Olympic champion in the _?_ is sometimes called the "world's greatest athlete." The ten events require extraordinary talent, strength, and stamina.

_______________ 15. Before a kicker attempts an important _?_, the opposing team may call a timeout to give the kicker time to think and to become nervous.

Number correct _____ (total 15)

FOCUS ON: **The Language of Advertising**

Three thousand years ago, advertisements were carved on stones. Today, advertisements appear in newspapers, magazines, and catalogs, on radio and television—and on billboards alongside roads. A person may encounter as many as fifteen hundred ads in a single day. To be a smart buyer, therefore, you must learn the language of ads.

Informative Advertising

There are two basic types of ads: informative and persuasive. Informative ads, the kind you see in catalogs, give specific information about a product, especially its price. The information may be presented without emotional appeals; however, look out for **bargain words** when you check the price. For example, an ad may mention selling at "list price," or the price suggested by the manufacturer. However, since many products actually sell for much less than what the manufacturer suggests, paying the list price may not be a savings at all. Another word to look out for is "originally." An ad may state "originally $19.95, now only $17.95." *Originally* may mean five years ago. Moreover, if the product was overpriced to begin with, that $17.95 may not be a very good price.

Persuasive Advertising

To make their products seem different and attractive, advertisers create persuasive ads to sway your thinking. Sometimes advertisers use **purr words,** such as *mother, home,* and *success,* that suggest pleasant thoughts.

Another type of ad appeals to the desire to be like others. "Everybody loves Mama Mia's Pizza!" This kind of **bandwagon** ad entices you to join the happy crowd. Other ads use the opposite strategy, appealing to the need to be different. "Zaps—the distinctive candy bar for distinctive people." Such ads are based on **snob appeal.**

Companies sometimes hire celebrities to help sell products. By linking a product to a **celebrity,** advertisers hope that people will think "If this product is good enough for this star, then it's good enough for me." In truth, the celebrity may not even use the product or may know very little about it.

Still another type of appeal uses **scientific terms** or statistics. "The sportswear with polypropylene!" The clothing sounds great, but what *is* polypropylene? The ad often does not say. The term *polypropylene* is enough to impress people and persuade them to buy.

Identifying Advertising Techniques Identify the technique used in each of the following advertisements. Choose from among the following listed techniques.

bargain words	bandwagon	celebrity
purr words	snob appeal	scientific terms

______________ 1. Make your mother happy by eating Gag's Always-Fresh Spinach.

______________ 2. Come to the sale of the century. Everything in our store is selling for less than list price.

______________ 3. Stand out from the crowd. At Strange Department Store we have clothes for the one and only you.

______________ 4. Our cleanser is the only one with trinitrocresol—for really tough cleaning jobs.

______________ 5. Everyone in your class is using it—or will be soon. Blemish-Free Skin Cream, the unanimous choice!

______________ 6. Is bad breath getting in the way of your success? Fresh Mouth will get you through the day and make you a winner.

______________ 7. All of our stereos are selling for less than the original price. Buy one while they last!

______________ 8. When Olympic champion Diana Highstep isn't wearing a track uniform, she wears Romance Perfume.

______________ 9. Use SWAT, containing pyrophosphoric acid, to take care of your flies and mosquitoes.

______________ 10. Don't follow the herd. Plan your next vacation with Way-Out Travel Agency—designing adventures for the pathfinder in all of us.

Number correct _____ (total 10)

Writing Advertisements Choose a product you are familiar with. Write two ads for it, an informative ad and a persuasive ad.

Number correct in Vocab Lab _____ (total 25)

Special Unit Taking Standardized Vocabulary Tests

At various times during your years in school, you have taken standardized tests. These tests are given to large groups of students around the country. Teachers use the test scores to compare your knowledge and skills with those of other students who have completed the same number of years of school.

During the next few years you will be taking many other standardized tests. Because these tests usually contain vocabulary questions, it is to your advantage to spend time becoming familiar with the major types of vocabulary test questions. These types of questions include **synonyms, antonyms,** and **sentence completion**.

This special unit offers specific strategies for taking standardized tests, as well as additional practice.

Part A Synonyms

As you know, **synonyms** are words that have the same meaning. Standardized test questions covering synonyms are answered by selecting the word that is closest in meaning to the given word. A typical synonym question looks like this:

HURT: (A) poison (B) quit (C) injure (D) punch (E) benefit

To answer a synonym question, use the following guidelines:

1. Try to determine the meaning of the given word before you look at the answer choices. Pay attention to any prefix, suffix, or root that may help reveal the meaning.
2. Look carefully at the answer choices. Remember to look only for words with *similar* meanings. Do not be thrown off by *antonyms*—words that are opposite in meaning. In the example above, choice (E), *benefit,* is an antonym for the given word, *hurt.*
3. Keep in mind that many words have more than one meaning. For example, *hurt* means both "to cause pain" and "to offend." If none of the answer choices seems to fit your sense of the given word's meaning, think about other meanings.
4. If you cannot readily identify the correct answer, try to eliminate any obviously incorrect answers.
5. Remember that you are looking for the *best* answer, the word that is *closest* in meaning to the given word. In the example above, *poison* and *punch* have meanings related to bodily harm. However, choice (C), *injure,* is closest in meaning to *hurt.*

Exercise Write the letter of the word that is closest in meaning to the capitalized word.

____ 1. FORM: (A) argue (B) check (C) supervise (D) shape (E) govern

____ 2. EFFECTIVE: (A) serious (B) damaged (C) useful (D) weak (E) risky

____ 3. MISHAP: (A) discussion (B) fortune (C) illness (D) accident (E) event

____ 4. FORTUNATE: (A) deserving (B) private (C) unhappy (D) lucky (E) friendly

____ 5. ATTENTIVE: (A) intelligent (B) alert (C) clumsy (D) fast (E) unconcerned

____ 6. CONFERENCE: (A) meeting (B) result (C) situation (D) society (E) decision

____ 7. JOINTLY: (A) thoroughly (B) entirely (C) quickly (D) together (E) separately

____ 8. UTTER: (A) share (B) suspect (C) collect (D) decrease (E) express

____ 9. DECLARE: (A) move (B) announce (C) own (D) deserve (E) fight

____ 10. EXERTION: (A) guarantee (B) decline (C) effort (D) increase (E) request

Number correct ______ (total 10)

Part B ***Antonyms***

As you know, **antonyms** are words that are opposite in meaning. Standardized test questions covering antonyms are answered by selecting the word that is most nearly opposite in meaning to a given word. A typical question looks like this:

> ANXIOUS: (A) calm (B) bored (C) alone (D) angry (E) worried

To complete an antonym question, use the following guidelines:

1. Try to determine the meaning of the given word before you look at the answer choices. Pay attention to any prefix, suffix, or root that may help reveal the meaning.

2. Look carefully at the answer choices. Remember that you must find a word that is opposite in meaning. Do not be thrown off by *synonyms* —words that are similar in meaning. In the example above, choice (E), *worried,* is a synonym for the given word, *anxious.*
3. Keep in mind that many words have more than one meaning. For example, *anxious* means both "worried" and "eager." If none of the answer choices seems to fit your sense of the opposite meaning, think about other meanings for the given word.
4. If you cannot readily identify the correct answer, try to eliminate any obviously incorrect answers.
5. Remember that you are looking for the *best* answer, the word that is *most nearly opposite* in meaning. In the example above, *bored* has a meaning related to lack of anxiety. However, choice (A), *calm,* is most nearly opposite in meaning to *anxious.*

Exercise Write the letter of the word that is most nearly *opposite* in meaning to the capitalized word.

____ 1. EXTERIOR: (A) outside (B) near (C) distant (D) interior (E) difficult

____ 2. FORBID: (A) permit (B) question (C) complain (D) sell (E) inspire

____ 3. DEMOLISH: (A) deceive (B) build (C) destroy (D) trust (E) win

____ 4. ASSIST: (A) give (B) borrow (C) help (D) oppose (E) mock

____ 5. CONSTANT: (A) changeable (B) steady (C) secure (D) silly (E) thoughtless

____ 6. DISAGREEMENT: (A) pleasure (B) difference (C) participation (D) silence (E) harmony

____ 7. ISOLATE: (A) separate (B) unite (C) celebrate (D) invite (E) betray

____ 8. CONCEAL: (A) remove (B) show (C) make (D) lie (E) hide

____ 9. EASE: (A) recovery (B) comfort (C) vacation (D) defeat (E) hardship

____ 10. BRILLIANT: (A) starry (B) smart (C) dependent (D) dark (E) solitary

Number correct ______ (total 10)

Part C **Sentence Completion**

Sentence completion questions test your ability to use words and to recognize relationships among parts of a sentence. A sentence completion question gives you a sentence in which one or two words are missing. You must then choose the word or set of words that best completes the sentence. A typical sentence completion question looks like this:

> A __?__ of the class needed extra instruction on the homework assignment, but only a __?__ of the students stayed after school for help.
> (A) student ... few (B) part ... portion (C) majority ... few
> (D) teacher ... minority (E) leader ... group

To answer sentence completion questions, use the following guidelines:

1. Read the entire sentence carefully, noting key words. Pay particular attention to words such as *but* and *however,* which indicate contrast. Note any words that might indicate similarity, such as *and, the same as,* and *another.* Also look for words that might indicate cause and effect, such as *because, as a result,* and *therefore.* In the example above, the word *but* suggests that the correct word pair may contain words that are opposite in meaning.
2. Try each of the choices in the sentence. Eliminate those choices that make no sense or those that contradict some other part of the statement. In a sentence with two blanks, the right answer must correctly fill *both* blanks. A wrong answer choice often includes one correct and one incorrect word.
3. After choosing an answer, reread the entire sentence to make sure that it makes sense. Be sure that you have not ignored an answer that would create a more logical sentence than your choice.

Exercise Write the letter of the word or words that best completes the sentence.

____ 1. The peacock spread its tail feathers, showing its __?__ colors to the __?__ crowd of onlookers.
(A) dull ... bored (B) vivid ... threatening
(C) disappointing ... pleased (D) brilliant ... delighted
(E) dim ... thrilled

____ 2. No one noticed the shy, __?__ man standing at the back of the room.
(A) friendly (B) quiet (C) violent (D) embarrassing
(E) noisy

____ 3. When playing basketball, she combines the __?__ of a ballerina, the __?__ of a prizefighter, and the speed of a sprinter.
(A) beauty ... popularity (B) strength ... stupidity
(C) charm ... agony (D) admiration ... dislike
(E) grace ... toughness

____ 4. The magician's clever and amusing act __?__ the children, who sat in their chairs as if spellbound.
(A) fascinated (B) annoyed (C) bored (D) scared
(E) tempted

____ 5. Though the parents objected to the __?__ of the music, they were pleased to see the students __?__ themselves.
(A) lyrics ... hurting (B) loudness ... enjoying
(C) rhythm ... challenging (D) sound ... defending
(E) message ... annoying

____ 6. The hauntingly __?__ cry of the loon filled the sky with sad music.
(A) ugly (B) silent (C) beautiful (D) forgettable
(E) joyful

____ 7. Though Elyssa __?__ after the accident, she still felt __?__ several weeks later.
(A) laughed ... cheerful (B) moaned ... sad
(C) cried ... tired (D) recovered ... pain (E) slept ... sick

____ 8. The Civil War was indeed __?__; it took more American lives than any other war.
(A) interesting (B) tragic (C) dull (D) avoidable
(E) exciting

____ 9. In ancient times, Sumerian men wore __?__ skirts, __?__ the men of Crete, who wore very short skirts.
(A) lengthy ... despite (B) beautiful ... fighting
(C) long ... unlike (D) short ... criticizing
(E) woolen ... mocking

____ 10. The audience __?__ wildly when the two popular heroes escaped from danger.
(A) cheered (B) moved (C) hissed (D) jeered
(E) laughed

Number correct ______ (total 10)

Number correct in unit ______ (total 30)

Part D **General Strategies**

No matter what type of question you are answering, certain strategies can be applied to any part of a standardized test. Keep the following guidelines in mind. They can help you increase your chance of success. Remember, too, that a good mental attitude, plenty of rest the night before a test, and the ability to relax will further improve your test performance.

Basic Strategies for Taking Standardized Tests

1. **Read and listen to directions carefully.** This may seem obvious, but many students do poorly on tests because they misunderstand the directions or fail to read each item completely. For each question, read all of the choices before choosing an answer.
2. **Budget your time carefully.** Most standardized tests are timed, so it is important that you not spend too much time on any single item.
3. **Complete the test items you know first.** Skip items that you do not know the answer for, but mark them so that you can return to them later. After you have answered the items that you know, go back and tackle the more difficult items.
4. **Mark the answer sheet carefully and correctly.** Most standardized tests make use of computerized answer sheets. Students are required to fill in a circle corresponding to the correct answer in the test booklet, as follows:

   10. (A) (B) (C) (D) (E)

   When using such computerized answer sheets, follow these guidelines:
   a. Always neatly fill in the circle for the correct answer.
   b. Periodically check your numbering on the answer sheet, especially if you skip an item. Make sure your answer matches the number of the test item.
   c. Never make notes or stray marks on the answer sheet. These could be misread as wrong answers by the scoring machine. Instead, write on the test booklet itself or on scratch paper, whichever is indicated in the directions.
5. **Make guesses only if you can eliminate some of the answer choices.** Random guessing is unlikely to improve your score. In fact, on some standardized tests, points are subtracted for incorrect answers. In such cases it is a better idea to leave an item blank rather than to guess wildly. However, if you can eliminate one or more of the choices, then your chance of guessing the correct answer is increased.

UNIT 9

Part A Target Words and Their Meanings

1. calculate (kal′ kyə lāt′) v.
2. classify (klas′ ə fī′) v.
3. collapse (kə laps′) v., n.
4. concentrate (kän′ sən trāt′) v., n.
5. contract (kən′ trakt′) v., (kän′ trakt′) n.
6. core (kôr) n.
7. create (krē āt′) v.
8. develop (di vel′ əp) v.
9. exceptional (ik sep′ shen əl) adj.
10. expand (ik spand′) v.
11. explore (ik splôr′) v.
12. extreme (ik strem′) adj., n.
13. gravity (grav′ ə tē) n.
14. mercy (mʉr′ sē) n.
15. produce (prə do͞os′) n., (präd′ o͞os,)v.

Inferring Meaning from Context

For each sentence write the letter of the word or phrase that is closest in meaning to the word or words in italics. Use context clues to help you choose the correct answer. (For information about how context helps you understand vocabulary, see pages 1–6.)

____ 1. Lupita could not *calculate* the cost of the art supplies in her head. She needed paper and pencil to add so many numbers.
a. increase b. remember c. profit from d. figure

____ 2. Canoeists *classify* rivers by how difficult or dangerous the rivers are. A Class I river is easy; a Class VI river is extremely dangerous.
a. grade b. prefer c. assault d. learn

____ 3. The park ranger worried that the old silver mine might *collapse,* injuring visitors.
a. increase b. open c. fall in d. vary

____ 4. "*Concentrate on* your race," my coach said. "Don't worry about the crowd or how cold it is."
a. Focus your attention on b. Struggle in c. Pay no attention to d. Argue about

____ 5. Because of the cold weather, the air inside my bike tires had *contracted.* The tires were almost flat.
a. become compressed b. increased c. frozen d. exploded

____ 6. Scientists believe the earth's *core* is very hot. They've drilled deep into the earth, and the temperature increased as they drilled deeper.

a. climate b. destination c. outer surface d. center

____ 7. Tornadoes sometimes form during powerful thunderstorms. The tornadoes are often more dangerous than the storms that *create* them.

a. dispose of b. cause c. invite d. destroy

____ 8. The coach was given credit for *developing* an average basketball team into a state powerhouse.

a. forcing b. building c. talking d. destroying

____ 9. Anna Edson Taylor was *an exceptional* person. In 1901 she got into a barrel and plunged over Niagara Falls.

a. a fearful b. a courteous c. an unusual d. a cowardly

____ 10. More students attend our middle school each year. Classrooms are already crowded, but there is no money to *expand* the building.

a. close b. increase c. decrease d. open

____ 11. Taro and Matthew set out on their bikes to *explore* the park. Neither had been to the park before, and they were curious about it.

a. assault b. neglect c. investigate d. hide in

____ 12. Some animals, like the penguin, can live in the *extreme* cold of Antarctica. As for me, I don't ever want to go where it's that cold.

a. calm b. severe c. slight d. gentle

____ 13. *Gravity* is weaker on the moon than it is on earth. It would be a great place for basketball because you could jump really high.

a. Chemistry b. Carelessness c. The speed of light
d. The force that makes things fall

____ 14. The judge showed *mercy on* the young offender by lowering the fine.

a. cruelty to b. anger at c. disbelief of d. willingness to forgive

____ 15. The hurricane *produced* huge waves that grew larger as the storm came nearer.

a. made b. classified c. collapsed d. invented

Number correct ______ (total 15)

Part B Target Words in Reading and Literature

You should now have a general idea of the meaning of each target word. Sharpen your understanding by studying how these words are used in the following selection.

The Black Hole

Howard Peet

The crew of the spaceship Silver Chariot *think all is going well on their trip through outer space. Then they are mysteriously shaken and feel themselves being pulled toward a black hole!*

The giant spaceship *Silver Chariot* sped silently toward the star Capella, forty-five light years from Earth and the most brilliant star in the Auriga constellation. The navigator, Georgia Bartlet, glanced at her computer screen. Right on course, she thought. She was pleased with the new computer. It had been **developed** to help her spacecraft **explore** deep space. The computer constantly **calculated** the ship's exact position, speed, and route. The computer was especially useful on this trip to explore the Auriga star system because no ship had ever been this far from Earth before. The voyage of the *Silver Chariot* had already done much to **expand** scientists' knowledge of distant star systems.

Suddenly, the entire crew was thrown to the port[1] side of the ship. There was a sharp, unexpected increase in speed. An **exceptional** force from somewhere pulled the *Silver Chariot* off course. Alex Burness, the engineer, promptly turned the starboard[2] rocket to full blast. This **extreme** measure **produced** no effect. A tremendous pull of **gravity** sucked the ship closer to Capella. Then, in an instant, the brilliance of Capella was gone.

The voice of Captain Torrance came over the ship's loudspeaker. "Secure your seatbelts. It seems that Capella, **classified** as a type K5 star, has just become a black hole, and we are being pulled toward it. A black hole occurs when a dying star begins cooling at its **core.** As the core cools, the star **collapses** and **creates** a great suction, something like a whirlpool. Anything near the collapsing star **contracts** and is pulled into the powerful whirlpool. Everything—from spaceship to planets—disappears into the core of the collapsing star—gone forever. That's the theory anyway.

---

[1] port: the left side of a ship
[2] starboard: the right side of a ship

"Our only hope is to keep cool heads, **concentrate** on doing our jobs, and try to increase our speed until we reach the speed of light. At that point, we may be able to escape the pull and get away from the black hole. Brace yourselves." 30

The *Silver Chariot* shook and trembled. There was an ear-shattering roar. The whirling force was showing no **mercy.** Then, incredibly, the ship was again soaring through space, past familiar stars. With the force of a slingshot, it had been flung back from where it came.

The ship sped faster than the speed of light toward what appeared to 35 be Earth—an Earth, however, that seemed many times larger than it should have been. The *Silver Chariot* hurtled uncontrollably to the planet's surface. There was a series of crashes, a breaking of glass, a tumbling over what seemed like bushes, and finally, a thud.

The crew regained their senses and stared out the ship's portals into a 40 vast powder-blue field. The ship's computer soon had the "field" identified—dense rows of giant strands of woven wool. In the distance, at the far edges of this landscape, huge chairs and tables sat like mountains. The computer supplied more information, the ship's present location: a carpeted room in a home near San Diego, California. With horror, 45 Captain Torrance now realized the effect of the blackhole's force on the spaceship. Ship and crew had been shrunk to the size of a matchbox.

Several minutes later, the entire crew heard a giant call, "Johnny, time for your bath. Get your bath toys."

Among the toys that the Earth child grabbed was a tiny metal spaceship. 50

Refining Your Understanding

For each of the following items, consider how the target word is used in the passage. Write the letter of the word or phrase that best completes the sentence.

____ 1. Another example of the "pull of *gravity*" (line 15) would be a. an apple falling from a tree b. a rainbow c. an exploding star.

____ 2. The best way to *classify* (line 19) this reading selection is to describe it as a. nonfiction b. science fiction c. a play.

____ 3. "Anything near the collapsing star *contracts* (line 23)," means that the star causes things to a. expand b. get smaller c. go forward in time.

____ 4. When the captain asks crew members to *concentrate* on their jobs (line 27), he expects them to a. work a great deal faster b. worry about their situation c. think only about their assigned work.

____ 5. A good example of *mercy* (line 32) would be a person a. punishing a child by spanking b. walking to the bus station in the rain c. throwing a fish back in the water after catching it.

Number correct ______ (total 5)

Part C Ways to Make New Words Your Own

By now you are familiar with the target words and their meanings. This section presents activities that will help you make the words part of your permanent vocabulary.

Using Language and Thinking Skills

Understanding Multiple Meanings Each box in this exercise contains a boldfaced word with its definitions. Read the definitions and then the sentences that use the word. Write the letter of the definition that applies to each sentence.

contract
a. an agreement (n.)
b. to draw together; to become smaller; to shrink (v.)
c. to get or acquire (v.)

____ 1. According to the sales *contract,* the house will belong to Robin after January 1.

____ 2. Looking in the microscope, Sarah watched the organisms move toward one spot. In a matter of seconds, they would *contract* into a single mass.

____ 3. Under the workers' new *contract* with the owners, Saturdays and Sundays will always be considered nonworking days.

____ 4. When objects cool, they *contract;* as they become warmer, they expand.

____ 5. Since Jeremy started having a flu shot at the start of each winter, he has never *contracted* the flu.

concentrate
a. to bring together in one place (v.)
b. to give careful attention to (v.)
c. a substance that is especially strong, not weakened (n.)

____ 6. Jeff *concentrated* on reading the directions before he started assembling the model airplane.

____ 7. Officer Vorucci *concentrated* her police patrols in the area of the criminals' hide-out.

____ 8. Most of the population of Canada is *concentrated* within several hundred miles of the Canadian-United States border.

____ 9. The orange juice was a *concentrate,* so Lee added water to it before drinking it.

____ 10. It was so noisy in the lunchroom that Andrew could not *concentrate* on his book.

Number correct ________ (total 10)

Word's Worth: calculate

Can you imagine what it would be like if you had to use pebbles to solve your math problems? That is exactly how people performed calculations centuries ago, before the invention of the abacus. As a result, the *pebble* became associated with mathematics. The Latin word for *pebble* is *calculus,* from which we get the word *calculate* and other related words. Today's *calculators* are far superior to pebbles. With the aid of computer chips, calculators can solve complex equations almost instantly.

Practicing for Standardized Tests

Synonyms Write the letter of the word that is closest in meaning to the capitalized word.

____ 1. CORE: (A) conference (B) outside (C) reason (D) center (E) society

____ 2. CREATE: (A) make (B) undo (C) transfer (D) package (E) give

____ 3. PRODUCE: (A) manufacture (B) restore (C) dispose (D) separate (E) consume

____ 4. MERCY: (A) anger (B) messiness (C) knowledge (D) illness (E) kindness

____ 5. DEVELOP: (A) destroy (B) commit (C) grow (D) express (E) understand

Number correct ______ (total 5)

Analogies Determine the relationship between the pair of capitalized words. Then decide which other word pair expresses a similar relationship. Write the letter of this word pair.

____ 1. EXPLORE : EXPLORATION : : (A) concentrate : concentration (B) pull : trigger (C) teach : teacher (D) bake : kitchen (E) study : history

____ 2. GRAVITY : WEIGHT : : (A) fire : heat (B) path : trail (C) luxury : necessity (D) salt : pepper (E) laughter : weeping

____ 3. COLLAPSE : EXPAND : : (A) understand : know (B) shout : yell (C) forget : remember (D) make : assemble (E) stop : finish

____ 4. EXCEPTIONAL : UNUSUAL : : (A) gentle : tender (B) harmless : hurtful (C) broken : restored (D) bad : good (E) difficult : easy

____ 5. PRODUCE : DESTROY : : (A) trick : fool (B) hit : miss (C) start : begin (D) whittle : carve (E) talk : discuss

Number correct ______ (total 5)

Spelling and Wordplay

Word Maze Find and circle each target word in this maze.

C O L L A P S E L Q U F A G
O L E X C E P T I O N A L R
N M A G N E T A C V X G D A
C D C S U L P R O D U C E V
E K B O S X M A N O M R V I
N P E Y R I U L T W S E E T
T C M Q U E F V R N Q A L Y
R E E R E W Q I A F C T O T
A X R F X K X M C R H E P I
T P C V P P Y R T A J G H O
E L Y C A L C U L A T E Y N
J O A K N J Z A V E O I H A
A R L A D P E F G O R S O L
C E I N Z E X T R E M E B N

calculate
classification
collapse
concentrate
contract
core
create
develop
exceptional
expand
explore
extreme
gravity
mercy
produce

Part D **Related Words**

The words below are closely related to the target words. Use your knowledge of the target words and of word parts to determine the meanings of these words. (For information about word parts analysis, see pages 7–13.) Use your dictionary if necessary.

1. classic (klas′ ik) adj.
2. concentration (kän′ sən trā′ shən) n.
3. decrease (di krēs′) v., (dē′ krēs) n.
4. design (di zīn′) v., n.
5. exception (eg sep′ shən) n.
6. exit (ik′ zit, ek′ sit) n., v.
7. exploration (eks′ plə rā′ shən) n.
8. exterior (ik stîr′ ē ər) n., adj.
9. extinguish (ik stiŋ′ gwish) v.
10. progress (präg′ res′) n., (prə gres′) v.

Understanding Related Words

Sentence Completion Write the related word from the list on page 117 that best completes the meaning of the sentence. Do not use a related word more than once.

_______________ 1. "If we do not _?_ spending immediately," the mayor said, "this city will be broke within a week."

_______________ 2. The United States took a big leap forward in the _?_ of space when Neil Armstrong took the first step on the moon.

_______________ 3. Rafael and Bill made rapid _?_ down the river. The swift current helped move them along quickly.

_______________ 4. The house's wooden _?_ is in bad need of fresh paint. Many years of rain, snow, and sun have caused the old paint to crack and peel.

_______________ 5. Shakespeare's *King Lear* is a _?_ play. It is one of the most famous plays ever written.

_______________ 6. People who leave early should use the _?_ at the rear of the theater.

_______________ 7. Mark's _?_ was broken by the loud noise from the back of the classroom, and he had a difficult time getting his thoughts back on his exam.

_______________ 8. Tickets cost $5 each for all regular-season baseball games. The only _?_ is the last game, when tickets are half price.

_______________ 9. When you leave camp, _?_ your campfire completely. If you don't, it could start up again and cause a forest fire.

_______________ 10. Sachi is trying to _?_ a better tree house. She thinks there is a way to make one big enough for at least five people.

Number correct ______ (total 10)

Turn to **The Prefix *ex-*** on page 215 of the **Spelling Handbook.** Read the rule and complete the exercises provided.

Analyzing Word Parts

The Prefix *ex-* A common prefix, *ex-* usually means "out" or "out of." For example, the target word *explore* comes from a Latin word meaning "to search *out.*" The related word *exit* means "to go *out.*" Use a dictionary to learn the meanings of the other *ex-* words in the list below. Then write the word from the list that best completes the meaning of each sentence.

exaggerate   examine   excess   exploit   extraordinary

_______________ 1. Uncle Raymond tells many stories about his adventures. My favorite one is his __?__ in East Africa in which he helped capture ivory traders.

_______________ 2. Hideo wanted to __?__ the old steam engine more closely to see how it worked.

_______________ 3. "Don't __?__," Ben said. "Tell me what really happened."

_______________ 4. Michael Jordan is a magician on a basketball court. Some of his fakes and jumps are truly __?__.

_______________ 5. The scoutmaster warned his troops about packing __?__ gear. He said the scouts should take only things they really needed.

Number correct ______ (total 5)

The Latin Prefix *pro-* The prefix *pro-* is found in many English words. It comes from the Latin word meaning "forward." The target word *produce* comes from the Latin words *pro* and *ducere* ("to lead.") *Produce* literally means "to lead forward." The related word *progress* also includes the Latin word *pro. Progress* means "to go forward."

Match each of the following *pro* words with its definition. Write the word in the blank next to the correct definition. Use your dictionary if necessary.

profound   prolong   propel   protest   provoke

_______________ 1. to make angry

_______________ 2. to push; to make to go forward

_______________ 3. to cause to last longer

_______________ 4. to speak out against

_______________ 5. showing great thought; deeply felt

Number correct ______ (total 5)

Number correct in unit ______ (total 60)

The Last Word

Writing

Imagine that you are an astronaut *exploring* a distant planet. This strange world is filled with odd plants and animals. The *gravity* on the planet is only one-tenth that of the earth. Write a report to your home base describing your experiences and observations on this planet.

Speaking

If you were an artist and your community offered to pay you to *create* a work of art to represent your town, what would you make? Consider these questions: What makes your community different from other communities? What are the people in your town proud of? What is the town's history? What is the town's "personality"?

Write a summary of your planned artwork and read it to your class.

Group Discussion

Often some of the biggest arguments occur when an organization wants to *develop* a community's land in some way. The plan might call for building a new airport, a parking lot, or an apartment complex. Whatever the development is, some people will argue that it would hurt the community, while others will argue just as strongly that it is just what people need. In a group of four students, role play a discussion of a new development. Discuss the advantages and disadvantages of the development. Have two students argue for the development and two students argue against.

UNIT 10

Part A Target Words and Their Meanings

1. abandon (ə ban′ dən) v., n.
2. combat (käm′ bat) n., adj.
   (kəm bat′) v.
3. companion (kəm pan′ yən) n.
4. conscious (kän′ shəs) adj.
5. exhaust (ig zôst′) v., n.
6. experience (ik spîr′ ē əns) n., v.
7. furious (fyoor′ ē əs) adj.
8. interrupt (in′ tə rupt′) v.
9. persuade (pər swād′) v.
10. predict (pri dikt′) v.
11. progress (präg′ res) n. (prə gres′) v.
12. pursue (pər sōō′, -syōō′) v.
13. remarkable (ri märk′ ə b′l) adj.
14. site (sīt) n., v.
15. vicious (vish′ əs) adj.

Inferring Meaning from Context

For each sentence write the letter of the word or phrase that is closest in meaning to the word or words in italics. Use context clues to help you choose the correct answer. (For information about how context helps you understand vocabulary, see pages 1–6.)

____ 1. During the Dust Bowl period of the 1930's, many farmers on the Great Plains could not make a living, so they *abandoned* their farms and moved away.

a. possessed b. worked harder on c. stayed on d. left

____ 2. When we heard about the cease-fire and the signing of the peace treaty, we knew that the *combat* had finally ended.

a. fighting b. calmness c. party d. celebration

____ 3. I think Tomas should take *a companion* on the climb up the mountain, but he insists on going alone.

a. a detour b. a friend c. an easy route d. some hiking gear

____ 4. Li was *conscious* when her tonsils were removed. The medicine the surgeon gave Li prevented her from feeling pain, but it did not put her to sleep.

a. unaware b. courteous c. awake d. neglected

____ 5. The 26-mile marathon *exhausted* Barbara. When it was over, she did not have the energy to do anything but sleep.

a. wore out b. inspired c. restored d. angered

____ 6. Tony's first *experience* flying in a small plane was not pleasant. During the flight, he became sick to his stomach.

a. hazard b. collision c. fortune d. time

____ 7. The driver that Andrew cut off looked more than irritated. The driver was shaking his fist and appeared to be *furious*.

a. brilliant b. amused c. a little annoyed d. very angry

____ 8. We waited until the end of the lecture to ask questions and make comments, so that we would not *interrupt* the teacher.

a. understand b. cut in on c. assure d. hear

____ 9. Akiko's friends *persuaded* her to wear the gorilla costume. Even though she felt silly in it, she put it on.

a. convinced b. informed c. respected d. preferred

____ 10. Kate *predicted* that we would miss the beginning of the movie. When we got to the theater, the movie had already started. We realized Kate was right.

a. appreciated b. recalled c. forecast d. was not sure

____ 11. Because there was hardly any traffic on the highway, our *progress* home was rapid.

a. destination b. collision with c. struggle d. movement toward

____ 12. The police officers *pursued* the speeding driver until they caught up with him. Even though the driver offered excuses, the officers gave him a ticket.

a. chased b. waited for c. called for d. collided with

____ 13. Can you imagine a cannon shooting a person into the air? Some people think the human cannonball is the most *remarkable* circus event.

a. hopeless b. extraordinary c. ordinary d. boring

____ 14. The Jordans cannot decide on *a site* for their new home. Mrs. Jordan likes a plot of land in the country, but Mr. Jordan prefers a city location.

a. a map b. a picture c. a place d. the building materials

____ 15. If that lioness thinks you are threatening her cub, she may become *vicious* and come after you.

a. human b. very pleasant c. very aggressive d. somewhat withdrawn

Number correct ______ (total 15)

Part B **Target Words in Reading and Literature**

You should now have a general idea of the meaning of each target word. Sharpen your understanding by studying how these words are used in the following selection.

Hugh Glass and the Grizzly

James Coomber

This is a true story of a man's struggle to survive. In this account, we come to respect the fearsome nature of a grizzly bear—and the courage of a fur trapper attacked by the bear.

The grizzly bear is one of the most **vicious** animals of North America. Under the right conditions, it will attack even a powerful bull buffalo. A grizzly may weigh over four hundred pounds and have claws three inches long. Therefore, in serious **combat** with this exceptional creature, a human is likely to be the loser. 5

Hugh Glass's **experience** with a grizzly bear is one of the most memorable mishaps a person has had with an animal. In 1823, Glass was on a beaver-trapping trip in the area that is now Montana. One day at twilight, he and his **companions** pitched their camp at a **site** along a stream. Noticing nothing strange in the immediate vicinity, Glass went down to the 10 quiet stream and knelt to drink the clear, cool water. Suddenly an awful roar made him jump. A huge grizzly rushed toward him from across the stream.

What could he do? He took quick aim with his rifle and shot the bear. But the bear did not die. The wounded creature became **furious** and attacked Glass, nearly killing him. Then the creature **pursued** Glass's 15 companions. Somehow they escaped harm.

For two days after the merciless assault, the trappers made every effort to care for the wounded Hugh Glass, but he didn't improve.

"He'll never make it," one trapper **predicted.**

"We've got a long way to go," his companion reminded him. 20

"In my opinion, staying here can't be any benefit to a man who won't get better anyway," added the first.

The two trappers **persuaded** one another that they should **abandon** Glass. They continued on their way. Glass was left with only two things in his possession—a kettle of water and his wallet. 25

However, Hugh Glass did not die. When he became **conscious,** he realized he was all alone and severely injured. Where could he go? He knew of a trading post, but from his calculations he estimated the post was eighty miles away. He had no horse, and he could not walk.

The seriously injured man set out on his hands and knees for his desti- 30 nation, the distant trading post. He lived on roots and berries. **Progress**

was slow, and the effort that it took to crawl **exhausted** him. He tried not to become discouraged. He crawled for forty days. Finally, a band of Native Americans found Glass and cared for him. They fed him and dressed his wounds. When he became stronger, they took him to the trading post at the mouth of the Little Missouri River. 35

Several months later Glass's former companions were camping along the Missouri River. Suddenly, the clop-clop of horse hooves **interrupted** the quiet evening. Minutes later horse and rider came into view. The rider was the **remarkable** Hugh Glass. 40

Refining Your Understanding

For each of the following items, consider how the target word is used in the passage. Write the letter of the word or phrase that best completes the sentence.

____ 1. Of the following animals, the one you might expect to be *vicious* (line 1) is a. a sparrow b. a rabbit c. a rattlesnake

____ 2. When he *predicted* (line 19) that Glass would "never make it," the trapper was a. telling what he thought would happen b. telling what had already happened c. bothered by the wounds.

____ 3. A good example of the word *abandon* (line 23) would be a. to leave a car on the side of the road b. to help care for a sick friend c. to cook dinner for your family.

____ 4. A quiet evening might be *interrupted* (line 38) by a. a bright star b. rifle fire c. a soft breeze.

____ 5. Hugh Glass was *remarkable* (line 40) because he a. found his companions b. survived serious injuries c. trapped beavers.

Number correct ______ (total 5)

Part C **Ways to Make New Words Your Own**

By now you are familiar with the target words and their meanings. This section presents activities that will help you make the words part of your permanent vocabulary.

Using Language and Thinking Skills

True-False Decide whether each statement is true **(T)** or false **(F)**.

____ 1. By the time you are old, you will have had many *experiences.*

____ 2. Advertisers try to *persuade* us to buy things.

____ 3. Tourists often visit a historical *site.*

____ 4. A gift that you have always wanted will make you *furious.*

____ 5. If you don't want to listen to a salesperson on the telephone, you might *interrupt* the caller.

____ 6. A person in a deep sleep is *conscious.*

____ 7. A hungry snake is likely to *pursue* a mouse.

____ 8. You can usually *predict* how long it will take you to clean the garage.

____ 9. A traveler making *progress* is getting farther and farther from his destination.

____ 10. A puppy is considered a *vicious* animal.

Number correct ______ (total 10)

Understanding Multiple Meanings Each box in this exercise contains a boldfaced word with its definitions. Read the definitions and then the sentences that use the word. Write the letter of the definition that applies to each sentence.

combat
a. a battle or fight (n.)
b. to struggle against or try to get rid of something (v.)

____ 1. The fierce *combat* at Gettysburg left thousands of soldiers dead.

____ 2. Through his scientific research Louis Pasteur *combated* various contagious diseases.

____ 3. In the French and Indian Wars, the French engaged in *combat* against the British.

pursue
a. to follow, chase, or go after in order to catch (v.)
b. to seek or try to attain or achieve (v.)

____ 4. They who *pursue* knowledge will grow in wisdom.

____ 5. I would *pursue* him, but if he sees me coming after him, he'll only run faster.

Number correct ______ (total 5)

Practicing for Standardized Tests

Synonyms Write the letter of the word that is closest in meaning to the capitalized word.

____ 1. ABANDON: (A) stay (B) desert (C) oppose (D) assault (E) request

____ 2. COMPANION: (A) buddy (B) stranger (C) victim (D) explorer (E) navigator

____ 3. CONSCIOUS: (A) dishonest (B) asleep (C) excited (D) unsociable (E) aware

____ 4. EXHAUST: (A) deserve (B) excel (C) fatigue (D) lose (E) restore

____ 5. FURIOUS: (A) enraged (B) intelligent (C) pale (D) thorough (E) sociable

____ 6. PREDICT: (A) declare (B) foretell (C) expect (D) remember (E) pretend

____ 7. PROGRESS: (A) delay (B) excitement (C) fortune (D) advancement (E) action

____ 8. PURSUE: (A) retreat (B) disguise (C) follow (D) fight (E) watch

____ 9. REMARKABLE: (A) common (B) likable (C) sincere (D) extraordinary (E) sour

____ 10. VICIOUS: (A) serious (B) friendly (C) mean (D) private (E) thoughtful

Number correct ______ (total 10)

Spelling and Wordplay

Crossword Puzzle Read the clues and print the correct answer to each in the proper squares.

ACROSS

1. A laugh or exclamation
3. To convince to do or believe
8. A place to build on or use in some other specific way
10. A cardboard container
12. Abbr. Very important person
14. To go on doing something
16. May I have ___ apple?
17. Short for touchdown
18. To chase
20. To tell what you think will happen
24. Not off
26. The call of a dove
28. Abbr. North Carolina
29. I have; you have; she ___
31. Abbr. United States
32. Cubes with dots on their sides used in some games
33. Tired

DOWN

1. Slang for hello
2. He will be home ___ five o'clock.
4. You sit on it.
5. To leave behind
6. A wedding vow: I ___.
7. Something we have done or been through
8. Rescuing
9. Edward's nickname
11. Awake
13. A dog that is not full-grown; short for puppy
14. Automobile
15. Abbr. Italian
19. To consume, take in food
21. Measles cause this on your body.
22. Washington, ___
23. The tape will ____ you $8.
24. A story beginning: ____ upon a time
25. That girl
27. To total numbers
30. Used to split wood

Word's Worth: vicious

You know that *vicious* can be used to describe a charging, angry bear or a roaring lion on the attack. But did you know that *vicious* can also describe an ugly, hateful lie? In this sense, *vicious* means "something mean, intended to cause hurt." The word *vicious* comes from the Latin word *vitium,* meaning a "vice" or "fault." Consequently, *vicious* has also come to be used to describe something that is faulty or inaccurate, such as *vicious* thinking or a *vicious* statement.

Part D **Related Words**

The words below are closely related to the target words. Use your knowledge of the target words and of word parts to determine the meanings of these words. (For information about word parts analysis, see pages 7–13.) Use your dictionary if necessary.

1. bankrupt (baŋk′ rupt′, rəpt) n., adj., v.
2. combatant (käm′ bə tənt, kəm bat′ ’nt) n., adj.
3. companionable (kəm pan′ yən ə b’l) adj.
4. corrupt (kə rupt′) adj., v.
5. disrupt (dis rupt′) v.
6. exhaustion (ig zôs′ chən) n.
7. fury (fyoor′ ē) n.
8. interruption (in′ tə rup′ shən) n.
9. persuasion (pər swā′ zhən) n.
10. prediction (pri dik′ shən) n.
11. proceed (prə sēd′, prō-) v.
12. profess (prə fes′, prō-) v.
13. promote (prə mōt′) v.
14. protect (prə tekt′) v.
15. provide (prə vīd′) v.
16. unconscious (un kän′ shəs) adj.

Understanding Related Words

Sentence Completion Write the word from the list below that best completes the meaning of the sentence.

bankrupt	corrupt	exhaustion	interruption	prediction
combatants	disrupt	fury	persuasion	unconscious

________________ 1. The doctor told Mom that she was suffering from _?_ and that she should take it easy for several weeks.

________________ 2. Never give water to an injured person who is _?_. He might choke because he is unaware of needing to swallow.

________________ 3. On election day, November 2, 1948, many people made a _?_: Thomas Dewey would win the U.S. presidency. But they were wrong. The next morning the election results showed Harry Truman had been elected President.

________________ 4. The _?_ of an injured bear is one thing I hope I never experience!

________________ 5. Josh told Ms. Juarez that he was sorry for the _?_, but he had an urgent message for her from the office.

________________ 6. A successful salesperson must be good at _?_; she must be able to convince people to buy what she is selling.

_______________ 7. The company that Dad works for is __?__. It has no money left and will shut down next week.

_______________ 8. Many people were outraged by the news that the director of that charity is __?__. He has actually been stealing donations!

_______________ 9. Lena turned down the radio so that the music would not __?__ her studying.

_______________ 10. When the war was finally over, __?__ on both sides hoped that their countries would stay at peace for many years to come.

Number correct ______ (total 10)

Analyzing Word Parts

The Prefix *pro-* The prefix *pro-* has several meanings, including "before" *(prologue),* "forward" or "ahead" *(propel),* and "in favor of" *(pro-American).* The target word *progress* comes from the Latin *pro-,* meaning "before," and *gradi,* meaning "to step." The related words *proceed, profess, promote, protect,* and *provide* also contain the *pro-* prefix. Use your dictionary to learn the sources and meanings of these five related words. Then complete the exercise below by writing the related word that best completes the meaning of the sentence.

_______________ 1. In addition to wearing a helmet, what else can you do to __?__ yourself when skateboarding?

_______________ 2. "Please __?__ to the nearest exit," said the flight attendant calmly.

_______________ 3. As the hostess, Carmen will __?__ all the food for the party, but she asked that we bring our favorite dance music.

_______________ 4. In math class, David will often __?__ to know the answer, but I have found that frequently he is wrong.

_______________ 5. Mr. Payton will __?__ Linda to be the head waitress because she is such a hard worker.

Number correct ______ (total 5)

Number correct in unit ______ (total 60)

Turn to **The Letter *c*** on page 228 of the **Spelling Handbook.** Read the rules and complete the exercises provided.

The Last Word

Writing

Think about an interesting or unusual *experience* that you and a *companion* have shared. Where were you? What happened? What details about the experience have stayed with you? Write a few paragraphs describing the experience. Then, if possible, share what you have written with your companion. Does he or she remember the incident in the same way?

Speaking

Imagine that you have been *abandoned* on a deserted island. What five things would you like to have with you? Why is each of these things important? How will you use these things? After you have considered this situation, share your thoughts with your class. How many of your classmates chose the same things?

Group Discussion

How do we know when a particular nation is making *progress?* What are some of the signs of improved conditions? In a group, discuss these questions. List some of the things you think show that a country is advancing.

UNIT 11

Part A Target Words and Their Meanings

1. approximate (ə präk′ sə mit) adj.
   (ə präk′ sə māt′) v.
2. conduct (kən dukt′) v.
   (kän′ dukt′) n.
3. crisis (krī′ sis) n.
4. degree (di grē′) n.
5. erupt (i rupt′) v.
6. faithful (fāth′ fəl) adj.
7. fragment (frag′ mənt) n., v.
8. meaningful (mē′ niŋ fəl) adj.
9. process (präs′ es) n., v., adj.
10. reliable (ri lī′ ə b'l) adj.
11. require (ri kwīr′) v.
12. reservoir (rez′ ər vwär′, -vwôr′) n.
13. resident (rez′ i dənt) n., adj.
14. strategy (strat′ ə jē) n.
15. sufficient (sə fish′ 'nt) adj.

Inferring Meaning from Context

For each sentence write the letter of the word or phrase that is closest in meaning to the word or words in italics. Use context clues to help you choose the correct answer. (For information about how context helps you understand vocabulary, see pages 1–6.)

____ 1. What is the *approximate* number of teachers in your school? In other words, about how many teachers are there?
a. estimated b. smallest c. exact d. enormous

____ 2. Water is *conducted* through underground pipes into your home.
a. interrupted b. held back c. expanded d. carried

____ 3. When the pilot instructed us to position ourselves for a crash landing, we knew we were in the midst of *a crisis.*
a. an explosion b. an opportunity c. an emergency
d. a fortune

____ 4. I'm not surprised that we're sweating and feeling uncomfortable. The weather report just indicated that it's 99 *degrees* outside!
a. units of distance b. units of weight c. units of temperature
d. types of units

____ 5. When the volcano *erupted,* people living nearby left to avoid the lava, ash, and rock shooting from it.
a. died down b. blew open c. rumbled d. stopped moving

____ 6. Guide dogs are very *faithful* animals. They stand by their owners, helping when needed.

a. loyal b. angry c. lazy d. violent

____ 7. Jason hoped he would find a whole arrowhead buried in the ground. Unfortunately, he discovered only a few *fragments,* and he couldn't even tell if they were from the same arrowhead.

a. plants b. shovels c. boulders d. pieces

____ 8. Because Carlo wants to become a teacher, his grandmother's stories about her first pupils and her early teaching methods are especially *meaningful* to him.

a. unrelated b. boring c. important d. useless

____ 9. Do you understand how computers store information? I'd like to learn more about this fascinating *process.*

a. way something is done b. set of rules c. observation
d. group of issues

____ 10. Lawanda is very *reliable.* If she says she will volunteer at the nursing home every Saturday, she will do it.

a. private b. happy c. dependable d. suspicious

____ 11. Mr. Chang does not *require* written reports. We can give oral reports in his class.

a. demand b. investigate c. complete d. dislike

____ 12. Water that we collected during the rainy season will be held in the *reservoir* for use during the dry months.

a. atmosphere b. ocean c. streams d. storage place

____ 13. What city in California has the largest population? My guess would be that Los Angeles has more *residents* than any other city in the state.

a. accidents b. people living in a place c. tourists
d. tall buildings

____ 14. Our debate team won the competition because the members had agreed upon a *strategy.* They decided beforehand exactly how they would approach and handle each topic.

a. slogan b. plan c. contribution d. problem

____ 15. The amusement park charges a fifteen-dollar entrance fee. We'll also need a little extra money for food, so twenty dollars each should be *sufficient.*

a. too much b. illegal c. enough d. unnecessary

Number correct ______ (total 15)

Part B Target Words in Reading and Literature

You should now have a general idea of the meaning of each target word. Sharpen your understanding by studying how these words are used in the following selection.

Putting Geysers to Work for Us

James Coomber

An erupting geyser is exciting to watch. But what might be just as exciting are the contributions geysers could make in helping us solve our energy problems.

"There she blows." That cry sometimes pierces the quiet of Yellowstone National Park in Wyoming. Visitors often travel many miles to see the geysers, especially one popular and very **faithful** geyser—aptly named Old Faithful. About every 65 minutes this geyser gurgles and then shoots water high into the sky. It continues to create this hourly show, without interruption, year after year.

How do geysers work? The **process** begins with steam produced miles underground. The interior of the earth is extremely hot, with an **approximate** temperature of fifteen hundred **degrees**, three miles down. Such a temperature, because it is so high, is **sufficient** to transform water, which seeps down to the interior from the earth's surface, into steam. The steam is then **conducted** up to the surface through naturally formed tunnels. Many underground **reservoirs** of water are located in the vicinity of these tunnels. As the steam rises toward the surface, it forces up some of this stored water.

When the steam-and-water mixture—sometimes along with **fragments** of rock—reaches the surface, it shoots up into the air. Some geysers, like Old Faithful, **erupt** regularly. Most are much less **reliable.** But one prediction is usually true—sooner or later they will erupt. 30

Geysers may provide one solution to the energy **crisis. Residents** of Reykjavik, Iceland, heat their homes and other buildings with hot water produced by geysers and hot springs. Furnaces are not **required** for comfortable living in Reykjavik. 35

To make use of the energy given off by the earth's hot interior, other cities are trying similar **strategies.** The information gained from studying geysers may prove to be extremely **meaningful**, benefiting society by saving both energy and money.

Refining Your Understanding

For each of the following items, consider how the target word is used in the passage. Write the letter of the word or phrase that best completes the sentence.

____ 1. The geyser called Old Faithful can be described as *faithful* (line 6) because it a. is a popular geyser b. erupts regularly c. is located in Yellowstone National Park.

____ 2. If the earth's interior three miles below the surface has an "*approximate* temperature of fifteen hundred *degrees*" (lines 15–17), then the temperature might be a. one hundred degrees b. three hundred degrees c. fifteen hundred and fifty degrees.

____ 3. Examples of *reservoirs* (line 24) would include a. rainstorms b. blizzards c. lakes.

____ 4. Geysers that are "less *reliable*" (line 30) would a. not erupt at predicted times b. erupt less often than Old Faithful c. erupt every few minutes.

____ 5. A good example of a *crisis* (line 32) would be a. having a closet full of clothes b. running out of food and water c. getting a better job.

Number correct ______ (total 5)

Part C **Ways to Make New Words Your Own**

By now you are familiar with the target words and their meanings. This section presents activities that will help you make the words part of your permanent vocabulary.

Using Language and Thinking Skills

True-False Decide whether each statement is true **(T)** or false **(F)**.

____ 1. Many health problems result from getting *sufficient* amounts of nutrients.

____ 2. One thing that is quite *reliable* is the sun; in most parts of the world, it rises every morning and sets every evening.

____ 3. A *resident* of Detroit, Michigan, could live in Pennsylvania.

____ 4. Most people don't care about things that are *meaningful* to them.

____ 5. If a driver's license is *required* by law, then you must not drive a car without one.

____ 6. Careful studying is a good *strategy* for doing well on exams.

____ 7. You can make soup in a *fragment* of a pot.

____ 8. Buses are used to *conduct* passengers from one place to another.

____ 9. A happy celebration is an example of a *crisis*.

____ 10. It is best to set an alarm clock to an *approximate* time.

Number correct ______ (total 10)

Practicing for Standardized Tests

Analogies Determine the relationship between the pair of capitalized words. Then decide which other word pair expresses a similar relationship. Write the letter of this word pair.

____ 1. DEGREE : TEMPERATURE :: (A) problem : solution
(B) navigator : ship (C) site : location (D) mile : distance
(E) basement : attic

____ 2. SUFFICIENT : ENOUGH :: (A) courteous : rude
(B) extreme : slight (C) brilliant : dull (D) happy : happiest
(E) remarkable : extraordinary

____ 3. MEANINGFUL : MEANINGLESS :: (A) conscious : asleep
(B) prompt : immediate (C) funny : hilarious (D) fast : rapid
(E) angry : furious

____ 4. RESERVOIR : WATER :: (A) farmer : tractor (B) storm : damage (C) pool : concrete (D) barrel : oil (E) stroll : race

____ 5. WHOLE : FRAGMENT :: (A) country : nation (B) fraction : piece (C) cake : pie (D) one : one-tenth (E) race : victory

Number correct ______ (total 5)

Word's Worth: residence

What do you do at home, at your *residence?* Our word *residence* comes from the Latin word *residere.* Its prefix *re-* means "back," and the word *sedere* means "to sit." To the people of ancient Rome, a *residence* was a place where you "sat back" and took it easy. *Residence* means the same thing today, although at times our homes may be very busy places where we seem to have too little time to "sit back."

Spelling and Wordplay

Word Maze Find and circle each target word in this maze.

```
A E K Q C R I S I S F B M
H P R O C E S S R U L F E
P O P U L A R T V F R A A
D E G R E E R F N F E I N
S R D U O B E R U I S T I
T E C S L X L A W C I H N
R Q O Y H D I G C I D F G
A U N K P L A M J E E U F
T I D G X Q B E A N N L U
E R U P T A L N Z T T C L
G E C J O X E T M G E I X
Y A T R E S E R V O I R Z
```

approximate
conduct
crisis
degree
erupt
faithful
fragment
meaningful
process
reliable
require
reservoir
resident
strategy
sufficient

Part D Related Words

The words below are closely related to the target words. Use your knowledge of the target words and of word parts to help you determine the meanings of these words. (For information about word parts analysis, see pages 7–13.) Use your dictionary if necessary.

1. conductor (kən duk′ tər) n.
2. confine (kən fīn′) v. (kän′ fīn′) n.
3. eruption (i rup′ shən) n.
4. faith (fāth) n.
5. painful (pān′ fəl) adj.
6. reliability (ri lī′ ə bil′ ə tē) n.
7. requirement (ri kwīr′ mənt) n.
8. reside (ri zīd′) v.
9. residence (rez′ i dəns) n.
10. strategic (strə tē′ jik) adj.
11. suffice (sə fīs′, -fīz′) v.
12. thankful (thaŋk′ fəl) adj.

Understanding Related Words

Finding Examples Write the letter of the situation that best shows the meaning of the boldfaced word.

____ 1. **conductor**
   a. The orchestra leader signaled the musicians to get ready to play.
   b. The head mechanic at the garage repairs foreign cars.
   c. My aunt from Baltimore visited us for two weeks.

____ 2. **confine**
   a. Everyone giggled at Donna's silly joke.
   b. Mark read the entire book in one hour.
   c. Charles keeps his dog in a fenced yard.

____ 3. **painful**
   a. Martha said the wasp sting hurt a lot.
   b. Tom felt great after his nap in the hammock.
   c. Pauli didn't feel a thing when the splinter was removed.

____ 4. **thankful**
   a. Nobody on the team could agree on a practice time.
   b. All the players on the squad knew Terry had done his best, and they told him how much they appreciated it.
   c. The loss was difficult for us to accept.

____ 5. **residence**
   a. My mother shops at the market on First Avenue.
   b. Jeremy lives in an apartment on the third floor of that building.
   c. Peter works out at a gym a few blocks from here.

____ 6. **faith**

a. My grandfather trusts me to drive his car.
b. The landscape in the Southwest is beautiful.
c. The detective investigated the complaint.

____ 7. **eruption**

a. When I walked by, the tower that my sister was building collapsed.
b. When the nickel sank to the bottom of the pool, we dove in to retrieve it.
c. Just as Tina got the film loaded into her camera, the geyser began to spew water.

____ 8. **strategic**

a. Although she wasn't looking for it, Yoko found her missing watch.
b. Linda has figured out the most effective way to take a test.
c. Jonathon accidentally dropped the platter of food.

____ 9. **requirement**

a. You can take that Spanish class, even though you have no experience with foreign languages.
b. You must have a signed permission slip to go on the field trip.
c. I know I have a perfectly good coat, but I'd love to buy a new one.

____ 10. **suffice**

a. Stay inside so you don't get drenched.
b. We couldn't finish the test because we ran out of time.
c. Thirty people have enrolled in the class, so thirty chairs will be enough.

Number correct ______ (total 10)

Analyzing Word Parts

The Suffix *-ful* The suffix *-ful* means "full of" or "likely to." In this unit, the target words *faithful* and *meaningful* and the related words *painful* and *thankful* contain this suffix.

The suffix *-ful* can be added to many English words. In most cases, when you add *-ful* to a base word, you form an adjective.

Add *-ful* to the words in italics listed below. (Notice that the *-ful* ending has only one *l*.) Then use the new word you have created in a sentence.

1. full of *wonder* =

____

2. likely to *help* =

____

3. full of *beauty* =

____

4. likely to *forget* =

____

5. full of *joy* =

____

Number correct ______ (total 5)

The Latin Root *duct* The root *duct* means "lead." Both the target word *conduct* and the related word *conductor* contain this root. *Conduct* comes from the Latin word *conducere,* which is made up of *con-,* meaning "together," and *ducere,* meaning "to lead."

All the words listed below also contain the *duct* root. Use your dictionary to learn the part of speech, derivation, and meaning(s) of each word. Then write the word from the list that best completes the meaning of each sentence.

abduct deduct induct introduction product

______________ 1. Should we _?_ Carol as president of the Astronomy Club?

______________ 2. That game is the most popular _?_ that our store sells.

______________ 3. The kidnappers were caught before they could _?_ the child.

______________ 4. No one made a(n) _?_, so I have no idea who that person is.

______________ 5. Adam just gave you five dollars, so you should _?_ that from what he still owes you.

Number correct ______ (total 5)

Number correct in unit ______ (total 55)

Turn to **The Letter *g*** on page 228 in the **Spelling Handbook.** Read the rules and complete the exercises provided.

The Last Word

Writing

Answer each of the following questions in one sentence. Use the italicized words in your sentences.

1. What animal is the most *faithful* pet? Why?

   Sample starter: The most *faithful* pet is . . .

2. What was the cause of a *crisis* you have heard or read about?

3. If you were going to *conduct* some foreign students on a tour of your town, what would you show them first?

4. What would you do with a *fragment* of a meteorite if you found one?

5. What is the most *meaningful* book, story, or article you have ever read? What made it so *meaningful?*

6. Give an example of a *process* you could teach to others.

7. How do others know that you are a *reliable* person?

8. What are you *required* to do in your social studies class?

9. Of what community are you a *resident?*

10. How much sleep at night do you believe is a *sufficient* amount?

Group Discussion

What are some *strategies* for making and keeping friends? Are there some things you can do or ways you can behave toward people that will help you find and hold on to friends? In a group, discuss these questions. See if your group can come up with at least five general *strategies* for developing successful friendships.

UNIT 12: Review of Units 9–11

Part A Review Word List

Unit 9 Target Words

1. calculate
2. classify
3. collapse
4. concentrate
5. contract
6. core
7. create
8. develop
9. exceptional
10. expand
11. explore
12. extreme
13. gravity
14. mercy
15. produce

Unit 9 Related Words

1. classic
2. concentration
3. decrease
4. design
5. exception
6. exit
7. exploration
8. exterior
9. extinguish
10. progress

Unit 10 Target Words

1. abandon
2. combat
3. companion
4. conscious
5. exhaust
6. experience
7. furious
8. interrupt
9. persuade
10. predict
11. progress
12. pursue
13. remarkable
14. site
15. vicious

Unit 10 Related Words

1. bankrupt
2. combatant
3. companionable
4. corrupt
5. disrupt
6. exhaustion
7. fury
8. interruption
9. persuasion
10. prediction
11. proceed
12. profess
13. promote
14. protect
15. provide
16. unconscious

Unit 11 Target Words

1. approximate
2. conduct
3. crisis
4. degree
5. erupt
6. faithful
7. fragment
8. meaningful
9. process
10. reliable
11. require
12. reservoir
13. resident
14. strategy
15. sufficient

Unit 11 Related Words

1. conductor
2. confine
3. eruption
4. faith
5. painful
6. reliability
7. requirement
8. reside
9. residence
10. strategic
11. suffice
12. thankful

Inferring Meaning from Context

For each sentence write the letter of the word or phrase that is closest in meaning to the word or words in italics.

____ 1. Mrs. Cruz's dog, Charlie, was her only *companion* during her drive across the country.

a. fear b. friend c. problem d. comfort

____ 2. "No matter who is talking," Andrew said, "Bob always tries to *interrupt.*"

a. understand b. disagree c. cut in d. leave

____ 3. Most electrical wire is made of copper because copper *conducts* electricity very well.

a. stops b. carries c. makes d. contains

____ 4. Lisa's *strategy* was to wait until the sun came up and then explore the haunted house room by room.

a. plan b. wish c. solution d. mistake

____ 5. Lucinda always walked the long way to school because she didn't want to go near the house with the *vicious* dog.

a. friendly b. neglected c. huge d. very mean

____ 6. During the *crisis* in the Middle East, the President acted quickly and decisively.

a. peace conference b. meeting c. emergency d. celebration

____ 7. When the Glen Canyon dam was built, it created a huge *reservoir* where a beautiful canyon had been.

a. desert b. forest c. industry d. lake

____ 8. The directions for hooking up the VCR looked simple enough, but the *process* turned into a nightmare.

a. list of parts b. way of doing something c. effort d. issue

____ 9. The earth's *gravity* holds the moon in a steady orbit around the earth.

a. force that pulls objects toward each other b. force that produces light c. radio waves d. dense cloud cover

____ 10. A physical examination is *required for* students wishing to play on any school sports team.

a. useful for b. planned for c. demanded of d. optional for

Number correct ______ (total 10)

Using Review Words in Context

Using context clues, determine which word from the list below best completes each sentence in the story. Write the word in the blank. Each word will be used only once.

abandoned	combat	extreme	mercy	residents
approximate	developed	furious	reliable	site
collapsed	experiences	meaningful	remarkable	strategy

Lincoln's Totem

A totem is an animal or other natural object that has been chosen as a symbol for a family or group. Totems are often carved and painted on wooden posts called totem poles. These poles have been important and ______________ to the Native Americans of southeastern Alaska. Although totem poles do not give enough information about the details of these peoples' ______________ to provide a ______________ history, they do give an ______________ idea of their ways of life.

Before Alaska was purchased from Russia by the United States, Native Americans in the region belonged to one of two main groups. One group used the wolf or the eagle as its sign. The other group used the raven. Those people who took the wolf as their symbol were traders and warriors. During wars, the Wolves fought in a wild and ______________ manner. The Ravens, on the other hand, were fishers and woodcarvers. They did not want war but were often forced into ______________ with the Wolves, who usually won. The defeated Ravens could expect little in the way of kindness from the Wolves. Instead of showing ______________ to their enemies, the Wolves often made them slaves.

When the United States bought Alaska just after the American Civil War, U.S. soldiers set up a fort known as Fort Tongass. Shortly afterward, one group of Ravens, known as the Ganaxadi, ______________ their homes in order to move near the fort. By that time, slavery was against the law in the United States. The Ganaxadi believed that because they were ______________ of this new U.S. territory, the soldiers would keep them from being used as slaves by the Wolves. Indeed, the ______________ of moving near Fort Tongass turned out to be a clever idea, for the Wolves did not attack the Ganaxadi while they stayed near the fort.

To show the Ganaxadi's thankfulness, their leader, Chief Ebbetts, had an unusual totem pole carved. This ________________ pole had a raven at the bottom and a likeness of Abraham Lincoln at the top. The pole was very tall, with a height of about fifty feet.

As the nearby village of Ketchikan grew and ________________ into a city, the Ganaxadi people left their homes and the Lincoln totem pole for work in the city. The abandoned totem pole began to rot due to the ________________ rainfall and generally wet weather of the region. However, before the pole ________________ and fell, the figure of Lincoln was sawed off. It was carried away from the ________________ where it had stood for so many years. Now it can be seen in a glass case in a museum in Juneau, Alaska, where it serves as a silent reminder of freedom for all.

Number correct ______ (total 15)

Part B **Review Word Reinforcement**

Using Language and Thinking Skills

Sentence Completion Write the word from the list below that best completes the meaning of the sentence.

calculated	contract	explore	remarkable	site
companion	degrees	pursue	resident	vicious

________________ 1. It has been _?_ that Alaska's area of 586,400 square miles is one-fifth the size of the rest of the United States.

________________ 2. To someone from Florida, it seems _?_ that, in Minnesota, school is not called off when there are six inches of fresh snow on the ground.

________________ 3. People scurried home down the snowy and wind-whipped streets as the temperature fell to twelve _?_ below zero.

________________ 4. When wounded, the polar bear can be one of the most dangerous and _?_ animals on earth.

________________ 5. Most things _?_ as they get colder, but water does the opposite, which is why pipes sometimes burst in freezing weather.

________________ 6. On any hike into the wilderness, it's always best to go with a _?_ so you're not alone if you get hurt.

_______________ 7. Alaska is the _?_ of North America's highest mountain, Mt. McKinley.

_______________ 8. Wolves often _?_ moose for many miles across rugged, snow-covered land.

_______________ 9. Many people take cruise ships to Alaska so they can _?_ the area along its coast.

_______________ 10. The author Jack London wrote about Canada's Yukon Territory, where he was a _?_ for many years.

Number correct ______ (total 10)

Finding the Unrelated Word Write the letter of the word that is not related in meaning to the other words in the set.

____ 1. a. calculate b. multiply c. classify d. estimate

____ 2. a. expand b. decrease c. contract d. shrink

____ 3. a. ordinary b. common c. remarkable d. normal

____ 4. a. accept b. make c. produce d. provide

____ 5. a. faithful b. loyal c. trustworthy d. false

____ 6. a. sufficient b. scarce c. enough d. plenty

____ 7. a. investigate b. explore c. search d. abandon

____ 8. a. escape b. pursue c. chase d. follow

____ 9. a. reliable b. dishonest c. dependable d. trustworthy

____ 10. a. piece b. part c. whole d. fragment

Number correct ______ (total 10)

Practicing for Standardized Tests

Analogies Determine the relationship between the pair of capitalized words. Then decide which other word pair expresses a similar relationship. Write the letter of this word pair.

____ 1. CORE : SURFACE :: (A) night : twilight (B) yolk : shell (C) page : paper (D) anger : hate (E) robin : bird

____ 2. FRAGMENT : PIECE :: (A) segment : whole (B) speech : speaker (C) destiny : future (D) opponent : friend (E) twilight : daybreak

____ 3. RESIDENT : NEIGHBORHOOD :: (A) ocean : desert (B) tree : forest (C) ant : insect (D) reservoir : lake (E) rain : flood

____ 4. STRATEGY : PLAN :: (A) baseball : score (B) crime : criminal (C) paddle : boat (D) doctor : hospital (E) companion : partner

____ 5. COMBAT : SOLDIER (A) peace : war (B) love : hate (C) game : player (D) information : newspaper (E) battle : war

Number correct ______ (total 5)

Antonyms Write the letter of the word that is most nearly *opposite* in meaning to the capitalized word.

____ 1. CONSCIOUS: (A) awake (B) effective (C) active (D) asleep (E) reliable

____ 2. FURIOUS: (A) angered (B) wild (C) calm (D) negative (E) fierce

____ 3. MERCY: (A) judgment (B) benefit (C) pity (D) cruelty (E) sympathy

____ 4. PERSUADE: (A) discourage (B) convince (C) deceive (D) tempt (E) realize

____ 5. RELIABLE: (A) dependable (B) proven (C) faithful (D) active (E) undependable

Number correct ______ (total 5)

Synonyms Write the letter of the word that is closest in meaning to the capitalized word.

____ 1. ERUPT: (A) explode (B) invade (C) extinguish (D) fall (E) collide

____ 2. EXHAUSTED: (A) devoured (B) calmed (C) tired (D) assured (E) restored

____ 3. EXPAND: (A) increase (B) express (C) collide (D) collapse (E) shrink

____ 4. EXPLORE: (A) think (B) abandon (C) decide (D) investigate (E) navigate

____ 5. FAITHFUL: (A) negligent (B) cheerful (C) sociable (D) brilliant (E) loyal

____ 6. FRAGMENT: (A) separation (B) mission (C) piece (D) whole (E) crack

____ 7. CREATE: (A) demolish (B) complete (C) copy (D) make (E) decide

____ 8. REQUIRE: (A) need (B) possess (C) like (D) hold (E) oppose

____ 9. SITE: (A) factor (B) location (C) view (D) strategy (E) realization

____ 10. COLLAPSE: (A) invade (B) increase (C) cause (D) judge (E) fall

Number correct ______ (total 10)

Spelling and Wordplay

Fill-ins Spell the review word correctly in the blanks to the right of its definition.

1. nearly correct: a _ _ r _ _ _ _ _ _ _
2. to place in the correct group: c _ _ _ _ _ _ f _
3. to say what will happen: _ _ _ d _ c _
4. to pay close attention: _ _ n _ _ n _ _ _ _ _ _
5. an emergency: c _ _ s _ _
6. special and important: _ _ _ n _ _ _ f _ _
7. to look at carefully: _ x _ _ _ r _
8. something one lives through: _ _ p _ r _ _ _ _ _
9. kindness to an opponent: m _ _ c _
10. a way of doing something: p _ _ c _ _ _
11. forward movement: p _ _ g _ _ _ _
12. to demand or need: r _ q _ _ _ _
13. a place where water is stored: r _ _ _ _ v _ _ _
14. to blow open: e _ _ _ t
15. enough: s _ f _ _ _ _ _ _ _ _

Number correct ______ (total 15)

Part C **Related Word Reinforcement**

Using Related Words

Matching Definitions Match each word on the left with its definition. Write the letter of the definition in the blank.

____	1. bankrupt	a. extreme tiredness
____	2. proceed	b. to keep shut up in one place
____	3. conductor	c. to go on or to go forward
____	4. corrupt	d. unable to pay one's debts
____	5. confine	e. belief
____	6. exhaustion	f. the leader of a chorus or orchestra
____	7. fury	g. to give a better or more advanced job
____	8. exploration	h. a fighter
____	9. reside	i. extreme or violent anger
____	10. promote	j. an investigation of a new place or area
____	11. exterior	k. a model of its kind
____	12. combatant	l. the outside
____	13. faith	m. to live in or at
____	14. classic	n. a break or pause
____	15. interruption	o. dishonest

Number correct ______ (total 15)

Reviewing Word Structures

The Prefix *pro-* As you know, the Latin prefix *pro-* can mean "before," "ahead," or "forward." For each item below, combine *pro-* with the Latin word given to form one of the following words.

profess progress promote protect provide

_______________ 1. *Pro-,* meaning "forward," plus *movere,* meaning "to move."

_______________ 2. *Pro-,* meaning "before," plus *gradi,* meaning "to step."

_______________ 3. *Pro-,* meaning "before," plus *tegere,* meaning "to cover."

_______________ 4. *Pro-,* meaning "before," plus *videre,* meaning "to see."

_______________ 5. *Pro-,* meaning "before," plus *fateri,* meaning "to declare."

Number correct ______ (total 5)

Number correct in unit ______ (total 95)

FOCUS ON: **Foreign Words and Phrases**

Many English words and phrases come from foreign languages, including Latin, Greek, French, German, and Spanish. Listed below are some words and phrases that have made their way from foreign languages into English.

a la carte (ä′ lə kärt′, al′ ə) French, each item priced separately on a menu (as opposed to complete dinners). • None of the dinner specials appealed to Rick, so he ordered separate dishes *a la carte.*

a la mode (al′ ə mōd′, ä′ lə) French, made or served in a certain style, such as pie or cake with ice cream. • Michiko likes ice cream, so we served her peach pie *a la mode.*

apartheid (ə pärt′ hāt, -hīt) n. Afrikaans, a South African government policy of keeping white and nonwhite races separate. • Bishop Tutu, one of the most powerful opponents of *apartheid,* demanded an end to discrimination against South African blacks.

bon voyage (bän′ voi azh′) French, good-bye to a traveler about to go on a journey • *"Bon voyage!"* Kenji exclaimed to Rita as the loudspeakers announced the flight to Amsterdam.

c'est la vie (se lȧ vē′) French, such is life. • When times are tough, Angelita's grandmother exclaims, "C'est la vie."

chutzpah (hoots′ pə, khoots′-; -pä) n. Hebrew, extreme boldness. • When Jeremy jokingly asked his teacher, Mr. Masters, if he had read the assignment himself, Mr. Masters replied, "Yes, I have—and you have real *chutzpah!*"

deja vu (dā zhá vü′) French, the feeling that one has had a specific experience before. • As Juan gave his acceptance speech, he had a strong sense of *deja vu.* He felt that he had given this same speech before.

en masse (en mas′) French, in a group. • The students gathered *en masse* outside Ms. Tanaka's house to sing "Happy Birthday to You!".

esprit de corps (es prē′ dā kôr′) French, a sense of spirit shared by members of an organization or team. • The members of a sports team often develop *esprit de corps* from playing together.

incognito (in′ käg nēt′ ō, in käg′ ni tō) adv., adj. Italian, in disguise. • The rock star traveled *incognito* during his vacation so that no one would recognize him.

kibbutz (ki bo͞ots′, -bo͝ots′) n. Hebrew, a settlement in Israel in which many people work together. • Travelers to Israel are often impressed by how well members of a *kibbutz* work together.

kowtow (kou′ tou′, kō′-) v. Chinese, to show great respect and obedience • Bill naturally *kowtowed* to his grandfather, a wise old man.

status quo (stāt′ əs kwō′, stat′-) Latin, the way things are at present. • In all societies people who want change struggle against people who prefer the *status quo.*

vice versa (vī′ sē vʉr′ sə, vī′ sə, vīs′-) Latin, the other way around. • People who are responsible are dependable and *vice versa*.

wanderlust (wän′ dər lust′, wôn′-) n. German, the urge to travel. • Ms. Loomis, who has *wanderlust,* has taken several trips abroad.

Sentence Completion Complete each sentence below by writing the appropriate focus word.

______________ 1. The empress expected her subjects to ? to her.

______________ 2. The ? system in South Africa separates blacks and whites.

______________ 3. After the employees left the factory ?, all the exits from the parking lot were jammed.

______________ 4. Before the Maeda family left for Euope, friends stopped to wish them ?.

______________ 5. The apparent leader of the burglary ring was really a police officer working ?.

______________ 6. Ms. Patterson must have ? again; she'll soon be leaving for South America.

______________ 7. Mr. Washington wants to see some changes in his company's policies. He says he is tired of the ?.

______________ 8. My favorite dessert at Ted's Cafe is apple pie ?.

______________ 9. We were pleased that Carlotta and Penny got along so well; Carlotta admired Penny, and ?.

______________ 10. We admire Aunt Lou's composure. Even when things are going wrong, she just says, "?."

______________ 11. While the rest of the family ordered dinners, Marietta just ordered appetizers ?.

______________ 12. Bob decided he would join a ? in Israel.

______________ 13. The Jets won not only because of their skill but also because of their ?. During the season the players developed a spirit of togetherness.

______________ 14. When Sharon opened the door of the old house, she had a sense of ?. She felt she had been there before.

______________ 15. It would take real ? to ask the boss for a raise after only a week on the job.

Number correct _____ (total 15

FOCUS ON: **How Words Enter Our Language**

How do new words enter the English language? Linguists, scholars who study language, have identified several processes, including borrowing words from other languages, deriving words from names, compounding, clipping, and making acronyms.

Borrowed Words

The vast majority of English words have been borrowed from other languages, including Greek, Latin, and the Romance languages (especially French), which developed from Latin. Borrowed words seldom look or sound exactly the same in English as they do in their original languages. Sometimes, however, you can see striking similarities. For example, the English word *grand* comes from and resembles the Latin word *grandis.* Most dictionaries give the origins of thousands of borrowed words. The following chart gives examples of borrowed words.

Words Borrowed from Other Languages

Algonquian	powwow	**French**	bankrupt
Chinese	typhoon	**Russian**	troika
Hindi	jungle	**Italian**	spaghetti
German	hoodlum	**Spanish**	potato
Greek	melancholy	**Turkish**	horde

People and Place Names

Some English words derive from the names of interesting persons or places. Take the word *sandwich,* for example. The fourth Earl of Sandwich ate meat or cheese between slices of bread as a portable meal. The word *sandwich* comes from his name. Other familiar words that have come from names include *pasteurize, saxophone, vandal,* and *waterloo.*

Compounding , Clipped Words, and Acronyms

Sometimes two words are joined to form a new word, a process called compounding. For example, a mat that lies in front of a door is known as a *doormat.* Other examples of compounding include words like *pickpocket, earthquake, income, railroad, evergreen,* and *underestimate.*

Clipping is another means of forming new words. Take the word *omnibus,* for example. You rarely hear *omnibus* but often hear *bus,* the shortened form. In the same way *cabriolet* has become *cab,* and *periwig* has become *wig.* A *gymnasium* can be called a *gym,* and a *microphone* can be called a *mike.*

Acronyms are also a source of new words. Acronyms are formed from the beginnings of words in a series. The military term Absent Without Leave (that is leaving a base without permission) was abbreviated AWOL. A person who left without permission was labelled AWOL. Now AWOL may refer to unexcused absences outside the military or to absent persons. Other examples of acronyms include radar (Radio Detecting and Ranging), VIP (Very Important Person) and SWAT (Special Weapons and Tactics).

Identifying Word Origins Match each word with the way it entered the language. Check your dictionary if necessary.

____	1. photo	a. borrowing
____	2. sonar	b. compounding
____	3. birdhouse	c. clipping
____	4. frankfurter	d. names
____	5. transport	e. acronyms

Number correct ______ (total 5)

Finding Word Sources Use your dictionary to trace the source of each of the following words. If the word is borrowed, write the name of the language from which it comes. If the word is derived from the name of a person or place, write the name from which it comes.

1. denim: ______________________________
2. hazard: ______________________________
3. scoop: ______________________________
4. hamburger: ______________________________
5. mission: ______________________________
6. comedy: ______________________________
7. karate: ______________________________
8. malapropism: ______________________________
9. machismo: ______________________________
10. prairie: ______________________________

Number correct ______ (total 10)

Number correct in Vocab Lab ______ (total 30)

UNIT 13

Part A Target Words and Their Meanings

1. amateur (am′ ə chər, -toor) n., adj.
2. demand (di mand′) v., n.
3. individual (in′ di vij′ oo wəl, -vij′ əl) adj., n.
4. local (lō′ k'l) adj., n.
5. occasion (ə kā′ zhən) n., v.
6. officer (ôf′ ə sər, äf′-) n.
7. parallel (par′ ə lel′, -ləl) adv., adj.
8. right (rīt) n., adj., adv., v.
9. screech (skrēch) n., v.
10. section (sek′ shən) n., v.
11. shatter (shat′ ər) v.
12. supreme (sə prēm′, soo-) adj.
13. technique (tek nēk′) n.
14. vessel (ves′ 'l) n.
15. yarn (yärn) n.

Inferring Meaning from Context

For each sentence write the letter of the word or phrase that is closest in meaning to the word or words in italics. Use context clues to help you choose the correct answer. (For information about how context helps you understand vocabulary, see pages 1–6.)

____ 1. Juan pitches regularly on his school's baseball team. He may be just *an amateur* now, but he dreams of making his living as a major-league player some day.
a. a hard worker b. a champion c. a nonprofessional d. a bad player

____ 2. Kate didn't think it was fair that only Bob got to explain, so she *demanded* a chance to tell her side of the story.
a. strongly asked for b. quietly gave up c. laughed at d. ignored

____ 3. Yoki was tired; Angel was bored; I was getting a headache. We all had our own *individual* reasons for leaving the party early.
a. made-up b. personal c. exciting d. second-hand

____ 4. The people who live in the *local* area say The Crab Palace is the best restaurant around here. Many visitors eat there too and speak highly of it.
a. crowded b. nearby c. wealthy d. poor

____ 5. Jed hates to cook. There was only one *occasion,* as far as I can remember, when he made dinner.

a. dream b. future event c. time d. mistake

____ 6. The *officers* on the ship will give orders and make sure the crew members obey them.

a. passengers b. equipment c. persons in charge d. guests

____ 7. If we walk *parallel to* the fence, sooner or later we'll find the place where the horses have been getting out.

a. along the side of b. straight away from c. through d. across or over

____ 8. Every arrested criminal, no matter how serious the crime, has a *right to* a fair trial.

a. fear of b. good result of c. suspicion of d. legal claim to

____ 9. We heard Anna *screech* when Phil scared the daylights out of her by jumping out of the shadows in the dark hallway.

a. scream b. giggle c. whisper d. faint

____ 10. Which *section* of the stadium would you like to sit in? I prefer the bleachers, but you may like the area that has chairs.

a. room b. seat c. row d. part

____ 11. When I dropped the light bulb on the concrete floor, the bulb *shattered.* I swept up all the pieces so no one would get hurt.

a. rolled b. broke c. collapsed d. bounced

____ 12. Chris felt *supreme* joy when, to her surprise, she won first place in the contest.

a. ordinary b. familiar c. small d. great

____ 13. Your volleyball serves are always good, but I can't see how you're holding your hands. Can you show me your *technique for* serving?

a. score from b. way of c. reason for d. rules for

____ 14. I have been in a rowboat often, but sometime I would like to travel in the kind of *vessel* that can cross the ocean.

a. boat b. jet c. whale d. large building

____ 15. For an hour the children's eyes were big with excitement as Grandpa told them a *yarn* having to do with his days as a cowboy.

a. joke b. story c. recipe d. nightmare

Number correct ______ (total 15)

Part B **Target Words in Reading and Literature**

You should now have a general idea of the meaning of each target word. Sharpen your understanding by studying how these words are used in the following selection.

The Dogholes

Howard Peet

Along the rough and rocky coast of California in the mid-1800's, "doghole schooners" sailed in and out of inlets to collect logs for America's sawmills. In the following selection, you will find out why these sturdy little ships were given their odd name.

In the evenings, after dinner, we could sometimes persuade the captain to sit by the fireplace and tell **yarns** about his days as a ship's **officer** on a **vessel** called the *Artful Dodger*. No matter what other delights or joys the day had held for us, this was always the **supreme** pleasure. With each movement of his arms throwing dark shadows on the walls, and his white beard glowing in the firelight, the captain could hold our attention for hours. Now and then, a **screech** from an owl somewhere outside in the deep darkness would make us jump. 5

We each had our own **individual** favorites among his tales, and each of us felt we had a **right** to hear the ones we liked best. The ones I wanted most to hear were those that told about the work the *Artful Dodger* was built to do. She was the type of ship known as a doghole schooner, which carried logs down the dangerous coast of California. She had a crew of four and one officer, the captain. The crews of these schooners were usually men from Scandinavia, which is why the **local** people called the dogholers the "Scandinavian Navy." 10 15

The job of a doghole schooner was to sail **parallel** to the coast and slip into and out of the narrow inlets, known as dogholes. After entering the inlets, the crew would try to grab a load of logs and escape without being left high and dry by a falling tide or getting smashed by a sudden storm. The doghole inlets are no more than cuts in the cliffs. Most are so small that sailors claimed only a dog could turn around in one. A ship in such waters required a crew with a lot of experience. Other types of ships could take on and train several new sailors at once, but on board these doghole schooners there was little room for **amateurs**. 20 25

To load logs, the sailors used slides make of greased redwood. The slides had been built down the sides of the cliffs. Lumberjacks cut the trees in the coastal forests and prepared the logs for transport. The loading **technique** was remarkable. Huge logs were sent plunging down the slippery slides toward the tiny, bobbing doghole ship below. Timing was 30 the trick. As the log whizzed down the slide, it had to be slowed just before reaching the schooner. To allow this, 35 the last **section** of the slide, called the "clapper," was made so that it could be tipped upward. This had to be done at 40 just exactly the right moment. If the clapperman's timing was off, the log would slam right through the schooner 45 and **shatter** it. Such mishaps were not uncommon. Most doghole schooners went to the bottom after only three or four years at sea. On many **occasions** the *Artful Dodger* herself barely escaped destruction.

As soon as one story was finished, we would all **demand** another. 50 Once the captain had turned his mind to the past and started with his stories, he was often willing to give in when we insisted on more. Many times the clock struck midnight before exhaustion turned our attention away from life aboard the *Dodger* and toward our beds.

Refining Your Understanding

For each of the following items, consider how the target word is used in the passage. Write the letter of the word or phrase that best completes the sentence.

____ 1. *Yarns* (line 2) are a. colorful stories b. threads c. boring stories.

____ 2. The word *supreme* as it is used in line 4 means a. pleasant b. quite good c. greater than any other.

____ 3. The phrase "little room for *amateurs*" (line 25) suggests that there was no room for sailors who were a. not paid b. young c. not yet good at the job.

____ 4. The "loading *technique*" (line 29) refers to a. how the logs were loaded b. why the logs were loaded c. when the logs were loaded.

____ 5. If a log would *shatter* a schooner (line 46), it would a. dent it b. tear it apart c. scrape it.

Number correct ______ (total 5)

Part C **Ways to Make New Words Your Own**

By now you are familiar with the target words and their meanings. This section presents activities that will help you make the words part of your permanent vocabulary.

Using Language and Thinking Skills

Understanding Multiple Meanings Each box in this exercise contains a boldfaced word with its definitions. Read the definitions and then the sentences that use the word. Write the letter of the definition that applies to each sentence.

right
a. honest, moral, decent (adj.)
b. correct, not mistaken (adj.)
c. exactly (adv.)
d. to fix or correct (v.)
e. privilege or claim (n.)

____ 1. Your answer to the last math problem is *right.*

____ 2. In the United States, people have the *right* to say that they disagree with the government.

____ 3. *Right* at twelve o'clock the factory whistle blew.

____ 4. Can you *right* the spelling mistakes in your essay?

____ 5. Bill decided that telling his mother that he was the one who had lost the money was the *right* thing to do.

vessel
a. a bowl, pot, or other utensil made to hold things (n.)
b. a ship (n.)
c. a tube in the body through which blood or other fluids pass (n.)

____ 6. Fat that builds up in blood *vessels* can cause heart disease.

____ 7. Some *vessels* can carry cars across lakes or other bodies of water.

____ 8. Beside the stove was a *vessel* filled with homemade dill pickles.

____ 9. Our bodies contain an amazing system of *vessels.*

____ 10. The thirsty laborer asked for a *vessel* of water.

Number correct ______ (total 10)

Finding Examples Write the letter of the situation that best shows the meaning of the boldfaced word.

____ 1. **vessel**
a. The Pilgrims traveled to North America on the *Mayflower.*
b. We took the bus to the theater downtown.
c. Pedro and Sam walked by a wrecked car on their way home.

____ 2. **parallel**
a. First Street crosses Brooklyn Avenue about two blocks from here.
b. The highway and the railroad tracks run side-by-side for miles.
c. A triangle is made up of three lines.

____ 3. **screech**
a. The whispering behind me is really annoying.
b. The loud, high sound coming from the woods made us all shiver.
c. The sound of the waves hitting the shore almost put Letha to sleep.

____ 4. **local**
a. It is now believed that the first humans lived in Africa.
b. By the sound of the sirens, we could tell there was a fire nearby.
c. That nation's election for president is held every six years.

____ 5. **demand**
a. Ms. Jones insisted that I give her the names of the students who had played the trick.
b. My little brother stayed up an extra half hour.
c. Letisha mentioned that our supply of computer paper is low.

Number correct ______ (total 5)

Practicing for Standardized Tests

Synonyms Write the letter of the word that is closest in meaning to the capitalized word.

____ 1. TECHNIQUE: (A) result (B) method (C) factor (D) segment (E) effort

____ 2. SCREECH: (A) sob (B) gasp (C) whimper (D) shriek (E) scratch

____ 3. SHATTER: (A) hurry (B) smash (C) plunge (D) drop (E) utter

____ 4. SUPREME: (A) serious (B) wealthy (C) true (D) known (E) best

____ 5. YARN: (A) tale (B) needle (C) report (D) mishap (E) directions

____ 6. OFFICER: (A) sailor (B) professional (C) leader (D) worker (E) victim

____ 7. DEMAND: (A) insist (B) tell (C) demolish (D) rush (E) realize

____ 8. SECTION: (A) blast (B) segment (C) square (D) whole (E) city

____ 9. INDIVIDUAL: (A) common (B) weird (C) unexpected (D) popular (E) special

____ 10. AMATEUR: (A) storyteller (B) expert (C) beginner (D) worker (E) boss

Number correct _____ (total 10)

Spelling and Wordplay

Crossword Puzzle Read the clues and print the answers in the squares.

ACROSS
1. One part
3. A story
5. A privilege or claim
8. Abbr. vice president
10. Past tense of eat
11. Short for Albert
12. Abbr. southwest
13. To receive in your hands something tossed or thrown
16. Quiet; unmoving
17. Conjunction that shows a choice between two things
18. Antonym of out
19. Not a part, but the whole amount
21. Best; greatest
23. Suffix added to associate to form association
24. Abbr. the people who call strikes and balls
26. Breaks and comes apart
27. Another name for Papa

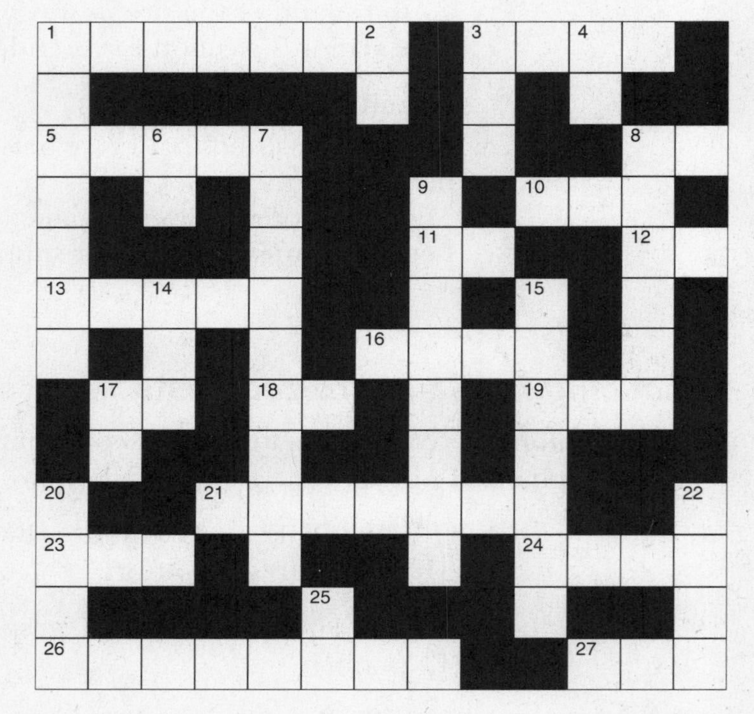

DOWN
1. A scream
2. Abbr. New Jersey
3. Soon but not _____
4. Abbr. railroad
6. Present tense of went
7. Method
8. A ship
9. Side-by-side, like railroad tracks
14. Sticky black material used on roofs
15. A nonprofessional
17. Exclamation a person might utter when surprised
20. What clothing that is the right size does
22. Second-hand
25. That man

Part D **Related Words**

The words below are closely related to the target words. Use your knowledge of the target words and of word parts to help you determine the meaning of these words. (For information about word parts analysis, see pages 7–13.) Use your dictionary if necessary.

1. demanding (di mand′ iŋ) adj.
2. individualism (in′ di vij′ oo wəl iz'm, -vij′ əl iz'm) n.
3. individualistic (in di vij′ oo wəl is′ tik) adj.
4. locality (lō kal′ ə tē) n.
5. occasionally (ə kā′ zhən 'lē, -ə lē) adv.
6. office (ôf′ is, äf′-) n.
7. supremacy (sə prem′ ə sē, soo-) n.
8. technical (tek′ ni k'l) adj.
9. technicality (tek′ nə kal′ ə tē) n.
10. technician (tek nish′ ən) n.
11. technocracy (tek näk′ rə sē) n.
12. technology (tek näl′ ə jē) n.

Understanding Related Words

Sentence Completion Write the word from the list below that best completes the meaning of the sentence.

demanding locality occasionally office supremacy

________________ 1. If you're not familiar with a certain area, you might have trouble finding a street in that __?__.

________________ 2. If you wish to talk with your principal, one place you would likely find her is in her __?__.

________________ 3. In most parts of North America, rain does not come every day, but only __?__.

________________ 4. Sarah is a very __?__ child. She insists that I play with her all the time.

________________ 5. When they had beaten all their enemies, the people enjoyed their __?__.

Number correct ______ (total 5)

Turn to **Words Ending in *y*** on page 217 of the **Spelling Handbook.** Read the rule and complete the exercises provided.

Analyzing Word Parts

The Greek Word *technē* In this unit the target word *technique* and the related words *technical, technicality, technician, technocracy,* and *technology* come from the Greek noun *technē*, meaning "an art." Use your dictionary to learn the meanings and parts of speech of the five related words listed above. Then choose the related word that best completes the meaning of each sentence below.

________________ 1. Because my dad knows a lot about computers, he understands computer books that contain ? language.

________________ 2. What would it be like if our democracy were replaced by a ? . I wonder if society's problems would be solved more easily.

________________ 3. Do you think someday we will have the ? that will make it possible for us to live in outer space?

________________ 4. The ? told me to hold still while she took an X-ray of my arm.

________________ 5. Joan said she understood most of the lecture, but she asked the speaker to explain one ? .

Number correct ______ (total 5)

Number correct in unit ______ (total 55)

Word's Worth: yarn

Yarn, which comes from the Old English word *gearn,* is a word with a colorful history and many meanings. It began as a medical term; specifically, it referred to the intestines. Later, *yarn* came to refer to a thin segment of animal intestine or gut that was used as string. Today we seldom use animal guts in weaving, but the spun fibers we weave with are still called *yarn.* "Spinning a *yarn*" in the sense of telling a story came into use in the early 1800's, probably from sailors who would tell stories while they made ropes from yarn. These stories were often long and exciting, and they usually stretched the truth in order to be more interesting. Can you see the connection between these different kinds of *yarn?*

The Last Word

Writing

Imagine you are a sailor on a ship like the *Artful Dodger.* Write a short *yarn* describing one of your exciting adventures.

Speaking

Think of a *technique* for doing or making something that you know well. Explain the technique to your class.

Group Discussion

What *rights* do citizens of the United States have? Which of these rights do you think are most important? Would you be willing to give up any of these rights? How might your life be different without these rights? In a group, discuss these questions. Give reasons to support your opinions.

UNIT 14

Part A Target Words and Their Meanings

1. associate (ə sō′ shē āt′, -sē-) v., n.
2. cloud (kloud) v., n.
3. foresight (fôr′ sīt′) n.
4. hardy (här′ dē) adj.
5. legend (lej′ ənd) n.
6. memorial (mə môr′ ē əl) n., adj.
7. migrate (mī′ grāt) v.
8. mysterious (mis tir′ ē əs) adj.
9. preserve (pri zurv′) v., n.
10. prohibit (prō hib′ it) v.
11. region (rē′ jən) n.
12. restless (rest′ lis) adj.
13. sacred (sā′ krid) adj.
14. secrecy (sē′ krə sē) n.
15. souvenir (sōō′ və nir′, sōō′ və nir′) n.

Inferring Meaning from Context

For each sentence write the letter of the word or phrase that is closest in meaning to the word or words in italics. Use context clues to help you choose the correct answer.

____ 1. What do you think of when you hear the name Washington, D.C.? Most Americans *associate* that name with the United States Capitol and the White House.

a. respect b. connect c. process d. oppose

____ 2. The rapidly changing events of war can *cloud* a newspaper reporter's understanding of events. Often, all the facts do not become clear until years later.

a. expand b. produce c. ease d. make unclear

____ 3. Brian showed no *foresight* when he went camping. The weather was cold, but he didn't think to bring matches so he could have a fire.

a. regret b. appreciation c. fear d. ability to plan ahead

____ 4. The pioneers were *hardy* people. They survived long, dangerous, exhausting trips in covered wagons to begin a new life in the West.

a. dependent b. strong c. fun-loving d. furious

____ 5. According to *legend*, the *Flying Dutchman* was a ship that sank in rough seas more than a hundred years ago. The story also says that the ship and its ghostly crew are still sailing the ocean.

a. a strategy b. a scene c. a law of long ago d. a story based on history

____ 6. In Washington, D.C., there is a wall that bears the names of those who died in the Vietnam War. One can see people gently touching the name of a loved one as they stand before this *memorial.*

a. judgment b. destination c. thing that gives support to a building d. thing that helps people remember

____ 7. People looking for a quieter life sometimes *migrate to* the country from the city; those looking for job opportunities often do the opposite.

a. move to b. stroll to c. look into d. rush to

____ 8. Even though no one lived in the house, Julio said he had seen lights go on and off and had heard thumping noises from inside it. We all wondered about these *mysterious* happenings.

a. helpful b. reliable c. strange d. gloomy

____ 9. The county decided to *preserve* the ghost town. Now the old buildings will remain for visitors to enjoy.

a. save b. build c. demolish d. neglect

____ 10. The park rangers decided to *prohibit* campfires in the state park because of the danger of fires spreading during the dry season.

a. encourage b. prefer c. not allow d. enjoy

____ 11. People often visit New England to see the trees when the leaves have changed color because this *region* is so beautiful in the fall.

a. weather b. city c. area d. state

____ 12. Meredith was *restless* as she waited for the game to begin. She walked back and forth, unable to calm down.

a. unable to be still b. ready to leave c. selfish d. faithful

____ 13. The Black Hills of South Dakota are *sacred* to Native Americans, who believe that the hills are peopled with spirits.

a. scenic b. financial c. holy d. disorderly

____ 14. Trina hadn't wanted anyone to know where her hideout was, but now there was no need for *secrecy.* The place had been discovered.

a. suspicion b. making known c. public attention d. not telling anyone

____ 15. When Mae visited Yellowstone National Park, she bought a statue of a bear to keep as *a souvenir.* Looking at it brings back memories of her trip.

a. a solution b. a temptation c. an experiment d. a reminder

Number correct ______ (total 15)

Part B **Target Words in Reading and Literature**

You should now have a general idea of the meaning of each target word. Sharpen your understanding by studying how these words are used in the following selection.

The Superstition Mountains

Howard Peet

This is a story of two nineteenth-century immigrants, one English, the other German. Both were important figures in the Southwest.

In the 1830's, two explorers, Darrel Duppa and Jacob Von Walzer, met in the goldfields of New Zealand. Duppa, a **restless** English traveler, and Von Walzer, a **hardy** German mining engineer, became friends. Little did they realize that their journeys would end halfway around the world in the American Southwest. 5

In 1862, Duppa and Von Walzer came to the United States—Duppa by way of San Francisco and Von Walzer through New York City. They both **migrated** to the Territory of Arizona, where they would spend the rest of their lives. Neither could have known it at the time, but each would become a popular symbol in the **region** of the Southwest. 10

No one knows for sure where Von Walzer went after he arrived. The best-known story says that he went to an area in Arizona near the Superstition Mountains. These mountains were believed to be the site of secret gold mines, dug long ago by Native Americans. When Von Walzer arrived, people told him that only the Apache Indians knew where the 15 mines were. The Apaches believed that the mountain area was **sacred,** and they **prohibited** other people from going there. However, this did not discourage Jacob Von Walzer. He immediately began his search through the Superstition Mountains in an effort to find the **mysterious** mines.

Soon Von Walzer was showing off a huge gold nugget as a **souvenir** 20 of his efforts. When asked where he had found it, he told many stories but never revealed the mine's location. In one story he said that he could easily see Weaver's Needle, a towering rock, from the opening of the mine. He also told about how the afternoon sun, just before twilight, created a brilliant light around the mine entrance. Far from helping 25 anyone locate the mine, however, these clues **clouded** the truth about where it could be found. Perhaps Von Walzer had the **foresight** to purposely provide details that would **preserve** the **secrecy** of the mine's location. Although many people searched for the mine, which came to be known as the Lost Dutchman Gold Mine, it was never found. 30

While Von Walzer was searching for gold, not far away Darrel Duppa was helping to build the village of Phoenix. It was Duppa who came up

with the name Phoenix, which he borrowed from a Greek myth about a bird that, after living for five hundred years, burned itself to death and then rose again from its ashes to live another long life. Duppa predicted that a great new city in the Salt River Valley would rise from ancient Indian ruins, and he was right. The city is a **memorial** to the man whose vision helped it come into being. 35

Von Walzer and Duppa both became well-known figures, but that is where the parallel ends. The little that we know of Von Walzer is based on **legend.** It seems that he lived a lonely life, trying to keep the secret of the gold mine he had discovered. Duppa, on the other hand, was loved and appreciated as the father of the city of Phoenix. Von Walzer is **associated** with a mine that may not even exist, while Duppa lives on in people's minds in connection with a lively and very real city. 40 45

Refining Your Understanding

For each of the following items, consider how the target word is used in the passage. Write the letter of the word or phrase that best completes the sentence.

____ 1. The passage uses the word *migrated* (line 8) to mean that Duppa and Von Walzer moved to Arizona a. for a brief visit b. for a long time c. every winter.

____ 2. The Apaches *prohibited* people from entering the Superstition Mountain area (line 17). However, Von Walzer went there anyway. This suggests that *prohibit* means a. prevent b. punish c. forbid.

____ 3. The mines are described as *mysterious* (line 19) because a. little is known about them b. they are quite dangerous c. they are in the Superstition Mountains.

____ 4. Von Walzer showed off a gold nugget he had as a *souvenir* (line 20). This suggests that he a. sold it b. kept it c. put it in a museum.

____ 5. The author's use of the word *foresight* in line 27 suggests that Von Walzer's stories may have been a. honest mistakes b. completely true c. deliberate lies.

Number correct ______ (total 5)

Part C **Ways to Make New Words Your Own**

By now you are familiar with the target words and their meanings. This section presents activities that will help you make the words part of your permanent vocabulary.

Using Language and Thinking Skills

True–False Decide whether each statement is true **(T)** or false **(F)**.

____ 1. A *restless* student will have a hard time sitting still in class.

____ 2. We collect *souvenirs* to help us forget events that were unpleasant.

____ 3. People *migrate* because they are happy where they are.

____ 4. A *memorial* reminds us of an important person or event.

____ 5. Many historians want to *preserve* places where important historical events took place.

____ 6. Libraries *prohibit* people from reading many different books.

____ 7. The most *mysterious* ghost stories are those in which there is a logical explanation for all the events.

____ 8. To *cloud* something is to explain it.

____ 9. If you have *foresight,* you will prepare for the future.

____ 10. People would probably protect something that was *sacred* to them.

Number correct ______ (total 10)

Practicing for Standardized Tests

Analogies Determine the relationship between the pair of capitalized words. Then decide which other word pair expresses a similar relationship. Write the letter of this word pair.

____ 1. SOUTHWEST : REGION :: (A) broccoli : vegetable (B) hero : story (C) poet : poem (D) past : future (E) dream : sleep

____ 2. CLOUD : HIDE :: (A) forget : remember (B) show : shine (C) forgive : explain (D) defend : protect (E) create : encourage

____ 3. PROHIBIT : STEALING :: (A) obey : obedience (B) encourage : honesty (C) support : cheating (D) help : aid (E) ignore : mistake

____ 4. BUTTERFLY : HARDY :: (A) lion : fierce (B) kitten : gentle (C) giraffe : short (D) wolf : wild (E) dolphin : intelligent

____ 5. PRESERVE : DEMOLISH :: (A) find : lose (B) talk : discuss (C) observe : watch (D) pursue : chase (E) erupt : explode

Number correct ______ (total 5)

Spelling and Wordplay

Word Maze Find and circle each target word in this maze.

M	Y	S	T	E	R	I	O	U	S	D	A	Q
E	H	O	D	S	E	C	R	E	C	Y	S	U
M	A	U	A	M	I	G	R	A	T	E	S	R
O	R	V	S	G	B	K	P	M	R	P	O	E
R	D	E	A	W	O	R	W	T	E	R	C	S
I	Y	N	C	D	J	Y	V	X	G	O	I	T
A	L	I	R	K	P	S	A	M	I	H	A	L
L	P	R	E	S	E	R	V	E	O	I	T	E
J	U	O	D	V	N	V	S	Y	N	B	E	S
F	O	X	I	L	C	L	O	U	D	I	G	S
C	N	Q	U	I	R	W	J	B	K	T	E	X
S	Y	F	B	O	L	E	G	E	N	D	B	Z
A	F	O	R	E	S	I	G	H	T	R	T	X

associate
cloud
foresight
hardy
legend
memorial
migrate
mysterious
preserve
prohibit
region
restless
sacred
secrecy
souvenir

Word's Worth: mystery

To most of us, *mystery* means a story or movie about a crime that needs to be solved. If we hear about something strange, we may also call it "a mystery." We think of mysteries as events that need a solution or explanation. The ancient Greeks had a different viewpoint, however. *Mystery* comes from the Greek word *myein,* which means "to shut the mouth or eyes." The Greeks believed that the common person was not ready for certain religious rituals. Only persons who were acceptable to the gods could attend. These special people had to promise not to tell anyone else what they saw or heard at the religious ceremonies. In other words, they had to keep their mouths shut. The ceremonies became known as mysteries because people didn't talk about them. Outsiders probably wanted an explanation of the mysteries, and so the meaning of the word evolved to our modern understanding of it.

Part D **Related Words**

The words below are closely related to the target words. Use your knowledge of the target words and of word parts to determine the meanings of these words. (For information about word parts analysis, see pages 7–13.) Use your dictionary if necessary.

1. association (ə sō′ sē ā′ shən, -shē-) n.
2. emigrate (em′ ə grāt′) v.
3. forefather (fôr′ fä′ *th*ər) n.
4. foreknowledge (fôr′ näl′ ij) n.
5. hindsight (hīnd′ sīt′) n.
6. immigrate (im′ ə grāt′) v.
7. legendary (lej′ ən der′ ē) adj.
8. migration (mī grā′ shən) n.
9. mystery (mis′ tə rē, -trē) n.
10. preservation (prez′ ər vā′ shən) n.
11. regional (rē′ jən'l) adj.
12. secret (sē′ krit) adj.

Understanding Related Words

Finding Examples Write the letter of the situation that best shows the meaning of the boldfaced word.

____ 1. **association**
   a. I remember how to spell *parallel* by mentally joining the sound of the word with the sound of "pair of *l*'s."
   b. Everything about our vacation was wonderful, from the train trip itself to the sights we saw in the national parks.
   c. Toni took classes in Spanish, woodworking, and public speaking.

____ 2. **forefather**
   a. Sarah's older sister moved to Nebraska last year.
   b. Sidney's brother is going to a baseball camp next summer.
   c. Maxine's great-grandfather came to the United States from Japan.

____ 3. **foreknowledge**
   a. No one told us that the stores would be closed over the holidays.
   b. Students knew the term paper was due the same day as the final test, so they planned ahead.
   c. Everyone met in the gym to hear the announcements.

____ 4. **hindsight**
   a. It is not easy to make all the right decisions.
   b. It is always best to plan for the unexpected.
   c. It is easy to see mistakes you've made after it's too late to change things.

____ 5. **legendary**

a. The story of George Washington crossing the Delaware is a mixture of fact and fiction.

b. George Washington was the first president of the United States.

c. George Washington died in 1799.

____ 6. **migration**

a. Every day of the week, the shopping malls are filled with people.

b. After the Civil War, great numbers of people left the South to look for work in Northern cities.

c. Each year, more people join teams in order to play organized sports.

____ 7. **mystery**

a. Jane Austen wrote novels about how people lived during the nineteenth century.

b. Davy Crockett was a hero in the Battle of the Alamo.

c. Sherlock Holmes was called in to find the missing necklace.

____ 8. **preservation**

a. It's important to keep some of our forests in their natural state.

b. It's a good idea to provide land where new businesses can build.

c. Many swamps have been drained so the land can be used for farming.

____ 9. **regional**

a. Members of the park commission will discuss how to use the land the city has just purchased.

b. The mayor has called for a meeting of the city council.

c. The governors from each state in the Great Lakes area will meet in January.

____ 10. **secret**

a. Vanna gave her speech on how to make friends in a new school.

b. Andrew wrote a story for the school paper about Saturday's football game.

c. Francisco promised Lori he would not tell anyone about the surprise party.

Number correct ______ (total 10)

Turn to **The Suffix *-ion*** on page 224 in the **Spelling Handbook.** Read the rule and complete the exercises provided.

Analyzing Word Parts

The Latin Root *migr* The target word *migrate* comes from the Latin word *migrare,* meaning to "to move." All of the following words come from this Latin word.

emigrate immigrate immigrants migrate migration

In your dictionary look up the definition of each word you do not know. Then use each word in one of the following sentences.

________________ 1. In the nineteenth century, Germans saw many people leave Germany to __?__ to North America.

________________ 2. In recent years, millions of __?__ from Southeast Asia have come into the United States.

________________ 3. In the spring, millions of ducks __?__ to Canada and Alaska, where they stay until fall.

________________ 4. The discovery of gold caused a great __?__ of people to California in the 1850's.

________________ 5. The Statue of Liberty in New York Harbor has welcomed many people as they __?__ into the United States.

Number correct ______ (total 5)

The Prefix *fore-* The prefix *fore-* comes from an Old English word meaning "first" or "in front." The target word *foresight* and the related words *forefather* and *foreknowledge* also use this prefix. This common prefix occurs in many other words as well, including *forehead, forecast,* and *foreground.* Using sentence clues and your knowledge of the prefix *fore-*, complete the following sentences with words from the list below. Use a dictionary if necessary.

forecast forefather foreground forehead foreknowledge

________________ 1. Allen bumped his __?__ just above his right eye.

________________ 2. Without her glasses, Teresa can see objects in the __?__ very clearly, but things farther away are blurry.

________________ 3. The weather __?__ says there will be rain tomorrow.

________________ 4. Matthew seemed to have __?__ of every question Sara asked and had all the answers on the tip of his tongue.

________________ 5. Cindy studied her family's history and learned that one __?__ was with the Pilgrims at Plymouth Rock.

Number correct ______ (total 5)

Number correct in Unit ______ (total 55)

The Last Word

Writing

Describe a particularly *hardy* person you know. What qualities does this person have that allow him or her to make it through difficult times? Is it the person's physical qualities that make him or her hardy? The person's personality? Both?

Group Discussion

If you could go anywhere, what *souvenir* would you bring back? Use your imagination and jot down notes about your ideas. Then meet with a group of your classmates and discuss the place you'd like to visit and the thing you'd bring back to help you remember your trip.

UNIT 15

Part A Target Words and Their Meanings

1. candidate (kan′ də dāt′, -dit) -n.
2. chemistry (kem′ is trē) n.
3. civilization (siv′ ə lə zā′ shən) n.
4. complicated (käm′ plə kāt′ id) adj.
5. economic (ē′ kə näm′ ik, ek′ ə-) adj.
6. engineer (en′ jə nir′) n., v.
7. establish (ə stab′ lish) v.
8. government (guv′ ər mənt, -ərn mənt) n.
9. league (lēg) n.
10. literature (lit′ ər ə chər, lit′ rə choor) n.
11. patent (pat′ ’nt) n., adj., v.
12. receipt (ri sēt′) n., v.
13. represent (rep′ ri zent′) v.
14. sincere (sin sir′) adj.
15. will (wil) n., v.

Inferring Meaning from Context

For each sentence write the letter of the word or phrase that is closest in meaning to the word or words in italics. Use context clues to help you choose the correct answer. (For information about how context helps you understand vocabulary, see pages 1–6.)

____ 1. Each *candidate* for the position of mayor hoped to be the one the voters would choose.
a. one who runs for public office b. one who votes in an election c. one who wins an election d. one who shows an interest in government

____ 2. Carlo likes *chemistry.* He especially enjoys doing experiments that show how two elements can be put together to make a new compound.
a. the science of stars and planets b. the science of rocks and fossils c. the science of matter and how it combines d. the science of navigation

____ 3. When you study ancient Egyptian *civilization,* you learn about the development of its government, customs, and religion.
a. warfare b. mathematics c. painting and music d. culture

____ 4. Setting the clock in our new car should be easy, but these lengthy directions make the process seem *complicated.*
a. thorough b. difficult c. urgent d. meaningful

____ 5. Our club is having *economic* problems; we have to increase our membership fees so we will have enough money to pay for activities.
a. financial b. private c. exceptional d. individual

____ 6. Imagine walking across a bridge that stands about one thousand feet above the river at the bottom of the Royal Gorge in Colorado. We visited the bridge to learn how the *engineers* designed it.
a. navigators b. residents of the area c. tourists
d. experts who plan and build things

____ 7. Because Mr. Lopez wanted his students to do well, he *established* an after-school study program for them.
a. set up b. predicted c. abandoned d. closed

____ 8. After visiting the Capitol and listening to the senators vote, Lisa said she wanted to learn more about how the *government* works.
a. fortune b. memorial c. transportation system
d. political system

____ 9. Sometimes countries join *a league.* As league members, they agree to help one another when necessary.
a. a site b. an association c. a display d. a region

____ 10. Yoko loves to read legends; in fact, she likes any kind of *literature.*
a. society b. collection of writings c. process d. list of names

____ 11. Mr. Lawrence had a wonderful invention, but he did not get *a patent.* Unfortunately, someone else copied his invention and got credit for it.
a. an estimate b. exclusive rights to make and sell a thing
c. an opportunity to buy something d. a technique

____ 12. When you return the new sweater, show the salesperson your *receipt* to prove you bought the sweater at that store.
a. money b. price tag c. written proof of payment d. label

____ 13. Native Americans used smoke signals to communicate over long distances. The puffs of smoke *represented* words.
a. stood for b. disposed of c. interrupted d. uttered

____ 14. You could tell your teacher that you really enjoyed the test that you failed, but you would not be *sincere.*
a. furious b. truthful c. mysterious d. conscious

____ 15. In her *will,* Grandmother said that when she died, I would get her diamond necklace.
a. paper that states someone's last wishes b. favorite story of a person's life c. report by a doctor d. application

Number correct ______ (total 15)

Part B Target Words in Reading and Literature

You should now have a general idea of the meaning of each target word. Sharpen your understanding by studying how these words are used in the following selection.

The Nobel Prizes

Howard Peet

The Nobel Prizes honor men and women whose work has had an important and lasting effect on life in the twentieth century.

The Nobel Prizes, named after Alfred Bernhard Nobel, are given each year to deserving leaders who have made exceptional contributions to society. The prizes in physics,[1] **chemistry,** medicine, **literature,** and peace, fields that **represent** the interests and concerns of Nobel, were first awarded in 1901. A sixth prize in **economics** was **established** in 1969. 5

Alfred Nobel was born in Stockholm, Sweden, in 1833. His father was an **engineer** who took a job developing steamships and underwater explosives for the Russian **government.** While his father worked for Czar Nicholas I, Alfred went to private teachers for his schooling. He was a 10 brilliant student. By the time he was sixteen, Alfred was an able chemist and could speak English, French, German, and Russian, in addition to Swedish. He studied in France and America before returning to Sweden to concentrate his attention on explosives. In 1867 his application for an English **patent** on dynamite was accepted. After **receipt** of the English 15 patent, he was granted a United States patent in 1868.

Although Nobel was responsible for inventing one of the most explosive materials known, he always had a **sincere** hope that the progress of **civilization** would bring peace to the world. It was with this hope that he placed in his **will** a gift of $9,200,000 to establish the Nobel Prizes. Alfred 20 Nobel died in 1896.

The first Nobel Prize was a physics award given to Wilhelm Roentgen of Germany. The judges chose him over the other **candidates** for his discovery of X-rays. Other Nobel Prize winners include Theodore Richards, Charles Huggins, and Francis Rous. Richards developed a **complicated** 25 but reliable technique to measure atomic weight. For this achievement he received the prize for chemistry in 1914. Huggins and Rous won the 1966 prize for medicine as a result of their efforts in cancer research.

---

[1] physics: the branch of natural science that deals with matter and energy and their inter-

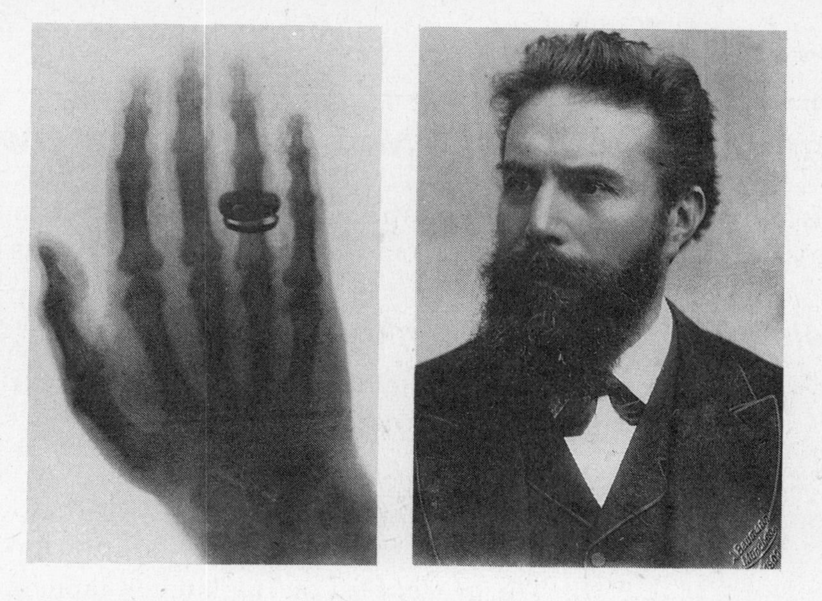

One of the first x-rays made by Wilhelm Roentgen in 1898.
The Bettmann Archive.

Wilhelm Roentgen, awarded the Nobel Prize in physics in 1901 for his discovery of x-rays.
The Bettmann Archive.

Ernest Hemingway's novel *The Old Man and the Sea* helped him win the prize for literature in 1954. In 1919, President Woodrow Wilson won the Nobel Peace Prize for his work in support of the **League** of Nations. The 1964 peace prize went to Martin Luther King, Jr., the famous civil rights leader. Another American, Dr. Linus Pauling, is the only individual to have won two Nobel Prizes by himself. He was awarded a Nobel in 1954 for chemistry and another for peace in 1962. 30 35

Each year there are new winners of the Nobel Prizes. Watch for this year's winners.

Refining Your Understanding

For each of the following items, consider how the target word is used in the passage. Write the letter of the word or phrase that best completes the sentence.

____ 1. In line 5, the word *economics* refers to a. the field of medicine b. Alfred Nobel's education c. the scientific study of how wealth is produced and used.

____ 2. Alfred Nobel's hope for peace was *sincere* (line 18), meaning it was a. dishonest b. real c. well-known.

____ 3. The phrase "after *receipt* of the English patent" (lines 15–16) indicates that Nobel a. was not given a patent in England b. was given a patent in England c. lost his English patent.

____ 4. Besides developing steamships, which of the following would an *engineer* (line 8) most likely do? a. find and explore new lands b. take care of sick people c. design a tower.

____ 5. In line 23, the word *candidates* refers to a. people in competition for a prize b. people running for public office c. judges.

Number correct ______ (total 5)

Part C **Ways to Make New Words Your Own**

By now you are familiar with the target words and their meanings. This section presents activities that will help you make the words part of your permanent vocabulary.

Using Language and Thinking Skills

Finding Examples Write the letter of the situation that best shows the meaning of the boldfaced word.

____ 1. **literature**
a. *The Adventures of Huckleberry Finn* is a wonderful book by Mark Twain.
b. The grocery list on the kitchen table has only three items on it.
c. My telephone conversation with Rose was brief.

____ 2. **patent**
a. Americans have the right to practice the religion of their choice.
b. After Louise invented an electric flyswatter, she applied for the right to sell it.
c. I'll give you written directions for driving from your house to mine.

____ 3. **economic**
a. Ed wrote a story about his experiences on a riverboat trip.
b. Ms. Morris told us to read the business section of the newspaper to find out about our government's financial situation.
c. You'll enjoy that magazine article; it's all about backpacking.

____ 4. **chemistry**
a. Jean read a book about magic and then tried to make her friend disappear!
b. To make the shelves, Maggie first sawed a board in two.
c. Jonah found out how to make water from hydrogen and oxygen.

____ 5. **candidate**
a. The prosecuting attorney is an important figure in a courtroom trial.
b. Ms. Gaffrey is running in this year's election for county sheriff.
c. Yvonne is president of our nature club.

____ 6. **receipt**
a. Misha was disappointed that the store had no chemistry sets in stock.
b. When Charles looked at the sales slip, he realized he had been overcharged for the books he had bought.
c. Andrew spent the day searching for the lost cat.

____ 7. **engineer**

a. Our next-door neighbor teaches English in a middle school.
b. Andrew's dad is a landscape artist; he creates beautiful gardens.
c. My cousin designed that new factory across town.

____ 8. **complicated**

a. Bill had trouble understanding his aunt's letter; it was filled with big words and long sentences.
b. Getting to the library from school is easy; just walk two blocks to the corner and you're there.
c. You can make pancakes in three quick steps.

____ 9. **establish**

a. Loons gather at the same spot in Minnesota each year before they fly south.
b. The Pilgrims started a colony in Massachusetts in the seventeenth century.
c. Rich has a legitimate reason for leaving school early today.

____ 10. **sincere**

a. Alexander promised never to use my computer without asking, but today he broke his word.
b. Mike congratulated Lashonda on her high grades, but behind her back he said that she was probably just lucky.
c. When Jonathan said he cared about what happened to Lin Su, he meant it.

Number correct ______ (total 10)

Practicing for Standardized Tests

Synonyms Write the letter of the word that is closest in meaning to the capitalized word.

____ 1. CANDIDATE: (A) victim (B) office-seeker (C) conductor (D) companion (E) winner

____ 2. CIVILIZATION: (A) society (B) experience (C) exploration (D) technology (E) foreknowledge

____ 3. ESTABLISH: (A) create (B) require (C) restore (D) demolish (E) prohibit

____ 4. LEAGUE: (A) crisis (B) legend (C) association (D) congregation (E) game

____ 5. SINCERE: (A) mysterious (B) loving (C) truthful (D) wrong (E) sociable

Number correct ______ (total 5)

Spelling and Wordplay

Word Maze Find and circle each target word in this maze.

C A N D I D A T E D R G C

O I S I N C E R E J E O K

M M V W Z H L T H M P V E

P A L I T E R A T U R E N

L T P L L M Q G K I E R G

I E A L E I U A M X S N I

C R T E A S Z V F B E M N

A I E N G T P A O P N E E

T A N V U R D W T Y T N E

E L T B E Y A S Q I Q T R

D E C O N O M I C Z O Z H

E S T A B L I S H A D N Y

A F W R E C E I P T X G B

candidate
chemistry
civilization
complicated
economic
engineer
establish
government
league
literature
patent
receipt
represent
sincere
will

Word's Worth: candidate

Candidate is derived from a Latin word that was associated with honesty. The Latin *candidatus* means "dressed in white." Candidates for office in ancient Rome wore white togas because Romans associated white with truthfulness. A related word, *candid,* comes from the Latin *candidus,* meaning "white." In English, candid means "frank" or "honest"—qualities that today's Americans, as much as the ancient Romans, want to see in candidates.

Turn to **Words with *ie* and *ei*** on pages 225 of the **Spelling Handbook.** Read the rules and complete the exercises provided.

Part D **Related Words**

The words below are closely related to the target words. Use your knowledge of the target words and of word parts to help you determine the meanings of these words. (For information about word parts analysis, see pages 7–13.) Use your dictionary if necessary.

1. chemical (kem′ i k'l) adj., n.
2. civil (siv′ 'l) adj.
3. civilize (siv′ ə līz′) v.
4. complicate (käm′ plə kāt′) v.
5. complication (käm′ plə kā′ shən) n.
6. economical (ē′ kə nom′ i k'l, ek′ ə-) adj.
7. economy (i kän′ ə mē) n.
8. establishment (ə stab′ lish mənt) n.
9. govern (guv′ ərn) v.
10. representation (rep′ ri zen tā′ shən) n.
11. sincerity (sin ser′ ə tē) n.
12. uncivilized (un siv′ ə līzd′) adj.

Understanding Related Words

True–False Decide whether each statement is true **(T)** or false **(F)**.

____ 1. Spitting on the sidewalk is *civil* behavior.

____ 2. Scientists who develop new medicines are familiar with *chemical* formulas.

____ 3. Having several people tell you different ways of doing something can *complicate* a task.

____ 4. A person who attends a conference provides *representation* for those who have sent him or her.

____ 5. The person with the least amount of experience is usually elected to *govern* a country.

Number correct ______ (total 5)

Matching Ideas Write the word from the list below that is most clearly related to the situation conveyed in the sentence. Three words are used twice.

civilize	establishment	complication	uncivilized
economical	economy	sincerity	

______________ 1. The financial situation in our town has improved since that factory opened and created many new jobs.

______________ 2. The pioneers worked hard to bring order to their settlement and to educate their children.

______________ 3. In the science fiction book I just read, one group of people was particularly ignorant and brutal.

_______________ 4. What was the first city founded in the West? Louis thinks it was Sante Fe, New Mexico.

_______________ 5. For thirty years Bonita Ricardo has run the town's most popular restaurant.

_______________ 6. Jennifer's plan nearly collapsed when she met with an unexpected obstacle.

_______________ 7. Jason genuinely appreciated Yoshiko's encouragement and told him so.

_______________ 8. If we refrigerate this leftover chili, we can keep it for lunch tomorrow rather than buy our lunch.

_______________ 9. Pierre and Maria are careful with their money; they always shop for the best buy.

_______________ 10. I believe Mr. Jacob; he is known for his truthfulness.

Number correct ______ (total 10)

Analyzing Word Parts

The Latin Root *plic* This root comes from the Latin verb *plicare,* which means "to fold." In this unit, the target word *complicated* and the related words *complicate* and *complication* come from *plicare.* Other words that come from *plicare* are *replicate, replica, reply,* and *implication.* Look up the words listed below in your dictionary to learn their meanings and parts of speech. Then choose the word from the list that best completes the meaning of each sentence.

complication   implication   replica   replicate   reply

_______________ 1. Though Cliff wasn't sure what Ms. Anderson meant by her comments, the _?_ seemed to be that she thought he wasn't working as hard as he could.

_______________ 2. We were disappointed to learn that the painting we bought at the auction was not an original but only a _?_ .

_______________ 3. Had we not handed out the wrong schedule, the meeting might have come off without a single _?_ .

_______________ 4. If you tell Sheri that the matter is urgent and you need to hear from her, I'm sure she will _?_ immediately.

_______________ 5. Mr. Kent needs a sign for the back door of his restaurant. Can you _?_ the sign on the front door?

Number correct ______ (total 5)

Number correct in unit ______ (total 55)

The Last Word

Writing

One of the main jobs of a newspaper editor is to rewrite material. An editor tries to use the right words in order to communicate in a simple, direct way. Each sentence below can be rewritten into a shorter, simpler sentence by using one of the target words from this unit. Write your shortened, revised sentences on a separate sheet of paper. When you are finished, check your spelling.

1. Marlene liked studying the behavior of molecules and the characteristics of different elements.
2. The clerk gave Jay a slip of paper showing that he had purchased the model airplane at that store.
3. Many students at that university want to become experts in designing and building things.
4. Jody is one of the students who is running for class president.
5. Aunt Ruth was fascinated by the art, language, government, religion, and economy of the Incas.

Speaking

What is your favorite work of *literature?* Choose a story or novel that you like and prepare a short talk about it for your class. Include a brief summary of the work, and tell why it is one of your favorites.

Group Discussion

1. Sincerity is an important character trait. How do you know that a person is or is not *sincere?* What are the signs that tell you? In a group, discuss these questions.
2. What qualities should a political *candidate* have? In a small group, list the traits you consider important. What traits are likely to tell you that a person would be a good leader? You might want to limit yourselves to a specific government position, such as mayor of your city, governor of your state, or president of the United States.

UNIT 16: Review of Units 13–15

Part A Review Word List

Unit 13 Target Words

1. amateur
2. demand
3. individual
4. local
5. occasion
6. officer
7. parallel
8. right
9. screech
10. section
11. shatter
12. supreme
13. technique
14. vessel
15. yarn

Unit 13 Related Words

1. demanding
2. individualism
3. individualistic
4. locality
5. occasionally
6. office
7. supremacy
8. technical
9. technicality
10. technician
11. technocracy
12. technology

Unit 14 Target Words

1. associate
2. cloud
3. foresight
4. hardy
5. legend
6. memorial
7. migrate
8. mysterious
9. preserve
10. prohibit
11. region
12. restless
13. sacred
14. secrecy
15. souvenir

Unit 14 Related Words

1. association
2. emigrate
3. forefather
4. foreknowledge
5. hindsight
6. immigrate
7. legendary
8. migration
9. mystery
10. preservation
11. regional
12. secret

Unit 15 Target Words

1. candidate
2. chemistry
3. civilization
4. complicated
5. economic
6. engineer
7. establish
8. government
9. league
10. literature
11. patent
12. receipt
13. represent
14. sincere
15. will

Unit 15 Related Words

1. chemical
2. civil
3. civilize
4. complicate
5. complication
6. economical
7. economy
8. establishment
9. govern
10. representation
11. sincerity
12. uncivilized

Inferring Meaning from Context

For each sentence write the letter of the word or phrase that is closest in meaning to the word or words in italics.

____ 1. I always *associate* California with Yosemite National Park. Ever since we visited the park, it is the first thing I think of when I hear someone mention the state of California.

a. estimate b. assume c. link d. explore together

____ 2. Mickey thinks Ms. Marene should win the election, but I think the other *candidate* would make the best governor for our state.

a. voter b. nominee c. senator d. officer

____ 3. After several minutes of trying to get his students to pay attention, the teacher *demanded* that everyone listen.

a. insisted b. hinted c. declared d. wished

____ 4. Because the nearest hospital was many miles away, some wealthy individuals *established* a medical clinic for the residents of the small town.

a. set up b. shut down c. neglected d. visited

____ 5. Because we all wanted to live in a warmer climate, our family *migrated* from Alaska to Georgia.

a. drove b. escaped c. hitchhiked d. moved

____ 6. The famous diplomat described *an occasion* when he met the Queen of England.

a. a legend b. a moment c. a time d. an opportunity

____ 7. At Wilson Middle School, holding club meetings during the school day is *prohibited.* Students may participate in club activities before or after school only.

a. not allowed b. allowed c. preserved d. required

____ 8. I know Tanya was *sincere* when she said she liked my new coat. She bought one just like it yesterday!

a. restless b. truthful c. vicious d. honorable

____ 9. That calendar would make a perfect *souvenir* of our trip. Each time we flip through the pictures, we will remember the sites we visited.

a. reminder b. movie c. mission d. segment

____ 10. James just built another great campfire. Next time I'll have to watch how he does it, so I can learn his *technique.*

a. method b. display c. destination d. experience

Number correct ______ (total 10)

Using Review Words in Context

Using context clues, determine which word from the list below best fits in each blank. Write the word in the blank. Each word in the list will be used only once.

complicated	hardy	migrate	receipt	restless
economic	local	officer	region	right

A Success Story

The Great Depression of the 1930's was a time of great hardship throughout the United States. Whatever _______________ of the country one lived in—North, South, East, or West—the economy was on the edge of collapse. The _______________ problems were so _______________ that they could not be solved quickly.

Each section of the United States tried to solve its _______________ community problems in the most effective way. Experiencing great difficulty during the Depression, some of the Mexican residents of Los Angeles were offered the opportunity to _______________ back to Mexico. If they agreed to go, they had the legal _______________ to make their request to an _______________ of the county government for travel expenses. Upon _______________ of the request, the county would guarantee the total travel expenses for each person.

The Nava family, living in the Mexican community, decided to return to Mexico. Once they had made up their minds to go, they were eager to get started. Before they left, however, they decided to attend a farewell party thrown in their honor by their neighbors.

It was an ordinary party with a lot of food. Because this was a true celebration, everybody ate as much as they pleased. As a result, no one noticed little Julian Nava devouring everything in sight. What fun it was to consume whatever he wanted! To Julian, it seemed like heaven.

Before long, the party was over, and little Julian, along with his seven brothers and sisters, went to bed. It was a _______________ night for all because they kept thinking about tomorrow's trip. Everyone except Julian. He was thinking about his terrible stomachache.

Soon it became clear that Julian had more than an ordinary stomachache. The Navas rushed Julian directly to the local hospital. He had to be operated on immediately for a ruptured appendix.

The Navas never did go back to Mexico. Little Julian helped his family pick fruit in the summer. They lived in a tent on the farm and cooked their food over an open wood fire. It was a hard life, but the Navas were _______________ people who could withstand it.

Julian was educated in the Los Angeles public schools. During World War II, he served in the United States Navy. After the war, he went on to college and earned a Ph.D. in history from Harvard University.

Today, Julian is a writer and teacher who has made a valuable contribution to American education. Thanks to the hard work of his family and to his own persistence and dedication, Julian was able to overcome economic difficulty and has become a successful leader in his field.

Number correct ______ (total 10)

Part B **Review Word Reinforcement**

Using Language and Thinking Skills

Sentence Completion Write the word from the list below that best completes the meaning of the sentence.

civilization	economic	governments	preserved	screech
cloud	foresight	legend	represent	sincere

_______________ 1. Giving someone too much information can _?_ his or her understanding of the most important facts.

_______________ 2. The United States and Mexico enjoy close _?_ ties. Most of Mexico's imports come from the United States, and most of its exports go to the United States.

_______________ 3. Because the owner of the auto plant had the _?_ to hire more workers as car sales rose, she was able to produce and sell more cars.

_______________ 4. If you are _?_ about improving your grades next quarter, then you should study more and remember to do your homework.

_______________ 5. Representatives from the _?_ of the two countries met to discuss the peace treaty.

_______________ 6. Have you heard the _?_ of Paul Bunyan? According to the story, Paul was a lumberjack who could do amazing things.

_______________ 7. If you visit Chichén Itzá in Mexico, you can explore the ruins and learn a lot about the Mayan _?_ that existed there hundreds of years ago.

_______________ 8. What do the stars on this map _?_ ? Yoko says they indicate capital cities.

_______________ 9. Residents of the town were upset to hear that the town hall was to be demolished, so the city manager ordered that it be _?_.

_______________ 10. Just as the wolf got ready to pounce, the owl gave a high-pitched _?_ and took to the air.

Number correct _____ (total 10)

Matching Ideas Write the word from the list below that is most clearly related to the situation conveyed in the sentence.

chemistry	local	memorial	patent	secrecy
individual	literature	parallel	sacred	yarn

_______________ 1. The Summit Theater in our little town is crowded every weekend night. Even though there is a newer theater not too far away, most people in our community prefer the Summit.

_______________ 2. People of most religions consider their place of worship to be holy.

_______________ 3. Chris set up the test tubes and chemicals in the laboratory. As soon as her partner arrived, they were ready to begin the experiment.

_______________ 4. Mary and Rita do not agree on that issue. Let each girl explain her view.

_______________ 5. The English class will study poems, short stories, and novels.

_______________ 6. When Phyllis bought the gift, she made her little brothers promise not to tell her parents what it was.

_______________ 7. The sunken remains of the U.S.S. *Arizona* lie in Pearl Harbor, Hawaii—a silent reminder of the sailors who died there on December 7, 1941.

_______________ 8. The two roads run side by side.

________________ 9. All inventors want a government permit that protects their rights to their inventions.

________________ 10. Most people enjoy spinning a good story about their experiences.

Number correct ______ (total 10)

Practicing for Standardized Tests

Analogies Determine the relationship between the pair of capitalized words. Then decide which other word pair expresses a similar relationship. Write the letter of this word pair.

____ 1. PATENT : INVENTION :: (A) copyright : book (B) occasion : time (C) sickness : medicine (D) vessel : ship (E) screech : whisper

____ 2. AMATEUR : PROFESSIONAL :: (A) story : plot (B) solution : answer (C) winner : loser (D) quarterback : football (E) civilization : culture

____ 3. CHEMISTRY : SCIENCE :: (A) souvenir : souvenir shop (B) crisis : emergency (C) soccer : sport (D) technique : method (E) profit : loss

____ 4. SECTION : PART :: (A) solution : problem (B) league : association (C) twilight : sunrise (D) leg : table (E) government : democracy

____ 5. COMPLICATED : SIMPLE :: (A) right : wrong (B) furious : angry (C) hardy : strong (D) mysterious : unexplainable (E) difficult : hard

Number correct ______ (total 5)

Antonyms Write the letter of the word that is most nearly *opposite* in meaning to the capitalized word.

____ 1. SUPREME: (A) best (B) sacred (C) hardy (D) worst (E) sincere

____ 2. PROHIBIT: (A) preserve (B) allow (C) produce (D) represent (E) cloud

____ 3. SACRED: (A) holy (B) mysterious (C) private (D) discourteous (E) unholy

____ 4. HARDY: (A) strong (B) weak (C) painful (D) reliable (E) faithful

____ 5. ESTABLISH: (A) demolish (B) create (C) erect
(D) produce (E) preserve

____ 6. FORESIGHT: (A) fortune (B) faith (C) hindsight
(D) secrecy (E) prediction

____ 7. MYSTERIOUS: (A) sincere (B) strange (C) private
(D) explainable (E) complicated

____ 8. PRESERVE: (A) save (B) destroy (C) establish (D) display
(E) create

____ 9. RESTLESS: (A) calm (B) troubled (C) honest
(D) nervous (E) effortless

____ 10. SINCERE: (A) truthful (B) open (C) mysterious
(D) dishonest (E) dishonorable

Number correct ______ (total 10)

Synonyms Write the letter of the word that is closest in meaning to the capitalized word.

____ 1. CANDIDATE: (A) governor (B) applicant (C) officer
(D) amateur (E) companion

____ 2. MEMORIAL: (A) secret (B) reservoir (C) process
(D) legend (E) reminder

____ 3. REGION: (A) area (B) landscape (C) scene (D) view
(E) house

____ 4. VESSEL: (A) train (B) automobile (C) ship (D) mission
(E) officer

____ 5. YARN: (A) cloth (B) struggle (C) suit (D) technique
(E) story

Number correct ______ (total 5)

Spelling and Wordplay

Fill-ins Spell the target word correctly in the blanks to the right of its definition.

1. nonprofessional: a __ __ __ __ __ __

2. the science of matter and how it combines and separates:

   c __ __ __ __ __ __ __ y

3. culture: c __ __ __ __ __ z __ __ __ __ __

4. difficult: c _ _ p _ _ _ _ t _ _
5. expert that plans and builds things: e _ _ _ _ _ _ _
6. the established political rule:

   g _ v _ _ _ _ _ _ _
7. an association of nations: l _ _ g _ _
8. something to preserve the memory of an individual or an event:

   m _ _ _ _ _ a _
9. a ship: v _ _ _ _ l
10. a scream: s _ _ _ e _ _
11. a document that states someone's last wishes: _ i _ _
12. a remembrance or reminder: s _ _ _ _ _ _ r
13. to break and come apart: s _ _ _ t _ _
14. a method: t _ _ _ _ _ _ _ _
15. top-ranking; highest: s _ _ _ _ _ e

Number correct ______ (total 15)

Part C Related Word Reinforcement

Using Related Words

Sentence Completion Write the word from the list below that best completes the meaning of the sentence.

association	civil	mystery	representation	office
chemical	hindsight	preservation	occasionally	secret

______________ 1. According to an old saying, " ? is 20/20." It means that when you look back at things, you can see more clearly what would have been the best action.

______________ 2. Every good investigator loves a ? .

______________ 3. In the U.S. House of Representatives, ? is based on population. The greater the population of a state, the more representatives that state has in Congress.

_______________ 4. If you want to meet other young writers, you should join that new writer's _?_.

_______________ 5. The counselor told John to wait in the hall outside her _?_ until it was time for his appointment.

_______________ 6. Because Ms. Thomas was embarrassed by the bad language her children were using in public, she asked them to be _?_.

_______________ 7. You can trust Ricardo to keep a _?_. He never repeats what he hears.

_______________ 8. You should always make yourself aware of the _?_ compounds contained in any medicine you take.

_______________ 9. When city hall proposed to build a shopping mall on the site of the local park, angry townspeople got together to work for the _?_ of the park.

_______________ 10. Foods that are high in fat should be eaten not often, but only _?_.

Number correct _____ (total 10)

Reviewing Word Structures

The Word Parts *tech*, *migr*, *fore-*, and *plic* Review these word parts in Units 13–15. Then complete each sentence below with the word from the Related Words List on page 184 that best completes the meaning of the sentence. Use the directions in the parentheses following each sentence to help you choose the correct word.

_______________ 1. The language in that medical journal is so _?_ that I'm sure only a doctor or nurse could understand it. (Use a word with *tech.*)

_______________ 2. Ken is fascinated by the _?_ of salmon from the ocean back to their birthplace. (Use a word with *migr.*)

_______________ 3. If we had only had _?_ of the storm, we would never have planned the picnic for today. (Use a word with *fore-.*)

_______________ 4. Putting the wrong date on the invitations was just the first _?_ that occurred as we attempted to organize the party. (Use a word with *plic.*)

_______________ 5. Mr. and Mrs. Chang _?_ from China in 1975. (Use a word with *migr.*)

_______________ 6. After the examination, Dr. Juarez told Carol to see the __?__, who would take a sample of blood. (Use a word with *tech.*)

_______________ 7. Mark's great-grandmother told him that one of his __?__ was an Arapaho chief. (Use a word with *fore-*.)

_______________ 8. Make a list of what we need for dinner, and then ask each person to bring something on the list. Allowing everyone to bring whatever they want will only __?__ things. (Use a word with *plic.*)

_______________ 9. If the United States were a __?__, the president might be a great scientist. (Use a word with *tech.*)

_______________ 10. The people who were sworn in as new citizens at the special ceremony were happy they had __?__ to America. (Use a word with *migr.*)

Number correct ______ (total 10)

Number correct in unit ______ (total 95)

Vocab Lab 4

FOCUS ON: Behavior

What you do and say tells others a lot about who you are. Many words in English describe personality traits and human behavior. Some of these words are listed below.

abnormal (ab nôr′ m'l) adj. not normal or typical. • Sleeping more than twelve hours a day is *abnormal.* Most people require only eight to ten hours of sleep.

clique (klēk, klik) n. a small group that keeps to itself. • Ms. Kinoshita discussed the dangers of *cliques* and asked her students to be friendly to everyone.

conform (kən fôrm′) v. to make one's behavior similar to that of others. • "Be yourself!" the guidance counselor urged. "Don't *conform* to the ways of others. Do what you think is right for you."

congenial (kən jēn′ yəl) adj. nice; agreeable. • Pedro is easy to get along with—he is one of the most *congenial* students in our class.

depression (di presh′ ən) n. a feeling of sadness and gloom. • Some sadness is normal, but anyone who feels constant *depression* should seek help.

devious (dē′ vē əs) adj. dishonest; deceiving. • Because Tom was *devious,* his friends did not believe what he said.

docile (däs′ 'l) adj. obedient; manageable. • Our dog responds well to commands. She is a very *docile* pet.

dominant (däm′ ə nənt) adj. controlling by exercising power over others. • Mary Sue, a *dominant* person, often gets her friends to do what she wants.

erratic (i rat′ ik) adj. unpredictable; strange. • Mr. Morelli is concerned about Kari's *erratic* behavior. She bursts into tears or loses her temper for no apparent reason.

extrovert (eks′ trə vurt′) n. one who is interested in others rather than in just himself or herself. • Chuck enjoys activities with other people. He is an *extrovert.*

generous (jen′ ər əs) adj. eager to give or share with others. • Many teachers are *generous* with their time.

introvert (in′ trə vurt′) n. one who is interested more in self than in others. • Ms. Thomas was concerned that Shane was too much of an *introvert.* She arranged class activities to get him involved with others.

irrational (i rash′ ən 'l) adj. failing to make sense. • People at football games may be *irrational* at times, saying and doing foolish things.

petty (pet′ ē) adj. small-minded; focusing on unimportant matters. • Only a *petty* person would complain about being shortchanged a penny.

reticent (ret′ ə s'nt) adj. tending to be private; not sharing thoughts or feelings. • I'm never sure what's on Tanya's mind. She is such a *reticent* person.

Sentence Completion Complete each sentence below by writing the appropriate focus word.

_______________ 1. Sheila is _?_, and works well with others.

_______________ 2. It is probably because Paul is insecure that he often _?_ to the expectations of others.

_______________ 3. Kevin's friends know he is _?_, so they often encourage him to express his ideas and feelings.

_______________ 4. Among her friends, Erika is _?_. They usually do what she wants.

_______________ 5. Jake's muttering about seeing flying cows and birds as large as airplanes was _?_.

_______________ 6. Ms. Lee, a(n) _?_ person, gives much of her time and money to those in need.

_______________ 7. People came to mistrust Molly because she was _?_. She would say one thing to your face but another thing behind your back.

_______________ 8. Most people act pretty much the same from day to day. But Chad puzzles people because his conduct is _?_—you never know what he will do or say next.

_______________ 9. Rita, Novie, and Beth formed a _?_ in their eighth-grade class. They were friendly to one another but not to anyone else.

_______________ 10. The camp counselor, who was concerned that Len was too much of a(n) _?_, encouraged him to join in activities with the other campers.

_______________ 11. Under Ms. Diaz's training, Rusty, an Irish setter, changed from being undisciplined to _?_.

_______________ 12. After feeling very sad for several weeks, Ginger sought Dr. Ito's help for _?_.

_______________ 13. Daily headaches are _?_ and should be checked by a doctor.

_______________ 14. It is _?_ to focus on little things and minor irritations.

_______________ 15. Everybody needs time alone—even a(n) _?_.

Number correct ______ (total 15)

FOCUS ON: **Word Games**

The first thing some people turn to in a newspaper is the crossword puzzle. They enjoy the challenge of figuring out the right words and filling in the missing letters. In addition to being fun, crossword puzzles and other word games strengthen vocabulary.

This Vocab Lab features four games you can play at home or at school. The rules for playing them are easy, and all you need is a pencil, some paper, and a dictionary.

Words Within Words

Write a fairly long word, one with eight to twelve letters, at the top of your paper. Then see how many smaller words you can find within that long word. You may switch the order of letters, but use a given letter only as many times as it appears in the word.

The object of the game is to see how many words you can make from the letters in the original word. If you are playing the game with a friend, whoever writes down more words wins the game.

Notice some of the words that can come from the word *complicate: mop, cat, lie, ate, eat, oat, ample, pleat, tea, team, come, pat, peat, polite, place.*

Exercise A On the lines below, write at least ten words that you can make from the letters in the word *ignorance.*

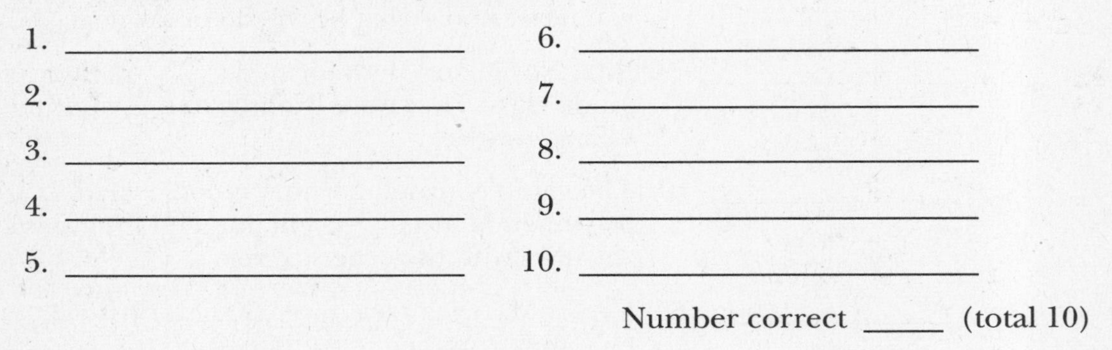

1. ____________________ 6. ____________________

2. ____________________ 7. ____________________

3. ____________________ 8. ____________________

4. ____________________ 9. ____________________

5. ____________________ 10. ____________________

Number correct _____ (total 10)

Letter Additions

One letter can make a great difference in a word. This is one reason spelling is so important. In this game, you change each word in the list into a different word by adding one letter at the beginning, the middle, or the end of the original word. For example, you can add *-e* to *pin* and get *pine.* Add an *-i* to *trade* and get *tirade.* Making a word plural does not count. Have your dictionary handy as you play the letter additions game.

Exercise B Make a new word from each of the following words by adding a letter.

11. rain ____________________ 13. race ____________________

12. win ____________________ 14. bake ____________________

15. pane ______________________ 18. steam ______________________

16. hot ______________________ 19. train ______________________

17. grim ______________________ 20. fright ______________________

Number correct _____ (total 10)

Anagrams

Have you ever taken a word and rearranged the letters so that it became another English word? If so, you made an anagram. Two words are anagrams only if the new word contains each letter of the original word. For example, *state* and *taste* are anagrams. So are *tip* and *pit.* For this game, too, you will want to keep your dictionary handy.

Exercise C Write an anagram for each of the following words. Remember that words may have more than one anagram.

21. pot ______________________ 26. rate ______________________

22. lame ______________________ 27. mad ______________________

23. tale ______________________ 28. adder ______________________

24. mesa ______________________ 29. trail ______________________

25. lane ______________________ 30. mane ______________________

Number correct _____ (total 10)

Pyramids

Word pyramids are an old word game. On the top line write one letter. On the second line write that letter and add another letter to make a two-letter word. On the third line add a third letter to make a three-letter word. Keep this process going until you have as long a word as you can write at the bottom. Look at the example below. Note that the letters do not have to be in the same order in each line.

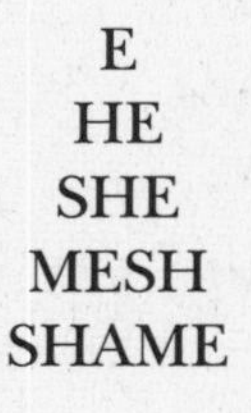

Exercise D Make three pyramids of your own. Use the letters *t, b,* and *h* for starting letters. If necessary, use your dictionary for help.

Number correct in Vocab Lab _____ (total 45)

Units 1–8 **Standardized Vocabulary Test**

The following questions test your comprehension of words studied in the first half of the book. Test questions have been written in a way that will familiarize you with the typical standardized test format. The questions are divided into the following categories: **synonyms, sentence completion, antonyms,** and **analogies.**

Synonyms

Each question below consists of a word in capital letters followed by five lettered words. In the blank, write the letter of the word that is closest in meaning to the word in capital letters. Because some of the questions require you to distinguish fine shades of meaning, consider all the choices before deciding which is best.

____ 1. COURTEOUS: (A) polite (B) advantageous (C) kind (D) opportune (E) sociable

____ 2. EFFECTIVE: (A) serious (B) brilliant (C) useful (D) dense (E) prompt

____ 3. MISHAP: (A) victim (B) plan (C) illness (D) accident (E) safety

____ 4. DISADVANTAGE: (A) discouragement (B) handicap (C) opportunity (D) suspicion (E) disturbance

____ 5. ATTENTION (A) dependence (B) notice (C) love (D) memory (E) opposition

____ 6. CONFERENCE: (A) meeting (B) result (C) party (D) society (E) class

____ 7. JOINTLY: (A) thoroughly (B) entirely (C) quickly (D) together (E) alone

____ 8. UTTER: (A) share (B) suspect (C) smile (D) decrease (E) speak

____ 9. PROMPT: (A) fat (B) negligent (C) quick (D) tardy (E) musical

____ 10. BENEFIT: (A) mishap (B) help (C) effort (D) display (E) request

____ 11. ASSAULT: (A) collision (B) assurance (C) victim (D) opinion (E) attack

____ 12. VICINITY: (A) neighborhood (B) identity (C) privacy (D) house (E) land

____ 13. POSITION: (A) career (B) destiny (C) suspicion (D) job (E) salary

____ 14. OPPORTUNITY: (A) estimate (B) chance (C) completion (D) opinion (E) density

____ 15. DENSE: (A) brilliant (B) thin (C) thick (D) round (E) long

____ 16. SLOGAN: (A) picture (B) joke (C) saying (D) speech (E) segment

____ 17. CAREER: (A) work (B) destiny (C) collision (D) fortune (E) result

____ 18. DISGUISE: (A) show (B) disband (C) dispose (D) wait (E) conceal

____ 19. EXPRESS: (A) extinguish (B) communicate (C) solve (D) think (E) travel

____ 20. OPINION: (A) opponent (B) question (C) answer (D) judgment (E) knowledge

Number correct ______ (total 20)

Sentence Completion

Each sentence below has one or two blanks. Each blank indicates that a word has been omitted. Beneath the sentence are five lettered words or pairs of words. In the blank to the left of each sentence, write the letter of the word or pair of words that *best* fits the meaning of the sentence.

____ 1. The members did not _?_ what a wonderful _?_ Jason had made to the club until after he quit.
(A) think . . . destination (B) realize . . . contribution
(C) agree . . . majority (D) possess . . . career
(E) return . . . result

____ 2. All over the city, lights in houses were turned on at _?_.
(A) landscape (B) surplus (C) profit (D) twilight
(E) fortune

____ 3. To show how her business had earned a(n) _?_, Ms. Juarez prepared a(n) _?_ report.
(A) fortune . . . financial (B) disadvantage . . . indirect
(C) issue . . . negligent (D) conference . . . dense
(E) application . . . sociable

____ 4. There must be a more _?_ way to reach our _?_; this route is taking too much time.

(A) severe . . . position (B) immediate . . . mishap
(C) direct . . . destination (D) interesting . . . oppression
(E) indirect . . . society

____ 5. The puppy _?_ to get out of the kitchen, but it did not succeed because its owner had done a(n) _?_ job of blocking the doorway.

(A) struggled . . . thorough (B) asked . . . urgent
(C) wished . . . negligible (D) cried . . . ineffective
(E) wanted . . . terrible

____ 6. From the confused look on Mark's face, I _?_ he didn't understand the joke.

(A) appreciate (B) deserve (C) wish (D) pose (E) suspect

____ 7. Bob is so hungry, he may _?_ everything in the refrigerator.

(A) transfer (B) devour (C) rearrange (D) straighten
(E) extinguish

____ 8. The students set up a(n) _?_ for their parents showing the _?_ kinds of work they had done in school that year.

(A) mission . . . troubled (B) observation . . . negative
(C) conference . . . prompt (D) display . . . various
(E) opportunity . . . pitiful

____ 9. If you _?_ the amount of time you spend studying, I bet you will be _?_ happy with your next report card.

(A) reduce . . . very (B) remember . . . indirectly
(C) dissolve . . . jointly (D) disregard . . . quickly
(E) increase . . . especially

____ 10. Mary thinks Charles was trying to _?_ her, so she intends to _?_ his story.

(A) insult . . . appreciate (B) inform . . . realize
(C) deceive . . . investigate (D) soothe . . . oppose
(E) suspect . . . write

____ 11. When Jeff was not chosen for the basketball team, he felt _?_.

(A) extinct (B) informative (C) discouraged (D) successful
(E) sociable

____ 12. The _?_ of the crime felt _?_ to all the people who had helped him after the horrible experience.

(A) opponent . . . hateful (B) invader . . . joyful
(C) informer . . . discourteous (D) contributor . . . judgmental
(E) victim . . . indebted

____ 13. Tina bounced on the diving board and then ? into the pool.
(A) plunged (B) rolled (C) walked (D) ran (E) dissolved

____ 14. If no one ? the money after two weeks, you may have it.
(A) demolishes (B) claims (C) restores (D) transforms
(E) prefers

____ 15. I ? James has some ? on the plans for our class trip since he was at the last planning meeting.
(A) doubt . . . ideas (B) remember . . . segments
(C) assume . . . information (D) hope . . . completion
(E) think . . . transformation

Number correct ______ (total 15)

Antonyms

Each question below consists of a word in capital letters followed by five lettered words. In the blank, write the letter of the word that is most nearly *opposite* in meaning to the word in capital letters. Because some of the questions require you to distinguish fine shades of meaning, consider all the choices before deciding which is best.

____ 1. SERIOUS: (A) significant (B) useless (C) comical
(D) unsociable (E) wrong

____ 2. SEVERE: (A) dense (B) brilliant (C) mild (D) negative
(E) harsh

____ 3. DEMOLISH: (A) lie (B) build (C) destroy (D) use (E) win

____ 4. SOLUTION: (A) reward (B) effort (C) person
(D) participation (E) problem

____ 5. OPPOSE: (A) support (B) solve (C) assault (D) deserve
(E) extinguish

____ 6. TROUBLED: (A) tempting (B) judgmental (C) discouraged
(D) carefree (E) sociable

____ 7. IMMEDIATE: (A) prompt (B) delayed (C) careful
(D) extinct (E) effective

____ 8. DISPLAY: (A) hide (B) show (C) make (D) devour
(E) disband

____ 9. RESULT: (A) effect (B) estimate (C) cause (D) solution
(E) factor

____ 10. BRILLIANT: (A) starry (B) smart (C) dependent
(D) dark (E) uncommon

Number correct ______ (total 10)

Analogies

Each question below consists of a pair of capitalized words followed by five pairs of words that are lettered. Determine the relationship between the pair of capitalized words. Then decide which lettered word pair expresses a similar relationship. In the blank, write the letter of this word pair.

____ 1. LANDSCAPE : SCENERY :: (A) mountain : trail (B) issue : question (C) vase : water (D) lid : pan (E) morning : night

____ 2. DISGUISE : COSTUME :: (A) discourage : discouragement (B) chase : escape (C) socialize : sociology (D) wash : soap (E) shop : food

____ 3. NAVIGATOR : RADAR :: (A) chicken : meat (B) professor : teacher (C) barber : scissors (D) cook : restaurant (E) envelope : letter

____ 4. TRANSFORM : CHANGE :: (A) assure : promise (B) give : love (C) press : wrinkle (D) help : grow (E) break : fix

____ 5. LACK : POSSESS :: (A) restore : finish (B) smile : grin (C) demolish : solve (D) disband : dissolve (E) lead : follow

Number correct ______ (total 5)

Number correct in Units 1–8 Test _____ (total 50)

Units 9–16 **Standardized Vocabulary Test**

The following questions test your comprehension of words studied in the second half of the book. Test questions have been written in a way that will familiarize you with the typical standardized test format. The questions are divided into the following categories: **synonyms, sentence completion, antonyms,** and **analogies.**

Synonyms

Each question below consists of a word in capital letters followed by five lettered words. In the blank, write the letter of the word that is closest in meaning to the word in capital letters. Because some of the questions require you to distinguish fine shades of meaning, consider all the choices before deciding which is best.

____ 1. SITE: (A) reservoir (B) movie (C) vision (D) location (E) conductor

____ 2. COMBAT: (A) complication (B) flight (C) departure (D) reward (E) fighting

____ 3. CONSCIOUS: (A) troubled (B) alive (C) awake (D) popular (E) thankful

____ 4. REQUIRE: (A) demand (B) represent (C) take (D) establish (E) contract

____ 5. CORE: (A) region (B) technician (C) center (D) agent (E) density

____ 6. SHATTER: (A) share (B) break (C) stumble (D) support (E) repair

____ 7. ABANDON: (A) visit (B) leave (C) strengthen (D) assure (E) return

____ 8. EXCEPTIONAL: (A) unusual (B) meaningful (C) hardy (D) unhappy (E) serious

____ 9. STRATEGY: (A) rule (B) struggle (C) story (D) plan (E) mystery

____ 10. PRESERVE: (A) choose (B) save (C) establish (D) abandon (E) help

____ 11. FAITHFUL: (A) supreme (B) thankful (C) loyal (D) sincere (E) sacred

____ 12. RELIABLE: (A) technical (B) restless (C) old
(D) changeable (E) dependable

____ 13. SACRED: (A) local (B) holy (C) humble (D) peaceful
(E) faithful

____ 14. DEVELOP: (A) grow (B) investigate (C) neglect
(D) represent (E) demolish

____ 15. CLASSIFY: (A) cloud (B) study (C) group (D) learn
(E) identify

____ 16. FURIOUS: (A) fortunate (B) angry (C) strong
(D) courteous (E) remarkable

____ 17. VICIOUS: (A) mean (B) kind (C) extreme (D) conscious
(E) various

____ 18. YARN: (A) story (B) strategy (C) poem (D) memorial
(E) reservoir

____ 19. ESTABLISH: (A) express (B) associate (C) conduct
(D) ruin (E) create

____ 20. FRAGMENT: (A) technique (B) requirement (C) step
(D) piece (E) event

Number correct ______ (total 20)

Sentence Completion

Each sentence below has one or two blanks. Each blank indicates that a word has been omitted. Beneath the sentence are five lettered words or pairs of words. In the blank to the left of each sentence, write the letter of the word or pair of words that *best* fits the meaning of the sentence.

____ 1. During class Mr. Washington said, "The test tomorrow will _?_ you to _?_ the area of a rectangle and a triangle."
(A) ask . . . lose (B) require . . . calculate (C) tell . . . forget
(D) order . . . associate (E) allow . . . return

____ 2. When Jason slammed the door, my house of cards _?_.
(A) leaped (B) stumbled (C) dissolved (D) screeched
(E) collapsed

____ 3. Anne was in such _?_ pain from the injury that she cried on and off for most of the day.
(A) brilliant (B) little (C) extreme (D) unconscious
(E) enjoyable

____ 4. Blowing into the balloon will cause it to __?__.

(A) contract (B) interrupt (C) migrate (D) expand
(E) collide

____ 5. The __?__ weight of that turkey is nine to ten pounds; I'm sure that size turkey is not __?__ to feed thirty people Thanksgiving dinner.

(A) approximate . . . sufficient (B) direct . . . effective
(C) local . . . courteous (D) total . . . thorough
(E) conscious . . . complicated

____ 6. Paddling across the pond, the boys imagined the canoe was a huge __?__ and they were __?__ new lands.

(A) memorial . . . buying (B) vessel . . . exploring
(C) candidate . . . visiting (D) site . . . representing
(E) reservoir . . . building

____ 7. When Tim __?__ we would find our way out of this __?__, he did not know that you had lost our compass.

(A) promised . . . occasion (B) predicted . . . region
(C) said . . . patent (D) stated . . . league
(E) calculated . . . residence

____ 8. If we __?__ them for another mile at this speed, we will be __?__.

(A) oppose . . . economical (B) classify . . . parallel
(C) pursue . . . exhausted (D) watch . . . thankful
(E) call . . . late

____ 9. When Angelo __?__ to the state of Washington, he became a(n) __?__ of Seattle.

(A) migrated . . . resident (B) erupted . . . candidate
(C) expanded . . . establishment (D) walked . . . section
(E) went . . . souvenir

____ 10. To __?__ the land in the park, the park ranger __?__ walking on unmarked paths and picking flowers and other plants.

(A) save . . . encouraged (B) help . . . required
(C) develop . . . demanded (D) preserve . . . prohibited
(E) control . . . classified

____ 11. After __?__ of his high school diploma, Charles went on to college.

(A) return (B) load (C) hope (D) receipt (E) right

____ 12. Until the inventor got a(n) __?__ on his new machine, he insisted on __?__ and would not let his family discuss the invention with anyone.

(A) patent . . . secrecy (B) price . . . mercy
(C) officer . . . exploration (D) degree . . . gravity
(E) amateur . . . society

____ 13. Short stories are Lynn's favorite type of __?__.

(A) civilization (B) chemistry (C) literature (D) science
(E) history

____ 14. A(n) __?__ will soon inspect that __?__ of the ship, so the crew is hurrying to finish cleaning it.

(A) companion . . . factor (B) officer . . . section
(C) teacher . . . strategy (D) vessel . . . floor
(E) government . . . legend

____ 15. If you are going to vote in the election for president, you'd better find out all you can about the two __?__

(A) degrees (B) exceptions (C) mysteries (D) chemicals
(E) candidates

Number correct ______ (total 15)

Antonyms

Each question below consists of a word in capital letters followed by five lettered words. In the blank, write the letter of the word that is most nearly *opposite* in meaning to the word in capital letters. Because some of the questions require you to distinguish fine shades of meaning, consider all the choices before deciding which is best.

____ 1. REMARKABLE: (A) exceptional (B) ordinary (C) hardy
(D) corrupt (E) reliable

____ 2. EXPAND: (A) exhaust (B) divide (C) leave (D) contract
(E) increase

____ 3. PRODUCE: (A) make (B) provide (C) demolish
(D) establish (E) use

____ 4. AMATEUR: (A) hero (B) professional (C) forefather
(D) championship (E) opponent

____ 5. MEANINGFUL: (A) unimportant (B) mysterious (C) funny
(D) unnecessary (E) complicated

____ 6. FORESIGHT: (A) hindsight (B) stupidity (C) wisdom
(D) locality (E) fault

____ 7. COMPLICATED: (A) exceptional (B) silly (C) weak
(D) simple (E) strategic

____ 8. RESTLESS: (A) loud (B) sociable (C) fearful (D) angry
(E) calm

____ 9. HARDY: (A) foolhardy (B) weak (C) uneducated
(D) supreme (E) dense

____ 10. CLOUD: (A) represent (B) deceive (C) explain (D) confuse (E) predict

Number correct ______ (total 10)

Analogies

Each question below consists of a pair of capitalized words followed by five pairs of words that are lettered. Determine the relationship between the pair of capitalized words. Then decide which lettered word pair expresses a similar relationship. In the blank, write the letter of this word pair.

____ 1. GRAVITY : FORCE :: (A) dentist : drill (B) happiness : feeling (C) region : New England (D) picture : frame (E) closet : clothes

____ 2. PURSUE : CHASE :: (A) add : subtract (B) conduct : sing (C) sit : stand (D) live : die (E) migrate : move

____ 3. LEGEND : LITERATURE :: (A) child : adult (B) wall : bricks (C) Europe : North America (D) rose : flower (E) sweater : wool

____ 4. CRISIS : PANIC :: (A) candidate : election (B) calculator : buttons (C) exercise : stiffness (D) cardinal : bird (E) core : exterior

____ 5. VICIOUS : FRIENDLY :: (A) old : young (B) sincere : truthful (C) cold : pain (D) unconscious : unaware (E) near : familiar

Number correct ______ (total 5)

Number correct in Units 9–16 Test _____ (total 50)

SPELLING HANDBOOK

Knowing the meanings of words is essential to using language correctly. However, another important skill is knowing how to spell the words you use.

Almost everyone has at least some problems with spelling. If you have trouble spelling, you might be encouraged to know that many others like you have learned to avoid spelling errors by following these suggestions:

1. **Proofread everything you write.** Everyone occasionally makes errors through carelessness or haste. By carefully reading through what you have written, you will catch many of your errors.

2. **Look up difficult words in a dictionary.** If you are not sure about the spelling of a word, don't guess at it. Take the time to look up the word.

3. **Learn to look at the letters in a word.** Learn to spell a word by examining various letter combinations contained in the word. Note the prefix, suffix, or double letters. Close your eyes and visualize the word. Then write the word from memory. Look at the word again to check your spelling.

4. **Pronounce words carefully.** It may be that you misspell certain words because you do not pronounce them correctly. For example, if you write *probly* instead of *probably,* it is likely that you are mispronouncing the word. Learning how to pronounce words and memorizing the letter combinations that create the sounds will improve your spelling.

5. **Keep a list of your "spelling demons."** Although you may not think about it, you *do* correctly spell most of the words you use. It is usually a few specific words that give you the most trouble. Keep a list of the words you have trouble spelling, and concentrate on learning them. Also, look for patterns in the words you misspell and learn those patterns.

6. **Use memory helps, called mnemonic devices, for words that give you trouble.** *Stationery* has *er* as in *letter;* there is *a rat* in *separate; Wednesday* contains *wed.*

7. **Learn and apply the rules given in this section.** Make sure you understand these rules. Then practice using them until they become automatic.

Words with Prefixes

The Addition of Prefixes

A prefix is a group of letters added to the beginning of a word to change its meaning. When a prefix is added to a base word, the spelling of the base word remains the same. (For further information about word parts, see pages 7–13.)

con- + form = conform
dis- + courage = discourage
re- + store = restore
ex- + change = exchange
de- + frost = defrost
in- + dependent = independent

A prefix can be added to a root as well as to a base word. A root is a word part that cannot stand alone; it must be joined to other parts to form a word. A root can be joined with many different prefixes to form words with different meanings. **However, the spelling of the prefix and the root remains the same.**

pro- + duce = produce
in- + vite = invite
per- + mit = permit
re- + sult = result

Exercise A Add the prefixes as indicated, and write the new word.

1. *pro-* + vide = ______________
2. *ad-* + venture = ______________
3. *ex-* + press = ______________
4. *un-* + til = ______________
5. *in-* + trude = ______________
6. *com-* + pare = ______________
7. *de-* + liver = ______________
8. *dis-* + able = ______________
9. *re-* + call = ______________
10. *per-* + form = ______________

Number correct ________ (total 10)

Exercise B Using words from the following list, complete each sentence with two words that have the same root.

assumed	decrease	enclosed	inspected	received
confer	deserve	encouraged	insulted	result
consume	disclose	increase	prefer	suspected
deceived	discouraged	informed	preserve	transform

1. Martin was ________________ by the advertisement and ________________ something he would never use.

2. When Janice asked how she could ________________ her robot into a super athlete, she was ________________ that parts were not available.

3. Because Michael wanted to lose weight, he tried to ________________ the amount of food he ate and to ________________ the amount of exercise he got.

4. When the Westside Whales ________________ us by saying we couldn't play ball, we knew the big game would have only one ________________—we'd destroy them.

5. Blair ________________ she could not ________________ raw fish, and when she tried to eat some, she knew she had guessed right.

6. "When would you ________________ to talk about your schedule?" the counselor asked. "We can ________________ on Monday or Tuesday."

7. Enrique was not ________________ when he didn't catch any fish. In fact, he was ________________ because he had some bites.

8. The detective ________________ the scene of the crime and then delcared that he ________________ that the criminal lived nearby.

9. "According to the ________________ letter," Mark said, "I only have to return the post card, and the magazine will ________________ to me which prize I have already won!"

10. "We should ________________ the city park and not let a parking lot be built on it," Traci said, "because people ________________ to have a park close by to visit."

Number correct ________ (total 20)

The Prefix *ad-*

When some prefixes are added to certain words, the spelling of the prefix changes. The prefix *ad-* changes in the following cases to create a double consonant:

ac- before *c*	*ag-* before *g*	*an-* before *n*	*ar-* before *r*	*at-* before *t*
af- before *f*	*al-* before *l*	*ap-* before *p*	*as-* before *s*	

Examples:

ad- + cept = accept
ad- + fect = affect
ad- + gravation = aggravation
ad- + low = allow
ad- + nouncement = announcement
ad- + pear = appear
ad- + rive = arrive
ad- + sist = assist
ad- + sign = assign
ad- + tend = attend

Exercise Add the prefix *ad-* to each of the roots or base words below. Change the spelling of the prefix as appropriate, and write the word.

1. *ad-* + vantage = ________________
2. *ad-* + sault = ________________
3. *ad-* + cident = ________________
4. *ad-* + nex = ________________
5. *ad-* + proximate = ________________
6. *ad-* + firm = ________________
7. *ad-* + plication = ________________
8. *ad-* + ray = ________________
9. *ad-* + sume = ________________
10. *ad-* + tain = ________________
11. *ad-* + prove = ________________
12. *ad-* + equate = ________________
13. *ad-* + gression = ________________
14. *ad-* + test = ________________
15. *ad-* + locate = ________________
16. *ad-* + curate = ________________
17. *ad-* + sure = ________________
18. *ad-* + verb = ________________

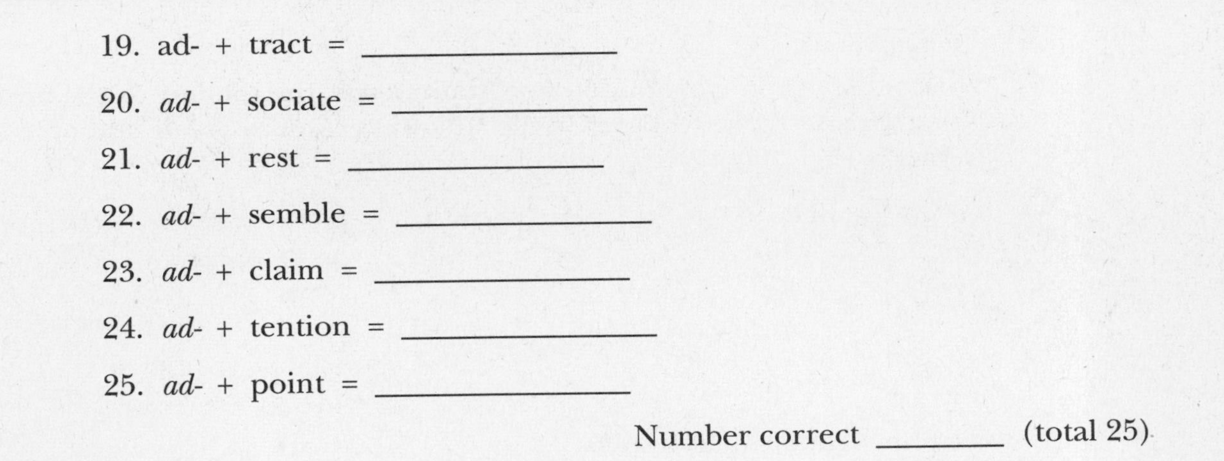

19. ad- + tract = ________________

20. *ad-* + sociate = ________________

21. *ad-* + rest = ________________

22. *ad-* + semble = ________________

23. *ad-* + claim = ________________

24. *ad-* + tention = ________________

25. *ad-* + point = ________________

Number correct ________ (total 25)

The Prefix *com-*

The spelling of the prefix *com-* does not change when it is added to roots or words that begin with the letter *m, p,* or *b.*

com- + mon = common
com- + panion = companion
com- + parable = comparable
com- + bat = combat

The prefix *com-* changes to *con-* when added to roots or words that begin with the letter *c, d, g, j, n, q, s, t,* or *v.*

com- + science = conscience
com- + vene = convene
com- + nect = connect
com- + cert = concert

The prefix *com-* changes to *col-* when added to roots or words that begin with the letter *l,* to create a double consonant.

com- + lect = collect
com- + lide = collide

The prefix *com-* changes to *cor-* when added to roots or words that begin with the letter *r,* to create a double consonant.

com- + rection = correction
com- + rupt = corrupt

Exercise A Add the prefix *com-* to each of the roots or base words below. Change the spelling of the prefix as appropriate, and write the word.

1. *com-* + plication = ________________

2. *com-* + bine = ________________

3. *com-* + respond = ________________

4. *com-* + quer = ________________

5. *com-* + mand = ________________

6. *com-* + gress = ________________

7. *com-* + pose = ________________

8. *com-* + strict = ______________

9. *com-* + serve = ______________

10. *com-* + tempt = ______________

11. *com-* + rode = ______________

12. *com-* + mittee = ______________

13. *com-* + lapse = ______________

14. *com-* + centrate = ______________

15. *com-* + plete = ______________

Number correct ________ (total 15)

Exercise B Find the misspelled word in each group. Write the word correctly.

______________ 1. convey
complex
comceal
compass

______________ 2. comvince
contract
compromise
corrode

______________ 3. confine
comment
conplain
concentrate

______________ 4. complete
contribute
comceited
consume

______________ 5. compress
conduct
competition
comform

______________ 6. convince
collection
compartment
conmit

______________ 7. confer
comfirm
convention
contain

______________ 8. concern
company
comfidence
consist

______________ 9. computer
condition
convert
corfess

______________ 10. comtact
concrete
construction
commence

Number correct ______ (total 10)

The Prefix *in-*

The spelling of the prefix *in-* does not change, except in the following cases:

(a) The prefix *in-* changes to *im-* when added to roots or words beginning with *m, p,* or *b*.

in- + mediate = immediate

in- + mature = immature

in- + perfect = imperfect

in- + balance = imbalance

(b) The prefix *in-* changes to *il-* when added to roots or words beginning with *l*, to create a double consonant.

in- + legal = illegal   *in-* + logical = illogical

(c) The prefix *in-* changes to *ir-* when added to roots or words beginning with *r*, to create a double consonant.

in- + regular = irregular   *in-* + responsible = irresponsible

Exercise A Add the prefix *in-* to each of the roots or base words below. Change the spelling of the prefix as appropriate, and write the word.

1. *in-* + portant = ________________
2. *in-* + vasion = ________________
3. *in-* + replaceable = ________________
4. *in-* + personal = ________________
5. *in-* + literate = ________________
6. *in-* + effective = ________________
7. *in-* + possible = ________________
8. *in-* + jury = ________________
9. *in-* + formation = ________________
10. *in-* + sist = ________________
11. *in-* + legible = ________________
12. *in-* + mortal = ________________
13. *in-* + habit = ________________
14. *in-* + migration = ________________
15. *in-* + nocent = ________________
16. *in-* + polite = ________________
17. *in-* + crease = ________________
18. *in-* + removable = ________________
19. *in-* + pure = ________________
20. *in-* + attentive = ________________

Number correct ______ (total 20)

Exercise B Find the misspelled word in each group. Write the word correctly.

______ 1. inlustrate
immature
implore
impermanent

______ 2. import
inrigate
impose
impractical

______ 3. indeed
inherit
imply
imquire

______ 4. imperil
impression
inprison
independent

______ 5. insure
intent
inpact
insight

______ 6. indecent
inpulse
indent
indefinite

______ 7. immobilize
improve
inprint
intend

______ 8. irreligious
impoverish
inpartial
inspection

______ 9. inlegal
incline
interior
infect

______ 10. impair
imstruct
infant
ingredient

Number correct ______ (total 10)

The Prefix *ex-*

The spelling of the prefix *ex-* does not change when it is added to roots or words beginning with vowels or with the consonant *p, t, h,* or *c*.

ex- + press = express
ex- + treme = extreme
ex- + hale = exhale
ex- + cuse = excuse
ex- + it = exit
ex- + ample = example

Exception: *Ex-* becomes *ec-* before *c* in the word *eccentric.*

The prefix *ex-* changes to *ef-* when added to roots or words beginning with *f*.

ex- + fort = effort
ex- + fect = effect

The prefix *ex-* changes to *e-* before most other consonants.

ex- + motion = emotion
ex- + vent = event
ex- + ject = eject
ex- + lection = election

No common English words begin the letters *exs*. When the prefix *ex-* is joined to roots that begin with the letter *s*, the *s* is dropped.

ex- + sert = exert
ex- + sist = exist

Exercise A Find the misspelled word in each group. Write the word correctly.

______ 1. extinct
exhaust
exrase
explain

______ 2. ecchange
excite
exhibit
exceed

______ 3. elude
exceptional
emit
eterior

______ 4. explode
expose
evacuate
eccellent

______ 5. ecceptional
elect
expansion
expire

______ 6. exlevate
eminent
explore
extend

______ 7. ehaust
emergency
erode
extract

______ 8. exterior
eperience
evaporate
examine

______ 9. exercise
existence
eperiment
elapse

______ 10. expend
external
exhume
exsecute

Number correct ______ (total 10)

Exercise B Add the prefix *ex-* to each of the roots or base words below. Change the spelling of the prefix as appropriate, and write the word.

1. *ex-* + normous = ______
2. *ex-* + ducate = ______
3. *ex-* + pand = ______
4. *ex-* + migrate = ______
5. *ex-* + ception = ______
6. *ex-* + valuate = ______
7. *ex-* + pel = ______
8. *ex-* + dition = ______
9. *ex-* + plore = ______
10. *ex-* + spect = ______

Number correct ______ (total 10)

Words with Suffixes

Words Ending in *y*

A suffix is a group of letters added to the end of a word that changes the word's meaning.

When a suffix is added to a word ending in *y* preceded by a consonant, the *y* is usually changed to *i*.

strategy + *-es* = strategies
mystery + *-ous* = mysterious
twenty + *-eth* = twentieth
merry + *-ly* = merrily
carry + *-er* = carrier

Exceptions:

(a) When *-ing* is added, the *y* does not change.

satistify + *-ing* = satisfying
unify + *-ing* = unifying
carry + *-ing* = carrying
supply + *-ing* = supplying

(b) In some one-syllable words the *y* does not change.

dry + *-ness* = dryness
shy + *-ness* = shyness

When a suffix is added to a word ending in *y* preceded by a vowel, the *y* usually does not change.

employ + *-ed* = employed
destroy + *-er* = destroyer
enjoy + *-able* = enjoyable
joy + *-ful* = joyful

Exceptions: day + *-ly* = daily
gay + *-ly* = gaily

Exercise A In these sentences, find each misspelled word, and write the correct spelling on the line following the sentence. There may be more than one misspelled word in a sentence.

1. William's mother was annoyed that the earlyer William got up, the longer he delayed getting ready for school.

 ____

2. Brenda relayed her brother's message, but she knew her parents would never believe he was staing at school late just because he was studying.

 ____

3. While Julie looked at the pityful, lonely puppy, her mind was racing with a thousand strategyies for talking her mom into letting her keep it.

 ____

4. Ms. Lopez applied for the job as assistant libraryan by filling out an application and talking to the principal, Mr. Bradley.

 ____

5. According to the historycal record, the earliest settlers in America did not usually have a plentyful supply of food.

____

6. Albert was so busy playing with his dog and watching the geese flying north that he didn't notice that he had straied into the wildest part of the park.

____

7. Susan's father is always looking for business opportunityes in our county or in one of the two neighboring countyes.

____

Number correct ______ (total 10)

Exercise B Add the suffixes indicated, and write the word in the blank.

1. entry + *-es* = ________________
2. display + *-ed* = ________________
3. sixty + *-es* = ________________
4. society + *-es* = ________________
5. pity + *-ing* = ________________
6. easy + *-ly* = ________________
7. busy + *-est* = ________________
8. frenzy + *-ed* = ________________
9. study + *-ing* = ________________
10. story + *-es* = ________________
11. laboratory + *-es* = ________________
12. pray + *-ing* = ________________
13. supply + *-er* = ________________
14. factory + *-es* = ________________
15. multiply + *-ing* = ________________
16. dismay + *-ed* = ________________
17. qualify + *-ing* = ________________
18. fancy + *-ful* = ________________
19. reality + *-es* = ________________
20. mutiny + *-ed* = ________________

21. necessary + *-ly* = ________________
22. vary + *-able* = ________________
23. pay + *-ment* = ________________
24. magnify + *-ing* = ________________
25. play + *-er* = ________________

Number correct ______ (total 25)

The Final Silent *e*

When a suffix beginning with a vowel is added to a word ending in a silent *e*, the *e* is usually dropped.

reverse + *-al* = reversal
circulate + *-ion* = circulation
dispose + *-able* = disposable
explore + *-er* = explorer
finance + *-ed* = financed
dissolve + *-ing* = dissolving

When a suffix beginning with a consonant is added to a word ending in a silent *e*, the *e* is usually retained.

tame + *-ness* = tameness
strange + *-ly* = strangely
hope + *-ful* = hopeful
purpose + *-less* = purposeless
amaze + *-ment* = amazement
whole + *-ness* = wholeness

Exceptions:

true + *-ly* = truly
argue + *-ment* = argument
whole + *-ly* = wholly
awe + *-ful* = awful

Exercise A In these sentences, find each misspelled word, and write the correct spelling on the line following the sentence. There may be more than one misspelled word in a sentence.

1. Andrew bravly plungeed ahead, forcing his way through the densely overgrown forest.

   ____

2. Sarah's greatest advantages over her teammates were her accuracy and her dazzleing speed.

   ____

3. An observer reported that the earthquake had left many people homless.

   ____

4. When the popular singer arrived, the excited crowd erupted into cheers and everyone began pushing and shoveing to get closer.

____

5. The gratful winners promised they would work hard to prove they deserved the award.

____

6. In the empty house, chains rattleed at midnight, and footsteps echoed in the lonly hall.

____

7. Michita stumbled across the dry and featurless land searching for water.

____

8. Following the investigateion, police officers decided that Joanne was blamless.

____

9. When he heard the applause, Mark was truely happy he had chosen to join the drama club.

____

10. Even Rosa was surprised at her rapid improvment after only a few days of studying.

____

11. Sandra's feeblness gradually disappeared as she exercised the leg that had been brokeen.

____

12. Raoul paged quickly through the newspaper searching for the announcment telling who had won the contest.

____

13. Ann pasted the pieces from the broken pot back together, hopeing she could still use it.

____

14. Elston's singlness of purpose as he shot basket after basket puzzld his younger brother.

____

15. Bret glanced at his watch and, because of the latness of the hour, decided to call his mom and ask for a ride home.

____

Number correct ______ (total 20)

Exercise B Add the suffixes indicated, and write the new word in the blank.

1. collide + *-ing* = ________________
2. expense + *-ive* = ________________
3. navigate + *-ion* = ________________
4. reserve + *-ation* = ________________
5. cease + *-less* = ________________
6. move + *-able* = ________________
7. decrease + *-ed* = ________________
8. immediate + *-ly* = ________________
9. glide + *-ing* = ________________
10. lame + *-ness* = ________________
11. hate + *-ful* = ________________
12. restore + *-ation* = ________________
13. determine + *-ation* = ________________
14. entire + *-ly* = ________________
15. involve + *-ment* = ________________
16. stole + *-en* = ________________
17. confine + *-ment* = ________________
18. solve + *-ing* = ________________
19. complete + *-ing* = ________________
20. celebrate + *-ion* = ________________
21. severe + *-ly* = ________________
22. educate + *-ion* = ________________
23. whole + *-some* = ________________
24. grade + *-ation* = ________________
25. invade + *-er* = ________________

Number correct ____________ (total 25)

Doubling the Final Consonant

In one-syllable words that end with a single consonant preceded by a single vowel, double the final consonant before adding a suffix beginning with a vowel.

pin + *-ing* = pinning   fat + *-er* = fatter

Before adding a suffix beginning with a vowel to a word of two or more syllables, double the final consonant only if both of the following conditions exist:

1. The word ends with a single consonant preceded by a single vowel.
2. The word is accented on the last syllable.

ex pel′ + *-ed* = ex pelled′   re fer′ + *-al* = re fer′ ral

be gin′ + *-er* = be gin′ ner   per mit′ + *-ing* = per mit′ ting

com mit′ + *-ed* = com mit′ ted   oc cur′ + *-ence* = oc cur′ rence

Note in the examples above that the syllable accented in the new word is the same syllable that was accented before adding the suffix.

If the newly formed word is accented on a different syllable, the final consonant is not doubled.

re fer′ + *-ence* = ref′ er ence   pre fer′ + *-ence* = pref′ er ence

Exercise A Each word below is divided into syllables. Determine which syllable in each word is accented, and insert the accent mark. Then add the suffix indicated, writing the new word in the blank. Repeat with the second suffix.
Example: e mit′ + *-ed* = emitted + *-ing* = emitting

1. de vel′ op + *-ed* = ____________ + *-ing* = ____________
2. e quip′ + *-ed* = ____________ + *-ing* = ____________
3. ad mit′ + *-ed* = ____________ + *-ance* = ____________
4. vis′ it + *-ed* = ____________ + *-ing* = ____________
5. re fer′ + *-ed* = ____________ + *-ence* = ____________
6. pre tend′ + *-er* = ____________ + *-ing* = ____________
7. be stir′ + *-ed* = ____________ + *-ing* = ____________
8. dif′ fer + *-ed* = ____________ + *-ence* = ____________
9. re gret′ + *-ed* = ____________ + *-ing* = ____________
10. ex′ it + *-ed* = ____________ + *-ing* = ____________
11. be gin′ + *-er* = ____________ + *-ing* = ____________
12. prof′ it + *-ed* = ____________ + *-ing* = ____________
13. con fer′ + *-ed* = ____________ + *-ence* = ____________
14. con trol′ + *-ed* = ____________ + *-ing* = ____________

15. sub mit′ + *-ed* = ______________ + *-able* = ______________

Number correct ______________ (total 30)

Exercise B Add the suffixes indicated, and write the new word in the blank.

1. protect + *-ed* = ______________
2. drop + *-ing* = ______________
3. omit + *-ed* = ______________
4. split + *-ing* = ______________
5. recover + *-ed* = ______________
6. slim + *-est* = ______________
7. transmit + *-ance* = ______________
8. disturb + *-ance* = ______________
9. propel + *-ed* = ______________
10. transfer + *-ence* = ______________

Number correct ______________ (total 10)

Words Ending in *-ize* or *-ise*

The suffix *-ize* is usually added to base words to form verbs meaning "to make" or "to become."

neutral + *-ize* = neutralize (to make neutral)
memory + *-ize* = memorize (to make into a memory)

The *-ise* ending is less common. It is usually part of the base word itself rather than a suffix.

advertise surprise televise

Exercise Decide whether *-ize* or *-ise* should be added to each word or letter group. Then write the complete word in the blank.

1. general ______________
2. civil ______________
3. exerc ______________
4. organ ______________
5. desp ______________
6. real ______________
7. public ______________
8. social ______________
9. dev ______________
10. superv ______________
11. individual ______________
12. magnet ______________
13. disgu ______________
14. comprom ______________
15. modern ______________

Number correct ______ (total 15)

The Suffix *-ion*

The *-ion* suffix changes verbs to nouns.

locate + *-ion* = location
discuss + *-ion* = discussion
attract + *-ion* = attraction
separate + *-ion* = separation
object + *-ion* = objection
complete + *-ion* = completion

In the examples above, *-ion* is either added directly to the verb form, or the final *e* is dropped before *-ion* is added.

Some verbs when made into nouns have irregular spellings.

compose + *-ion* = composition
assume + *-ion* = assumption
persuade + *-ion* = persuasion
proclaim + *-ion* = proclamation

In the case of words that do not follow regular spelling patterns, you must memorize their spellings.

Exercise A Add *-ion* to each of the following words. Then write the new word.

1. inspect ______________
2. navigate ______________
3. violate ______________
4. correct ______________
5. investigate ______________
6. confuse ______________
7. contribute ______________
8. express ______________
9. isolate ______________
10. participate ______________
11. calculate ______________
12. except ______________
13. interrupt ______________
14. illustrate ______________
15. suggest ______________

Number correct ______ (total 15)

Exercise B Each of the following nouns is formed by adding the *-ion* suffix to a verb. Write the verb from which the word was formed. Use a dictionary when needed.

1. description ______________
2. permission ______________
3. invasion ______________
4. demolition ______________
5. temptation ______________
6. collision ______________
7. application ______________
8. information ______________
9. observation ______________
10. solution ______________
11. suspicion ______________
12. invitation ______________
13. expectation ______________
14. provision ______________
15. qualification ______________

Number correct ______ (total 15)

Other Spelling Problems

Words with *ie* and *ei*

When the sound is long *e* (ē), it is spelled *ie* except after *c*. If the vowel combination sounds like a long *a* (ā), spell it *ei*.

i* before *e

thief	grief	niece
chief	believe	relieve
yield	brief	fierce

except after *c*

ceiling	perceive	deceit
deceive	receive	receipt

or when sounded as *a*

neighbor weigh reign

Exceptions:

either	weird	seize	financier
neither	species	leisure	

You can remember these words by combining them into the following sentence: *Neither financier seized either weird species of leisure.*

Exercise A In these sentences, find each misspelled word, and write the correct spelling on the line following the sentence.

1. Jason shreiked when he accidentally moved the 500-piece puzzle he had just finished.

 ____

2. Mrs. Sanchez asked her niece to clean the spider webs from the corners of the cieling.

 ____

3. Michelle got only a breif look at the thief running from her neighbor's house, but she knew something was weird and called the police.

 ____

4. "Don't deceive yourselves," the coach began, "that either of you will acheive a place on this team without earning it."

 ____

5. John seized the passed ball with both hands, shielded it with his body, and began running feircely toward the goal.

 ____

6. Sam sighed with relief after setting down the exercise wieghts he was moving into the garage.

____

7. Susan's nieghbor forgot to keep his receipt, so he couldn't return the shirt he'd purchased.

____

8. Mr. Foster shielded his eyes from the fierce sun and gazed across the feild at his ripening corn.

____

9. After the heavy snow, everyone in the neighborhood went to the park to go sliegh riding.

____

10. Who could believe that neither Sandra nor Rena would recieve a part in the school play?

____

Number correct _____ (total 10)

Exercise B Fill in the blanks with *ie* or *ei*.

1. __ __ ght
2. w __ __ gh
3. y __ __ ld
4. f __ __ rce
5. dec __ __ ve
6. sl __ __ gh
7. soc __ __ ty
8. gr __ __ f
9. l __ __ sure
10. w __ __ rd
11. p __ __ ce
12. handkerch __ __ f
13. rec __ __ ve
14. r __ __ gn
15. th __ __ ves

Number correct _____ (total 15)

Words with the "Seed" Sound

One English word ends in *sede:* supersede

Three words end in *ceed:* exceed proceed succeed

All other words ending in the sound of *seed* are spelled with *cede:*

accede concede precede recede secede

Exercise A Find each misspelled word, and write the correct spelling on the line.

1. According to the map, if we proceed through the gate, walk six steps east, and dig down two feet, we will succede in finding the treasure.

   ____

2. The governor said he would acceed to the mayor's demand for more money so the city could proceed in buying land for the park.

   ____

3. "This new rule supercedes any other rules," the principal said, "so don't exceed the time limit on use of the playing field."

   ____

4. The senator conceeded that winning reelection was unlikely, but he said he would proceed with his effort.

   ____

5. The rebel leader said his island would secede from the United States and procede in setting up a separate government.

   ____

6. Marie not only succeeded in selling more scout cookies than Carla, she even exceded the troop record for sales in one month.

   ____

7. The lake began to receed as the leak in the dam proceeded to get worse.

   ____

8. In 1991, people in the republic of Russia succeeded in voting to seceed from the Soviet Union.

   ____

9. As John rubbed his sore leg, he conceded that a brief warm-up should preceed any hard exercise.

   ____

10. Helen said her plan for exploring the cave should superseed Andre's because she has succeeded in exploring caves before.

    ____

Number correct ______ (total 10)

Exercise B Put a check by the five correctly spelled words below.

1. accede ____
2. excede ____
3. precede ____
4. succede ____
5. concede ____
6. intercede ____
7. prosede ____
8. receed ____
9. secede ____
10. superseed ____

Number correct ______ (total 10)

The Letter *c*

When the letter *c* has a *k* sound, it is usually followed by the vowel *a, o,* or *u,* or by any consonant except *y*.

*c*alendar *c*ollide cir*c*ulate predi*c*t

When the letter *c* has an *s* sound, it is usually followed by an *e*, an *i*, or a *y*.

re*c*ent differen*c*e *c*irculate *c*ycle

The Letter *g*

When the letter *g* has a hard sound, as in the word *go*, it is usually followed by the vowel *a, o,* or *u,* or by any consonant except *y*.

*g*arage *g*ar*g*le *g*oal *g*uard

When the letter *g* has a *j* sound, it is usually followed by an *e*, an *i*, or a *y*.

*g*enuine mer*g*e ri*g*id *g*ymnasium

Exceptions: *g*iggle *g*ill *g*irl *g*ive

Exercise A Decide if the *c* in each word below has a *k* sound or an *s* sound. Write *k* or *s* in the blank.

1. caught ____
2. vicinity ____
3. contain ____
4. decent ____
5. privacy ____
6. courteous ____
7. nice ____
8. current ____
9. musical ____
10. race ____
11. cellar ____
12. custom ____
13. December ____
14. crisis ____
15. clothes ____

Number correct ______ (total 15)

Exercise B Decide if the *g* in each word has a *j* sound or a hard sound, as in the word *go*. Write *j* or *go* in the blank.

1. great ____
2. plunge ____
3. navigate ____
4. courage ____
5. advantageous ____
6. sugar ____
7. progress ____
8. engine ____
9. urgent ____
10. investigate ____
11. guide ____
12. struggle ____
13. page ____
14. figure ____
15. judge ____

Number correct ______ (total 15)

Exercise C Write the missing letter in each word.

1. g __ ade
2. pic __ ure
3. neg __ te
4. g __ gantic
5. c __ remony
6. sc __ ssors
7. leg __ nd
8. polic __
9. orig __ nal
10. nec __ ssary
11. loc __ l
12. safeg __ ard
13. lodg __
14. c __ rrect
15. foc __ s

Number correct ______ (total 15)

Spelling Review

Exercise A Add the prefix or suffix indicated, and write the new word.

1. *in-* + mediate = ________________
2. *ad-* + tainable = ________________
3. *com-* + servation = ________________
4. navigate + *-ion* = ________________
5. *ad-* + prove = ________________
6. move + *-able* = ________________
7. *un-* + troubled = ________________
8. civil + *-ize* = ________________
9. *dis-* + like = ________________
10. *ad-* + sure = ________________
11. *ex-* + rupt = ________________
12. *in-* + possible = ________________
13. qualify + *-ing* = ________________
14. suggest + *-ion* = ________________
15. home + *-ly* = ________________
16. *re-* + ceive = ________________
17. severe + *-ity* = ________________
18. *in-* + resistible = ________________
19. necessary + *-ly* = ________________
20. invade + *-ion* = ________________

Number correct ______ (total 20)

Exercise B Three of the words in each row follow the same spelling pattern. Circle the word that does not follow that pattern.

1. invasion immigration impossible impersonal
2. explode elevate exceed explain
3. factories employment studied easily
4. conserve conquer confer correspond
5. protected beginner admitted equipped

6. grief believe receipt thief
7. attain affirm advantage accurate
8. correction expression exception description
9. exercise generalize memorize socialize
10. movable navigation immediately deserving

Number correct ______ (total 10)

Exercise C Find the misspelled words in these sentences, and spell them correctly on the line after the sentence. There may be more than one misspelled word in a sentence.

1. Many people are curious about mysteryous sightings of the Loch Ness Monster, Big Foot, and other wierd creatures.

   ____

2. Martha shreiked when the door slammed unexpectedly in the big, dark house.

   ____

3. Although Don had a spliting headache, he proceded with his plans to shop.

   ____

4. No one expected the imexperienced players to win many games.

   ____

5. While eploring the West, Lewis and Clark were often inperiled by bad weather.

   ____

6. Sean lost his compass and nearly panicked because he thought he'd never find his way out of the strangly dark and quiet forest.

   ____

7. Cindy's neighbor explained that his new telescope magnifyed stars so they were fifty times larger than when seen with the naked eye.

   ____

8. After her fall, Melanie stood up, dusted the snow off, and climbed to the top of the slope for another wild sliegh ride.

   ____

9. After striking out the third time, Jo heard an aweful silence hanging over the ball park.

   ____

10. Rosa confered with her teammates before making her decision about quiting the team.

    ____

11. Neither Terri nor Rachel could explain why she felt so exmotional about the school play.

____

12. Mr. Brewer adsigned forty-four pages of reading to be conpleted by next Friday.

____

13. Henry took conmand of the team and led them to a successful completion of the course.

____

14. The rich dessert was inresistible, and Matt kept returning for more.

____

15. Amazeingly, Lucinda's performance was flawless even though she was sick with the flu.

____

Number correct ______ (total 20)

Exercise D Find the misspelled word in each group. Write the word correctly in the blank.

__________ 1. dismayed
studious
multiplying
mutinyed

__________ 2. blameless
migration
livly
wholly

__________ 3. suggestion
participation
information
observetion

__________ 4. congress
complication
comvey
concentrate

__________ 5. intruder
inpractical
immeasurable
immodest

__________ 6. precede
supercede
secede
exceed

__________ 7. accident
adsume
accurate
attract

__________ 8. transmiting
uttered
conferring
invention

__________ 9. exterior
excellent
erode
exnormous

__________ 10. realize
despise
socialise
supervise

Number correct ______ (total 10)

Number correct in Spelling Handbook ______ (total 445)

Commonly Misspelled Words

abbreviate
accidentally
achievement
all right
altogether
amateur
analyze
anonymous
answer
apologize
appearance
appreciate
appropriate
arrangement
associate
awkward
bargain
beginning
believe
bicycle
bookkeeper
bulletin
bureau
business
calendar
campaign
candidate
certain
changeable
characteristic
column
committee
courageous
courteous
criticize
curiosity
cylinder
dealt
decision
definitely
dependent
description
desirable
despair
desperate
dictionary
different
disappear
disappoint
discipline
dissatisfied
efficient
eighth
eligible
embarrass
emphasize
enthusiastic
environment
especially
exaggerate
exhaust
experience
familiar
fascinating
February
financial
foreign
fourth
fragile
generally
government
grammar
guarantee
guard
gymnasium
handkerchief
height
humorous
imaginary
immediately
incredible
influence
intelligence
knowledge
laboratory
lightning
literature
loneliness
marriage
mathematics
medicine
minimum
mischievous
missile
mortgage
municipal
necessary
nickel
ninety
noticeable
nuclear
nuisance
obstacle
occasionally
occur
opinion
opportunity
outrageous
parallel
particularly
permanent
permissible
persuade
pleasant
pneumonia
politics
possess
possibility
prejudice
privilege
probably
pronunciation
psychology
realize
recognize
recommend
reference
referred
rehearse
repetition
representative
restaurant
rhythm
ridiculous
sandwich
scissors
separate
sergeant
similar
sincerely
sophomore
souvenir
specifically
success
syllable
sympathy
symptom
temperature
thorough
throughout
together
tomorrow
traffic
tragedy
transferred
truly
Tuesday
twelfth
undoubtedly
unnecessary
vacuum
vicinity
village
weird

Commonly Confused Words

The following section lists words that are commonly confused and misused. Some of these words are homonyms, words that sound similar but have different meanings. Study the words in this list and learn how to use them correctly.

accent (ak′sent) n.—emphasis in speech or writing
ascent (ə sent′) n.—act of going up
assent (ə sent′) n.—consent; v.—to accept or agree

accept (ək sept′, ak-) v.—to agree to something or receive something willingly
except (ik sept′) v.—to omit or exclude; prep.—not including

adapt (ə dapt′) v.—to adjust; make fitting or appropriate
adept (ə dept′) adj.—skillful
adopt (ə däpt′) v.—to choose as one's own; accept

affect (ə fekt′) v.—to influence; pretend
affect (af′ekt) n.—feeling
effect (ə fekt′, i-) n.—result of an action
effect (ə fekt′, i-) v.—to accomplish or produce a result

all ready adv. (all) and adj. (ready)—completely prepared
already (ôl red′ē) adv.—even now; before the given time

any way adj. (any) and n. (way)—in whatever manner
anyway (en′ē wā′) adv.—regardless

appraise (ə prāz′) v.—to set a value on
apprise (ə prīz′) v.—to inform

bibliography (bib′lē äg′rə fē) n.—list of writings on a particular topic
biography (bī äg′ rə fē, bē-) n.—written history of a person's life

bazaar (bə zär′) n.—market; fair
bizarre (bi zär′) adj.—odd

coarse (kôrs) adj.—rough; crude
course (kôrs) n.—route; progression; part of a meal; class or unit of instruction in a subject

costume (käs′to͞om, -tyo͞om) n.—special way of dressing
custom (kus′təm) n.—usual practice or habit

decent (dē′s′nt) adj.—proper
descent (di sent′) n.—a fall; a coming down
dissent (di sent′) n.—disagreement; v.—to disagree

desert (dez′ərt) n.—dry region
desert (di zʉrt′) v.—to abandon
dessert (di zʉrt′) n.—sweet course served at the end of a meal

device (di vīs′) n.—a piece of equipment for a special purpose
devise (di vīz′) v.—to plan

elusive (i lo͞o′siv) adj.—hard to catch or understand
illusive (i lo͞o′siv) adj.—misleading; unreal

emigrate (em′ə grāt′) v.—to leave a country and take up residence elsewhere
immigrate (im′ə grāt′) v.—to enter a country and take up residence

farther (fär′*th*ər) adj.—more distant (refers to space)
further (fʉr′*th*ər) adj.—additional (refers to time, quantity, or degree)

flair (fler) n.—natural ability; knack; sense of style
flare (fler) v.—to flame; erupt; n.—a blaze of light

lay (lā) v.—to set something down or place something
lie (lī) v.—to recline; tell untruths; n.—an untruth

moral (môr′əl, mär′-) n.—lesson; adj.—relating to right and wrong
morale (mə ral′, mô-) n.—mental state of confidence, enthusiasm

personal (pʉr′s'n əl) adj.—private
personnel (pʉr′ sə nel′) n.—persons employed in an organization

precede (pri sēd′) v.—to go before
proceed (prə sēd′, prō-) v.—to advance; continue

profit (präf′it) v.—to gain earnings; n.—financial gain on investments
prophet (präf′it) n.—predictor, fortuneteller

quiet (kwī′ ət) adj.—not noisy; n.—a sense of calm; v.—to soothe
quit (kwit) v.—to stop
quite (kwīt) adv.—very

step (step) n.—footfall; dance movement; one of a series of acts; v.—to move the foot as in walking
steppe (step) n.—large, treeless plain

team (tēm) n.—group of people working together on a project
teem (tēm) v.—to swarm or be full of

than (*th*an, *th*en; *unstressed* *th*ən, *th*'n) conj.—word used in comparison
then (*th*en) adv.—at that time, next in order of time; n.—that time

thorough (thʉr′ ō, -ə) adj.—complete
through (thro͞o) prep.—by means of; from beginning to end; adv.—in one side and out the other

Glossary

A

abandon (v.) to leave; to give up something; (n.) unrestrained freedom of action or emotion; p. 121.

amateur (n.) one lacking in experience; (adj.) not professional; p. 154.

application (n.) relevance or practicality; a written request; putting to use; putting on; p. 25. *Related word:* applicable; p. 32.

appreciate (v.) to think highly of, value; p. 25. *Related words:* appreciative, unappreciative; p. 32.

approximate (adj.) nearly correct; (v.) to come near to; p. 131.

assault (n.) a sudden attack, either verbal or physical; (v.) to attack; p. 14.

associate (v.) to connect in thought; join with another; (n.) companion, partner, or friend; p. 164. *Related word:* association; p. 170.

assume (v.) to take for granted; take upon oneself; p. 70. *Related word:* assumption; p. 76.

assure (v.) to tell positively; make a person sure of something; p. 60. *Related word:* assurance; p. 67.

attention (n.) care and thought; consideration; notice; p. 25. *Related words:* attentive, inattentive; p. 32.

B

benefit (n.) anything that is good for a person or thing; (v.) to do good to or for; p. 60. *Related word:* beneficial; p. 67.

brilliant (adj.) having great ability; shining brightly; p. 80. *Related word:* brilliance; p. 87.

C

calculate (v.) to find out beforehand by a process of reasoning; find out through a mathematical process; p. 110.

candidate (n.) one who seeks or is proposed for an office or honor; p. 174.

career (n.) one's progress through life or in one's work; job; occupation; p. 25.

chemistry (n.) the science that deals with substances and with the changes that take place when they combine; p. 174. *Related word:* chemical; p. 181.

civilization (n.) an advanced degree of social organization, in which sciences, government, etc., are developed; the total culture of a people, nation, period, etc.; p. 174. *Related words:* civil, civilize, uncivilized; p. 181.

claim (v.) to call for or require; deserve; (n.) a right or title to something; p. 60.

classify (v.) to arrange in groups or classes; p. 110. *Related word:* classic; p. 117.

cloud (v.) to make dark, unclear; (n.) a mass of fine drops of water floating in the air above the earth; p. 164.

collapse (v.) to fall down or fall to pieces; to cave in; (n.) failure or breakdown; p. 110.

collide (v.) to crash; strike violently against each other; p. 14. *Related word:* collision; p. 22.

combat (n.) a battle; any struggle or conflict (v.) to fight against; p. 121. *Related word:* combatant; p. 128.

common (adj.) ordinary; (n.) land owned or used by all the inhabitants of a place; p. 25. *Related word:* uncommon; p. 32.

companion (n.) one who often goes along with or accompanies another; p. 121. *Related word:* companionable; p. 128.

completion (n.) a finishing; process of completing; p. 14

complicated (adj.) quite involved; hard to untangle, solve, analyze, etc.; p. 174. *Related words:* complicate, complication; p. 181.

concentrate (v.) to pay close attention to; bring together in one place; make stronger; (n.) a substance that has been concentrated. p. 110. *Related word:* concentration; p. 117.

condition (n.) the state in which a person or thing is; (v.) to bring into a desired state of health; p. 60.

conduct (v.) to guide or lead; (n.) way of acting; p. 131. *Related words:* conductor, confine; p. 137.

conference (n.) a group joined together for discussion; p. 80. *Related word:* confer; p. 87.

conscious (adj.) awake; aware; p. 121. *Related word:* unconscious; p. 128.

contract (v.) to reduce in size, draw together, shrink; make a formal agreement with; (n.) an agreement; p. 110.

contribution (n.) something furnished or provided (knowledge, ideas, etc.); money or volunteer help given to a charity; an article, story, poem, etc., sent to a magazine for publication; p. 60.

core (n.) the central or most important part; p. 110.

courteous (adj.) polite; thoughtful; well-mannered; p. 25. *Related word:* discourteous; p. 32.

create (v.) to make a thing that has not been made before; p. 110.

crisis (n.) a time of great difficulty or danger; the turning point in a disease, toward life or death; p. 131.

D

deceive (v.) to mislead; make a person believe as true something that is false; p. 25.

degree (n.) unit for measuring temperature; amount; extent; a social, official or educational rank; p. 131.

demand (v.) to ask for as a right; (n.) a strong request; an urgent requirement or claim; p. 154. *Related word:* demanding; p. 161.

demolish (v.) to tear down or smash to pieces; p. 14. *Related word:* demolition; p. 22.

dense (adj.) closely packed together; thick; p. 70. *Related word:* density; p. 76.

dependent (adj.) relying on another person or thing for support; (n.) a person who is supported by another; p. 70. *Related words:* depend, dependence, independent; p. 76.

deserve (v.) to have a right to; be worthy of, p. 35. *Related word:* deserving; p. 44.

destination (n.) place to which a person or thing is going or being sent; p. 80. *Related word:* destiny; p. 87.

develop (v.) to work out in detail; grow; p. 110. *Related words:* decrease, design; p. 117.

devour (v.) to eat hungrily; p. 25.

direct (adj.) by the shortest way, straight; honest and straightforward; (v.) to manage or guide; p. 25. *Related words:* indirect, indirectly; p. 32.

disadvantage (n.) unfavorable condition; lack of advantage; p. 14. *Related words:* advantageous, disband, disorderly, dissolve; p. 22.

discourage (v.) to destroy the hopes of; prevent or try to prevent by disapproving; p. 80. *Related words:* discouragement, encourage; p. 87.

disguise (v.) to change one's appearance by looking like someone or something else; (n.) clothes or actions used to deceive; p. 25.

display (n.) a planned showing of a thing; (v.) to show; p. 35. *Related word:* disregard; p. 44.

dispose (v.) to get rid of, eliminate; make ready or willing; p. 70.

E

economic (adj.) having to do with the way people produce, distribute, and use wealth; p. 174. *Related words:* economical, economy; p. 181.

effective (adj.) producing the desired result; making a striking impression; p. 14. *Related words:* effect, ineffective; p. 22.

effort (n.) use of energy to do something; strong attempt; p. 60. *Related word:* effortless; p. 67.

engineer (n.) a person skilled in the planning or construction or machinery, roads, bridges, buildings, waterways, etc.; an operator of engines or technical equipment; (v.) to guide the course of; construct or manage; p. 174.

erupt (v.) to burst forth; p. 131. *Related word:* eruption; p. 137.

especially (adv.) particularly; more than others; p. 35.

establish (v.) to start; organize; prove; p. 174. *Related word:* establishment; p. 181.

estimate (n.) judgment or opinion; (v.) to form a judgment or opinion; make a general but careful guess; p. 14.

exceptional (adj.) unusual; out of the ordinary; p. 110. *Related word:* exception; p. 117.

exhaust (v.) to tire out; (n.) the discharge of used steam, gas, etc. from the cylinders of an engine; p. 121. *Related word:* exhaustion; p. 128.

expand (v.) to spread out; make larger; p. 110. *Related words:* exit, exterior, extinguish; p. 117.

experience (n.) knowledge gained by doing or seeing things; (v.) to feel; undergo; p. 121.

explore (v.) to travel for the purpose of discovery; examine; p. 110. *Related word:* exploration; p. 117.

express (v.) to put into words; (adj.) clear and direct; fast; (adv.) by express; (n.) an express bus, train, elevator, etc.; a method or means of swift transportation; p. 60. *Related word:* expression; p. 67.

extinguish (v.) to put out; destroy; p. 70. *Related words:* extinct, extinguisher; p. 76.

extreme (adj.) much more than usual; (n.) something more than usual; p. 110.

F

factor (n.) one element in a situation; p. 70.

faithful (adj.) loyal; true to fact; p. 131. *Related word:* faith; p. 137.

financial (adj.) having to do with money matters; p. 35. *Related word:* finance; p. 76.

foresight (n.) the power to see or know beforehand what may happen, p. 164. *Related words:* forefather, foreknowledge; p. 170.

fortune (n.) a great deal of wealth; success; luck; p. 35. *Related word:* fortunate; p. 44.

fragment (n.) a part of something that has been broken off; an incomplete part; (v.) to break into parts; p. 131.

furious (adj.) full of anger; p. 121. *Related word:* fury; p. 128.

G

government (n.) an established political system by which a nation, state, etc. is ruled; person or persons ruling a state, country, city, etc.; p. 174. *Related word:* govern; p. 181.

gravity (n.) the natural force that pulls objects toward the center of the earth; heaviness, weight; p. 110.

H

hardy (adj.) strong; able to withstand fatigue, discomfort, etc.; p. 164.

honorable (adj.) having a sense of what is right; p. 25. *Related word:* dishonorable; p. 32.

I

immediate (adj.) having nothing coming between; closest; nearest; without delay; p. 60.

increase (v.) to become greater in size number, power, etc.; (n.) amount added; p. 60. *Related word:* decrease; p. 67.

indebted (adj.) owing money or gratitude; obliged; p. 80.

individual (adj.) particular; of, for, or by one person or thing; (n.) a single person, animal, or thing; p. 154. *Related words:* individualism; individualistic; p. 161.

information (n.) knowledge given or received; news; p. 35. *Related words:* inform, informative; p. 44.

interrupt (v.) to break in upon; hinder; stop; p. 121. *Related words:* bankrupt, corrupt, disrupt, interruption; p. 128.

invader (n.) one who enters by force; p. 14. *Related words:* invade, invasion; p. 22.

investigate (v.) to search into; examine; p. 35. *Related word:* investigation; p. 44.

issue (n.) matter of concern; (v.) to send out; put forth; p. 60.

J

jointly (adv.) together; in common; p. 80.

judgment (n.) the power of comparing and deciding; good sense; an opinion; estimate; p. 70. *Related words:* judge, judgmental; p. 76.

L

lack (v.) to be deficient in or completely without; (n.) the fact or condition of not having enough; shortage; the thing that is needed; p. 80.

landscape (n.) view of scenery on land; (v.) to change the natural features of (a piece of land) so as to make it more attractive, as by adding lawns, bushes, or trees; p. 25.

league (n.) a union of persons or nations formed to help one another; an association; p. 174.

legend (n.) a story handed down for generations and believed by many to be based on actual events; p. 164. *Related word:* legendary; p. 170.

literature (n.) the writings of a particular time or place, especially those that have lasting value because of their beauty of style or thought; p. 174.

local (adj.) of or confined to a particular place; (n.) a resident of the local town or district; p. 154. *Related word:* locality; p. 161.

M

majority (n.) the greater part; larger number; more than half; p. 70.

meaningful (adj.) full of meaning; having significance; p. 131. *Related words*: painful, thankful; p. 137.

memorial (n.) something that is a reminder of an event or a person; p. 164.

mercy (n.) kindness; milder punishment; p. 110.

migrate (v.) to move from one place to settle in another; p. 164. *Related words:* emigrate, immigrate, migration; p. 170.

mishap (n.) an unlucky accident; p. 14.

mission (n.) a special purpose; errand; p. 14.

mysterious (adj.) hidden; hard to understand or explain; p. 164. *Related word:* mystery; p. 170.

N

navigator (n.) one who steers or plots the course for a craft; p. 14. *Related word:* navigate; p. 22.

neglect (v.) to give little attention to; (n.) act of giving little attention to; p. 70. *Related words:* negate, negative, negligent, negligible; p. 76.

O

observation (n.) the act or power of seeing; fact of being seen; a comment based on something observed; p. 35. *Related word:* observe; p. 44.

occasion (n.) a particular time; special event; (v.) to be the occasion of; cause; p. 154. *Related word:* occasionally; p.161.

officer (n.) a person who commands others, as in an army or a business; p. 154. *Related word:* office; p. 161.

opinion (n.) what one thinks; p. 80.

opportunity (n.) a good chance; favorable time; p. 35. *Related word:* opportune; p. 44.

oppose (v.) to be against; try to hinder; p. 60. *Related words:* opponent, opposition; p. 67.

P

parallel (adv.) in a parallel manner; (adj.) extending in the same direction and being the same distance apart; similar; p. 154.

participate (v.) to take part in; p. 60. *Related word:* participation; p. 67.

patent (n.) a government document that states that a person or company has exclusive rights to make, use, or sell a new invention; (adj.) protected by a patent; obvious; evident; (v.) to grant a patent to or for; p. 174.

persuade (v.) to win over to do or believe; p. 121. *Related word:* persuasion; p. 128.

plunge (v.) to throw or thrust with force; dive; (n.) a dive or downward leap. p. 80.

position (n.) a post of employment; job; office; the place where a thing or person is; rank; (v.) to put something or someone in a certain place; p. 35. *Related word:* pose; p. 44.

possess (v.) to own or have; p. 80. *Related word:* dispossess; p. 87.

predict (v.) to foretell; tell of an event beforehand; p. 121. *Related word:* prediction; p. 128.

prefer (v.) to like better; p. 80. *Related word:* preference; p. 87.

preserve (v.) to protect; maintain; keep from spoiling; p. 164. *Related word:* preservation; p. 170.

private (adj.) not for the public; secret; (n.) an enlisted person in either of the two lowest ranks in the U.S. Army; p. 35. *Related word:* privacy; p. 44.

process (n.) a set of actions or changes in a particular order; (v.) to prepare by, or subject to, a special method; (adj.) prepared in a special way; p. 131.

produce (v.) to bring about or forth; cause; (n.) what is produced; fresh fruits and vegetables; p. 110. *Related word:* progress; p. 117.

profit (v.) to make a financial gain; to benefit; (n.) what is gained; p. 35.

progress (n.) growth; development; improvement; (v.) to move forward; advance; p. 121. *Related words:* proceed, profess, promote, protect, provide; p. 128.

prohibit (v.) to forbid; p. 164.

prompt (adj.) on time; (v.) to cause to do something; p. 60.

pursue (v.) to follow in order to catch; chase; p. 121.

R

realize (v.) to understand clearly; achieve; p. 14. *Related word:* realization; p. 22.

receipt (n.) a receiving or being received; a written statement that money, a package, or some other item, has been received; (v.) to mark (a bill) paid; to write a receipt for (goods, etc.); p.174.

region (n.) any large part of the earth's surface; p. 164. *Related word:* regional; p. 170.

reliable (adj.) worthy of trust; able to be depended on; p. 131. *Related word:* reliability; p. 137.
remarkable (adj.) unusual; worthy of notice; p. 121.
represent (v.) to stand for; act in place of; be a symbol of; p. 174. *Related word:* representation; p. 181.
require (v.) to need; demand; order; p. 131. *Related word:* requirement; p. 137.
reservoir (n.) a place where water is collected and stored; p. 131.
resident (n.) a person living in a place; (adj.) having a residence in; present or existing (in); p. 131. *Related words:* reside, residence; p. 137.
restless (adj.) uneasy; unable to rest; p. 164.
restore (v.) to bring back to a former condition; p. 70.
result (n.) that which happens because of something; good or useful effect; (v.) to happen because of something else; p. 60.
right (n.) a just claim; (adj.) just; lawful; correct; proper; (v.) to make correct; (adv.) in a straight line; directly; in a way that is correct, proper, just or favorable; p. 154.

S

sacred (adj.) holy; connected with religion; worthy of reverence; p. 164.
screech (n.) a shrill scream; (v.) to cry out in a high voice; shriek; p. 154.
secrecy (n.) the condition of being kept secret; p. 164. *Related word:* secret; p. 170.
section (n.) any distinct or separate part; a part separated by cutting; slice; division; (v.) to cut or divide into sections; p. 154.
segment (n.) a piece or part cut off, marked off, or broken off; (v.) to divide into segments; p. 80.
serious (adj.) thoughtful; grave; not fooling; important; p. 25.
severe (adj.) serious; very strict; harsh; dangerous; p. 14.
shatter (v.) to break into pieces; destroy; p. 154.
sincere (adj.) free from pretense; honest; p. 174. *Related word:* sincerity; p. 181.
site (n.) a position or place; (v.) to place on a site; locate; p. 121.
slogan (n.) a motto; word or phrase used by a person or group to make known its purpose; p. 70.
society (n.) a group of persons joined together for a common purpose; human beings living together as a group; p. 60. *Related words:* associate, sociable, socialize, sociology; p. 67.
solution (n.) the solving of a problem; explanation; p. 35. *Related word:* solve; p. 44.
souvenir (n.) a keepsake; memento; p. 164.
strategy (n.) skillful planning of anything; the planning and directing of military operations; p. 131, *Related word:* strategic; p. 137.
struggle (v.) to work hard against difficulties; to contend or fight violently; to make great efforts; (n.) a great effort; fight; conflict; p. 35.
sufficient (adj.) as much as is needed; enough; p. 131. *Related word:* suffice; p. 137.
supreme (adj.) highest in degree; greatest; p. 154. *Related word:* supremacy; p. 161.
surplus (adj.) amount over what is needed; p. 70.
suspect (v.) to think likely; imagine to be so; (n.) a person suspected; (adj.) viewed with suspicion; p. 80. *Related word:* suspicion; p. 87.

T

technique (n.) method or level of skill in a human or mechanical operation;

p. 154. *Related words:* technical, technicality, technician, technocarcy, technology; p. 161.

temptation (n.) something that is exceptionally appealing; p. 35. *Related word:* tempt; p. 44.

thorough (adj.) complete; doing all that should be done; p. 70.

transform (v.) to change in form or appearance; p. 80. *Related words:* transfer, transfusion, transmit, transplant; p. 87.

troubled (adj.) distressed; worried; p. 25. *Related word:* untroubled; p. 32.

twilight (n.) the period of time from sunset to dark; (adj.) of or like twilight; p. 14.

U

urgent (adj.) demanding immediate action; p. 80.

utter (v.) to speak; make known; (adj.) complete; total; p. 70.

V

various (adj.) differing from one another; p. 70. *Related word:* vary; p. 76.

vessel (n.) a ship; large boat; tube carrying fluid; p. 154.

vicinity (n.) the region near or about a place; closeness; p. 14.

vicious (adj.) likely to attack or bite; evil; wicked; p. 121.

victim (n.) a person or animal injured or killed; a person badly treated or taken advantage of; p. 25.

W

will (n.) a legal document dealing with the distribution of a person's property after death; power of the mind to decide and do; (v.) to influence by the power of the will; desire; p. 174

Y

yarn (n.) tale; story; p.154.

Pronunciation Key

Symbol	Key Words
a	**a**sk, f**a**t, p**a**rrot
ā	**a**pe, d**a**te, pl**ay**
ä	**a**h, c**a**r, f**a**ther
e	**e**lf, t**e**n, b**e**rry
ē	**e**ven, m**ee**t, mon**ey**
i	**i**s, h**i**t, m**i**rror
ī	**i**ce, b**i**te, h**igh**
ō	**o**pen, t**o**ne, g**o**
ô	**a**ll, h**o**rn, l**aw**
o͞o	**oo**ze, t**oo**l, cr**ew**
o͝o	l**oo**k p**u**ll, m**oo**r
yo͞o	**u**se, c**u**te, f**ew**
yo͝o	**u**nited, c**u**re, glob**u**le
oi	**oi**l, p**oi**nt, t**oy**
ou	**ou**t, cr**ow**d, pl**ow**
u	**u**p, c**u**t, c**o**lor
ur	**ur**n, f**ur**, det**er**
ə	**a** in ago **e** in agent **i** in sanity **o** in comply **u** in focus
ər	p**er**haps, murd**er**

Symbol	Key Words
b	**b**ed, fa**b**le, du**b**
d	**d**ip, bea**d**le, ha**d**
f	**f**all, a**f**ter, o**ff**
g	**g**et, ha**gg**le, do**g**
h	**h**e, a**h**ead, **h**otel
j	**j**oy, a**g**ile, ba**dge**
k	**k**ill, ta**ck**le, ba**k**e
l	**l**et, he**ll**ow, ba**ll**
m	**m**et, ca**m**el, tri**m**
n	**n**ot, fla**nn**el, to**n**
p	**p**ut, a**pp**le, ta**p**
r	**r**ed, po**r**t, dea**r**
s	**s**ell, ca**s**tle, pa**ss**
t	**t**op, ca**tt**le ha**t**
v	**v**at, ho**v**el, ha**v**e
w	**w**ill, al**w**ays, s**w**ear
y	**y**et, on**i**on, **y**ard
z	**z**ebra, da**zz**le, ha**z**e
ch	**ch**in, cat**ch**er, ar**ch**
sh	**sh**e, cu**sh**ion, da**sh**
th	**th**in, no**th**ing, tru**th**
th	**th**en, fa**th**er, la**the**
zh	a**z**ure, lei**s**ure
ŋ	ri**ng**, a**n**ger, dri**n**k
'	abl**e** (a′ b'l)
′ ′	expedition (ek′ spə dish′ ən)

Inventory Test

These are all the target words in the book. Why not see how many you think you already know . . . or don't know?

- *If you're* sure *you know the word, mark the* **Y** *("yes") circle.*
- *If you think you* might *know it, mark the* **?** *(question mark) circle.*
- *If you have* no idea *what it means, mark the* **N** *("no") circle.*

Y ? N

❍ ❍ ❍ abandon
❍ ❍ ❍ amateur
❍ ❍ ❍ application
❍ ❍ ❍ appreciate
❍ ❍ ❍ approximate
❍ ❍ ❍ assault
❍ ❍ ❍ associate
❍ ❍ ❍ assume
❍ ❍ ❍ assure
❍ ❍ ❍ attention
❍ ❍ ❍ benefit
❍ ❍ ❍ brilliant
❍ ❍ ❍ calculate
❍ ❍ ❍ candidate
❍ ❍ ❍ career
❍ ❍ ❍ chemistry
❍ ❍ ❍ civilization
❍ ❍ ❍ claim
❍ ❍ ❍ classify
❍ ❍ ❍ cloud
❍ ❍ ❍ collapse
❍ ❍ ❍ collide
❍ ❍ ❍ combat
❍ ❍ ❍ common
❍ ❍ ❍ companion
❍ ❍ ❍ completion
❍ ❍ ❍ complicated
❍ ❍ ❍ concentrate
❍ ❍ ❍ condition
❍ ❍ ❍ conduct

That's the first 30 words.

Y ? N

❍ ❍ ❍ conference
❍ ❍ ❍ conscious
❍ ❍ ❍ contract
❍ ❍ ❍ contribution
❍ ❍ ❍ core
❍ ❍ ❍ courteous
❍ ❍ ❍ create
❍ ❍ ❍ crisis
❍ ❍ ❍ deceive
❍ ❍ ❍ degree
❍ ❍ ❍ demand

You're doing well.

❍ ❍ ❍ demolish
❍ ❍ ❍ dense
❍ ❍ ❍ dependent
❍ ❍ ❍ deserve
❍ ❍ ❍ destination
❍ ❍ ❍ develop
❍ ❍ ❍ devour
❍ ❍ ❍ direct
❍ ❍ ❍ disadvantage
❍ ❍ ❍ discourage
❍ ❍ ❍ disguise
❍ ❍ ❍ display
❍ ❍ ❍ dispose
❍ ❍ ❍ economic
❍ ❍ ❍ effective
❍ ❍ ❍ effort
❍ ❍ ❍ engineer
❍ ❍ ❍ erupt
❍ ❍ ❍ especially

Y ? N

❍ ❍ ❍ establish
❍ ❍ ❍ estimate
❍ ❍ ❍ exceptional
❍ ❍ ❍ exhaust
❍ ❍ ❍ expand
❍ ❍ ❍ experience
❍ ❍ ❍ explore
❍ ❍ ❍ express
❍ ❍ ❍ extinguish
❍ ❍ ❍ extreme
❍ ❍ ❍ factor
❍ ❍ ❍ faithful
❍ ❍ ❍ financial
❍ ❍ ❍ foresight
❍ ❍ ❍ fortune
❍ ❍ ❍ fragment
❍ ❍ ❍ furious
❍ ❍ ❍ government
❍ ❍ ❍ gravity
❍ ❍ ❍ hardy
❍ ❍ ❍ honorable
❍ ❍ ❍ immediate
❍ ❍ ❍ increase
❍ ❍ ❍ indebted
❍ ❍ ❍ individual
❍ ❍ ❍ information
❍ ❍ ❍ interrupt
❍ ❍ ❍ invader
❍ ❍ ❍ investigate
❍ ❍ ❍ issue

Take a break!

Y	?	N	
❍	❍	❍	jointly
❍	❍	❍	judgment
❍	❍	❍	lack
❍	❍	❍	landscape
❍	❍	❍	league
❍	❍	❍	legend
❍	❍	❍	literature
❍	❍	❍	local
❍	❍	❍	majority
❍	❍	❍	meaningful
❍	❍	❍	memorial
❍	❍	❍	mercy
❍	❍	❍	migrate
❍	❍	❍	mishap
❍	❍	❍	mission
❍	❍	❍	mysterious

Halfway through the alphabet.

Y	?	N	
❍	❍	❍	navigator
❍	❍	❍	neglect
❍	❍	❍	observation
❍	❍	❍	occasion
❍	❍	❍	officer
❍	❍	❍	opinion
❍	❍	❍	opportunity
❍	❍	❍	oppose
❍	❍	❍	parallel
❍	❍	❍	participate
❍	❍	❍	patent
❍	❍	❍	persuade
❍	❍	❍	plunge
❍	❍	❍	position

Y	?	N	
❍	❍	❍	possess
❍	❍	❍	predict
❍	❍	❍	prefer
❍	❍	❍	preserve
❍	❍	❍	private
❍	❍	❍	process
❍	❍	❍	produce
❍	❍	❍	profit
❍	❍	❍	progress
❍	❍	❍	prohibit
❍	❍	❍	prompt
❍	❍	❍	pursue
❍	❍	❍	realize
❍	❍	❍	receipt
❍	❍	❍	region
❍	❍	❍	reliable
❍	❍	❍	remarkable
❍	❍	❍	represent
❍	❍	❍	require
❍	❍	❍	reservoir
❍	❍	❍	resident
❍	❍	❍	restless
❍	❍	❍	restore
❍	❍	❍	result
❍	❍	❍	right

This list will end soon.

Y	?	N	
❍	❍	❍	sacred
❍	❍	❍	screech
❍	❍	❍	secrecy
❍	❍	❍	section
❍	❍	❍	segment

Y	?	N	
❍	❍	❍	serious
❍	❍	❍	severe
❍	❍	❍	shatter
❍	❍	❍	sincere
❍	❍	❍	site
❍	❍	❍	slogan
❍	❍	❍	society
❍	❍	❍	solution
❍	❍	❍	souvenir
❍	❍	❍	strategy

Only 20 more words.

Y	?	N	
❍	❍	❍	struggle
❍	❍	❍	sufficient
❍	❍	❍	supreme
❍	❍	❍	surplus
❍	❍	❍	suspect
❍	❍	❍	technique
❍	❍	❍	temptation
❍	❍	❍	thorough
❍	❍	❍	transform
❍	❍	❍	troubled
❍	❍	❍	twilight
❍	❍	❍	urgent
❍	❍	❍	utter
❍	❍	❍	various
❍	❍	❍	vessel
❍	❍	❍	vicinity
❍	❍	❍	vicious
❍	❍	❍	victim
❍	❍	❍	will
❍	❍	❍	yarn

Congratulations!

That was 180 words. How many of them *don't* you know? Highlight any words you marked **N**, write them on the Personal Vocabulary Log pages provided (beginning on page 261), and watch for them as you work through the book. You'll soon know them all!

Pretest Strategies

Use What You Already Know

There are many ways to figure out what a word you don't know might mean.

- It may contain a familiar **whole word.**
- It may be a **compound** of familiar words put together.
- You may recognize the **root**.
- You may recognize a **prefix** or **suffix**.
- There may be **context clues** to the meaning.

Try Everything

When you see a word you don't know, try taking it apart. Look at how this can work.

	Tim feels an unutterable happiness.	
	THOUGHTS	
unutterable	It describes happiness. Must be an adjective.	**a context clue**
un•utter•*able*	I see *utter* in there. It means "to say something."	**a whole word**
unutter•able	*-able* . . . like in *readable.* Something that can be *read* is *readable.*	**a familiar suffix**
un•*utterable*	The *un-* part is pretty easy. It just means "not." *Unhappy, unfold.*	**a familiar prefix**
	Let's see. Adjective. Not. Utter. Able. . . . Tim is so happy that he can't tell about it in words!	

Try It Yourself

_____ 1. presuppose (think about *prepaid* and *suppose*)
a. to guess b. to say again c. to be happy

_____ 2. unmistakable (think about *unwrap, mistake,* and *fixable*)
a. wrong b. happy c. very clear

_____ 3. overstate (think about *over* and *state*)
a. to write b. to embarrass c. to exaggerate

_____ 4. impermanent (think about *impossible* and *permanent*)
a. not real b. not lasting c. allowable

Score Yourself! *The answers are upside-down on the right.* Number correct: _____

2c, 4b, 1a, 3c

UNIT 1 Test Yourself

Part A Synonyms

Write the letter of the word that is closest in meaning to the capitalized word.

_____	1. ASSAULT:	(A) reward	(B) attack	(C) meeting	(D) problem
_____	2. DEMOLISH:	(A) wreck	(B) delay	(C) cover	(D) deliver
_____	3. DISADVANTAGE:	(A) luck	(B) accident	(C) mistake	(D) difficulty
_____	4. REALIZE:	(A) try	(B) measure	(C) understand	(D) guess
_____	5. MISSION:	(A) choice	(B) assignment	(C) problem	(D) flight

Part B Applying Meaning

Write the letter of the best answer.

_____ 6. You would expect someone to get a severe injury from
a. a bee sting. b. a paper cut. c. falling off a roof. d. falling off a chair.

_____ 7. If someone collides with you, he or she
a. likes you. b. agrees with you. c. works with you. d. runs into you.

_____ 8. At the completion of a meal, people
a. cook. b. eat. c. wash dishes. d. invite guests.

_____ 9. If you give an estimate, you give a
a. wild guess. b. good guess. c. perfect answer. d. silent nod.

_____10. A navigator would be needed by a
a. ship. b. school. c. hospital. d. courtroom.

_____11. During twilight, you would be able to see
a. nothing. b. many stars. c. the sun. d. objects nearby.

_____12. An invader is someone who goes where he or she is
a. welcome. b. not wanted. c. needed. d. in danger.

_____13. The vicinity of a library is
a. lending books. b. a librarian. c. the library's size. d. the area nearby.

_____14. If you dealt with a problem in an effective way, you would
a. solve it. b. make it worse. c. ignore it. d. avoid it.

_____15. An example of a mishap is a
a. home run. b. hurricane. c. bump on the head. d. surprise party.

Score Yourself! *The answers are on page 259.* Number correct: _____ Part A: _____ Part B: _____

UNIT 2 Test Yourself

Part A Matching Definitions

Match each word on the left with its definition on the right. Write the letter of the definition in the blank.

_____	1. courteous	a. straight; by the shortest way
_____	2. direct	b. a view of the scenery
_____	3. honorable	c. one who is killed or hurt
_____	4. victim	d. to eat in a very hungry way
_____	5. landscape	e. to hide what one really looks like
_____	6. disguise	f. having good manners; polite
_____	7. devour	g. doing what is right; honest

Part B Recognizing Meaning

Write the letter of the word or phrase that is closest in meaning to the word in italics.

_____ 8. a *troubled* look
a. mean c. kind
b. worried d. scared

_____ 9. a new *career*
a. job c. guess
b. circle d. way of thinking

_____10. to *deceive* someone
a. hate c. fool
b. laugh at d. talk with

_____11. a new *application* for a tool
a. use c. repair
b. covering d. price

_____12. to *appreciate* good food
a. eat c. expect
b. enjoy d. need

_____13. *common* people
a. ordinary c. loud
b. well-liked d. special

_____14. to have *serious* problems
a. small c. bad
b. funny d. unlucky

_____15. to get your *attention*
a. presence c. thankfulness
b. pardon d. notice

Score Yourself! *The answers are on page 259.* Number correct: _____ Part A: _____ Part B: _____

UNIT 3 **Test Yourself**

Part A **Recognizing Meaning**

Write the letter of the word or phrase that is closest in meaning to the word in italics.

_____ 1. to *profit* by an event
a. be hurt c. be confused
b. be helped d. be surprised

_____ 2. to find the *solution*
a. answer c. lost item
b. poison d. reason

_____ 3. to watch him *struggle*
a. win c. give up
b. do badly d. try hard

_____ 4. an interesting *display*
a. lesson c. hiding place
b. exhibit d. kind of work

_____ 5. a *position* as a teacher
a. job c. new chance
b. problem d. way of acting

_____ 6. to be *especially* funny
a. very c. loudly
b. rudely d. not very

_____ 7. during my *observation*
a. illness c. watching
b. reading d. short trip

_____ 8. to protect her *fortune*
a. riches c. secret
b. family d. place of safety

Part B **Matching Definitions**

Match each word on the left with its definition on the right. Write the letter of the definition in the blank.

_____ 9. deserve — a. a good chance
_____10. opportunity — b. knowledge; news
_____11. information — c. not for everyone; personal
_____12. private — d. to look at closely; examine
_____13. financial — e. having to do with money
_____14. temptation — f. to have a right to; earn
_____15. investigate — g. something that is desired

Score Yourself! *The answers are on page 259.* Number correct: _____ Part A: _____ Part B: _____

UNIT 5 Test Yourself

Part A Synonyms

Write the letter of the word that is closest in meaning to the capitalized word.

_____	1. BENEFIT:	(A) shame	(B) help	(C) party	(D) promise
_____	2. EFFORT:	(A) excuse	(B) idea	(C) try	(D) protection
_____	3. PROMPT:	(A) smart	(B) pretty	(C) quick	(D) important
_____	4. EXPRESS:	(A) say	(B) plan	(C) hope	(D) deliver
_____	5. CONDITION:	(A) kindness	(B) situation	(C) lie	(D) choice
_____	6. INCREASE:	(A) bend	(B) find	(C) help	(D) grow
_____	7. CONTRIBUTION:	(A) answer	(B) meeting	(C) gift	(D) decision
_____	8. CLAIM:	(A) enjoy	(B) take	(C) steal	(D) change

Part B Matching Definitions

Match each word on the left with its definition on the right. Write the letter of the definition in the blank.

_____	9. immediate	a. to take part in something
_____	10. assure	b. right away; without delay
_____	11. society	c. to tell positively
_____	12. result	d. to be against something
_____	13. oppose	e. people who live together as a group
_____	14. issue	f. something that happens because of something else
_____	15. participate	g. a matter of concern; something being considered

Score Yourself! *The answers are on page 259.* Number correct: _____ Part A: _____ Part B: _____

UNIT 6 **Test Yourself**

Part A **Recognizing Meaning**

Write the letter of the word or phrase that is closest in meaning to the word or words in italics.

_____ 1. a *dense* forest
a. thick c. scary
b. dark d. natural

_____ 2. to *utter* a few words
a. spell c. speak
b. think of d. understand

_____ 3. one *surplus* shoe
a. extra c. too big
b. heavy d. well-shined

_____ 4. to make the *judgment*
a. excuse c. mistake
b. decision d. suggestion

_____ 5. to *extinguish* a campfire
a. light c. need
b. enjoy d. put out

_____ 6. *the majority* will go
a. the winners c. the oldest ones
b. everyone d. more than half

_____ 7. to *restore* the floor's shine
a. ruin c. bring back
b. notice d. work hard on

_____ 8. there were *various* animals
a. wild c. useful
b. different d. interesting

Part B **Applying Meaning**

Write the letter of the best answer.

_____ 9. The factors in a traffic accident would be the
a. causes of it. b. people hurt. c. police. d. news reports.

_____10. If you assume an answer is right, you believe that it is right but you
a. are wrong. b. don't know for sure. c. can't find out. d. don't care.

_____11. Something that people need to dispose of is
a. food. b. photographs. c. garbage. d. money.

_____12. One reason a person might neglect something is that he or she is
a. smart. b. hard-working. c. forgetful. d. very careful.

_____13. One kind of animal that is usually dependent on human beings is a
a. gorilla. b. wasp. c. shark. d. pet dog.

_____14. You will often hear a slogan during a
a. concert. b. spelling bee. c. thunderstorm. d. commercial.

_____15. A thorough search for a lost item is one that is
a. quick. b. complete. c. successful. d. not successful.

Score Yourself! *The answers are on page 259.* Number correct: _____ Part A: _____ Part B: _____

UNIT 7 Test Yourself

Part A **Applying Meaning**

Write the letter of the best answer.

_____ 1. During the Olympics, which athletes plunge?
a. divers   swimmers   c. figure skaters   d. basketball players

_____ 2. You would be indebted to someone who
a. smiled at you.   b. scared you.   c. saved your life.   d. borrowed your book.

_____ 3. To whom is a destination most important?
a. a thief   b. a traveler   c. a storekeeper   d. a teacher

_____ 4. If you discourage someone, you take away that person's
a. hope.   b. fears.   c. bravery.   d. appetite.

_____ 5. What must married couples do jointly?
a. watch TV   b. eat dinner   c. take a walk   d. have a conversation

_____ 6. The thing that you prefer is the one you
a. are afraid of.   b. can't have.   c. like best.   d. already have.

_____ 7. A person who lacks food is probably
a. hungry.   b. a good cook.   c. overweight.   d. at the grocery store.

_____ 8. If you suspect that your brother did something, you
a. saw him do it.   b. hope he did it.   c. think he did it.   d. doubt he did it.

_____ 9. You'd use your opinion to decide which one of your friends is the
a. tallest.   b. fastest runner.   c. oldest.   d. nicest.

_____10. Which is usually considered the most urgent?
a. a soccer game   b. a house fire   c. an argument   d. a telephone call

Part B **Synonyms**

Write the letter of the word that is closest in meaning to the capitalized word.

_____11. TRANSFORM: (A) move   (B) fix   (C) change   (D) carry

_____12. SEGMENT: (A) color   (B) plant   (C) speed   (D) part

_____13. BRILLIANT: (A) smooth   (B) shining   (C) expensive   (D) unusual

_____14. CONFERENCE: (A) election   (B) building   (C) party   (D) meeting

_____15. POSSESS: (A) own   (B) give   (C) want   (D) chase

Score Yourself! *The answers are on page 259.*   Number correct: _____   Part A: _____   Part B: _____

UNIT 9 Test Yourself

Part A Recognizing Meaning

Write the letter of the word or phrase that is closest in meaning to the word in italics.

_____ 1. try to *concentrate*
a. move c. believe
b. be still d. think hard

_____ 2. to *create* something
a. copy c. invent
b. put away d. explain

_____ 3. when balloons *expand*
a. float c. swell
b. burst d. lose air

_____ 4. if buildings *collapse*
a. fall down c. look bad
b. stay open d. need fixing

_____ 5. to slowly *contract*
a. spoil c. get louder
b. feel cold d. get smaller

_____ 6. to *produce* a result
a. check c. expect
b. bring about d. demand

_____ 7. a boy with *exceptional* talent
a. little c. special
b. useful d. average

_____ 8. to *explore* the land
a. spoil c. go away from
b. enjoy d. look all around

Part B Matching Definitions

Match each word on the left with its definition on the right. Write the letter of the definition in the blank.

_____ 9. calculate
_____ 10. develop
_____ 11. mercy
_____ 12. core
_____ 13. classify
_____ 14. gravity
_____ 15. extreme

a. kindness; mildness
b. the center or most important part
c. to come into being; make
d. much more than usual; very great
e. to find out by doing math
f. to arrange into groups of things that go together
g. the force that pulls objects toward the earth's center

Score Yourself! *The answers are on page 259.* Number correct: _____ Part A: _____ Part B: _____

UNIT 10 Test Yourself

Part A Synonyms

Write the letter of the word that is closest in meaning to the capitalized word.

_____ 1. COMBAT: (A) scale (B) question (C) battle (D) reply

_____ 2. PURSUE: (A) kiss (B) chase (C) catch (D) punish

_____ 3. SITE: (A) part (B) place (C) town (D) statement

_____ 4. CONSCIOUS: (A) guilty (B) afraid (C) ashamed (D) awake

_____ 5. COMPANION: (A) partner (B) plan (C) problem (D) location

_____ 6. PERSUADE: (A) convince (B) forget (C) follow (D) guess

_____ 7. REMARKABLE: (A) nice (B) unusual (C) dull (D) needed

Part B Recognizing Meaning

_____ 8. to *exhaust* the other team
a. beat c. cheer for
b. wear out d. prepare for

_____ 9. a *furious* look
a. surprised c. scared
b. very angry d. slightly angry

_____10. to *abandon* a person
a. teach c. want to see
b. like d. leave behind

_____11. to *experience* something
a. want c. live through
b. hear about d. go away from

_____12. to *interrupt* the conversation
a. break into c. repeat
b. understand d. laugh at

_____13. making *progress*
a. sense c. a big change
b. trouble d. an advance

_____14. not able to *predict*
a. keep quiet c. make complete
b. refuse d. tell beforehand

_____15. if the animal is *vicious*
a. sick or hurt c. likely to attack
b. hungry d. hard to catch

Write the letter of the word or phrase that is closest in meaning to the word in italics.

Score Yourself! *The answers are on page 259.* Number correct: _____ Part A: _____ Part B: _____

UNIT 11 Test Yourself

Part A Matching Definitions

Match each word on the left with its definition on the right. Write the letter of the definition in the blank.

_____ 1. process
_____ 2. degree
_____ 3. erupt
_____ 4. resident
_____ 5. meaningful
_____ 6. reservoir
_____ 7. faithful

a. to burst forth; explode
b. remaining loyal; steady
c. a set of actions or changes that happen in order
d. having importance; full of meaning
e. a place where water is collected and kept
f. a unit for measuring temperature
g. a person living in a place

Part B Recognizing Meaning

Write the letter of the word or phrase that is closest in meaning to the word in italics.

_____ 8. to have *sufficient* clothing
a. fancy c. worn out
b. enough d. too small

_____ 9. to *conduct* electricity
a. need c. carry
b. pay for d. turn on

_____10. the *approximate* number
a. very large c. exactly right
b. very small d. close to right

_____11. a new *strategy*
a. plan c. direction
b. problem d. discovery

_____12. to *require* food
a. buy c. have to have
b. look for d. clearly enjoy

_____13. a major *crisis*
a. reason c. fight
b. emergency d. show of anger

_____14. a *reliable* girl
a. nice c. trustworthy
b. healthy d. very smart

_____15. just a small *fragment*
a. change c. accident
b. argument d. broken piece

Score Yourself! *The answers are on page 259.* Number correct: _____ Part A: _____ Part B: _____

UNIT 13 Test Yourself

Part A Recognizing Meaning

Write the letter of the word or phrase that is closest in meaning to the word in italics.

_____ 1. to *shatter* the bowl
a. fill c. bang on
b. crack d. totally break

_____ 2. a book's *sections*
a. parts c. facts
b. readers d. characters

_____ 3. his *supreme* mistake
a. greatest c. very stupid
b. dangerous d. not important

_____ 4. to let out a *screech*
a. laugh c. sob
b. high noise d. scared gasp

_____ 5. to *demand* an answer
a. want c. offer to give
b. dislike d. strongly ask for

_____ 6. a *local* store
a. small c. close-by
b. cheap d. well-known

_____ 7. make a wooden *vessel*
a. ship c. ramp
b. house d. set of steps

_____ 8. listen to her *yarn*
a. joke c. silly question
b. loud scream d. entertaining tale

Part B Applying Meaning

Write the letter of the best answer.

_____ 9. If you have a right to something, you
a. may do it. b. must do it. c. cannot do it. d. always do it.

_____10. Amateur bike riders are likely to
a. wobble. b. do tricks. c. go fast. d. lose their bikes.

_____11. The technique you use in drawing has to do with
a. why you draw. b. what you draw. c. how you draw. d. where you draw.

_____12. The officers of a bank are the people who
a. use it. b. run it. c. clean it. d. build it.

_____13. A person's individual likes and dislikes are those that are
a. well-known. b. like everyone's. c. silly or foolish. d. just his or hers.

_____14. One thing that always has parallel parts is
a. a set of train tracks. b. a set of dishes. c. a tree. d. an address.

_____15. A special occasion is a special
a. wish. b. event. c. reward. d. contest.

Score Yourself! *The answers are on page 259.* Number correct: _____ Part A: _____ Part B: _____

UNIT 14 Test Yourself

Part A Applying Meaning

Write the letter of the best answer.

_____ 1. A good souvenir of Washington, D.C., would be
a. the Capitol. b. the president. c. a new law. d. a postcard.

_____ 2. If you associate two things, you think of them
a. with fear. b. all the time. c. together. d. hardly ever.

_____ 3. Someone whose work uses secrecy is a
a. spy. b. pilot. c. wild animal trainer. d. carpenter.

_____ 4. Something a parent is likely to say to a restless child is,
a. "You're welcome." b. "Share." c. "Sit still." d. "It's time for bed."

_____ 5. A legend is a story that is
a. scary. b. based on the past. c. about animals. d. sad.

_____ 6. A memorial is something that is supposed to
a. help scientists. b. make money. c. honor someone. d. keep people safe.

_____ 7. Having foresight makes it easier to
a. plan. b. see a long distance. c. be polite. d. keep secrets.

_____ 8. To cloud the facts is to make them
a. known. b. wrong. c. interesting. d. hard to see.

Part B Synonyms

Write the letter of the word that is closest in meaning to the capitalized word.

_____ 9. MYSTERIOUS: (A) new (B) puzzling (C) untrue (D) pretend

_____10. MIGRATE: (A) appear (B) take (C) grow (D) move

_____11. HARDY: (A) lucky (B) happy (C) strong (D) friendly

_____12. SACRED: (A) holy (B) frightened (C) whole (D) cheerful

_____13. PRESERVE: (A) hide (B) enjoy (C) keep (D) plan

_____14. PROHIBIT: (A) break (B) forbid (C) warn (D) solve

_____15. REGION: (A) area (B) height (C) room (D) park

Score Yourself! *The answers are on page 259.* Number correct: _____ Part A: _____ Part B: _____

UNIT 15 Test Yourself

Part A Matching Definitions

Match each word on the left with its definition on the right. Write the letter of the definition in the blank.

_____ 1. will
_____ 2. patent
_____ 3. engineer
_____ 4. chemistry
_____ 5. represent
_____ 6. receipt
_____ 7. civilization
_____ 8. government
_____ 9. economic

a. a proof that something was paid for
b. the way of life of a people
c. the science that studies substances
d. to stand for or be a sign of something or someone
e. having to do with how money is used
f. a paper telling who gets one's belongings after death
g. the persons or system ruling a country or place
h. one who plans and builds things like machines and bridges
i. the right to be the only one to make or sell an invention

Part B Recognizing Meaning

Write the letter of the word or phrase that is closest in meaning to the word in italics.

_____10. a *sincere* apology
a. real c. fake
b. quick d. scared

_____11. a *complicated* plan
a. silly c. not simple
b. very smart d. dangerous

_____12. to *establish* a hospital
a. start c. need
b. work at d. design

_____13. each *candidate* in the election
a. voter c. commercial
b. decision d. person running

_____14. an interest in *literature*
a. good music c. written works
b. handwriting d. art and artists

_____15. the *league* of store owners
a. protection c. problems
b. hard work d. organized group

Score Yourself! *The answers are on page 259.* Number correct: _____ Part A: _____ Part B: _____

Score Yourself!

Unit 1

Part A

1. B
2. A
3. D
4. C
5. B

Part B

6. c
7. d
8. c
9. b
10. a
11. d
12. b
13. d
14. a
15. c

Unit 2

Part A

1. f
2. a
3. g
4. c
5. b
6. e
7. d

Part B

8. b
9. a
10. c
11. a
12. b
13. a
14. c
15. d

Unit 3

Part A

1. b
2. a
3. d
4. b
5. a
6. a
7. c
8. a

Part B

9. f
10. a
11. b
12. c
13. e
14. g
15. d

Unit 5

Part A

1. B
2. C
3. C
4. A
5. B
6. D
7. C
8. B

Part B

9. b
10. c
11. e
12. f
13. d
14. g
15. a

Unit 6

Part A

1. a
2. c
3. a
4. b
5. d
6. d
7. c
8. b

Part B

9. a
10. b
11. c
12. c
13. d
14. d
15. b

Unit 7

Part A

1. a
2. c
3. b
4. a
5. d
6. c
7. a
8. c
9. d
10. b

Part B

11. C
12. D
13. B
14. D
15. A

Unit 9

Part A

1. d
2. c
3. c
4. a
5. d
6. b
7. c
8. d

Part B

9. e
10. c
11. a
12. b
13. f
14. g
15. d

Unit 10

Part A

1. C
2. B
3. B
4. D
5. A
6. A
7. B

Part B

8. b
9. b
10. d
11. c
12. a
13. d
14. d
15. c

Unit 11

Part A

1. c
2. f
3. a
4. g
5. d
6. e
7. b

Part B

8. b
9. c
10. d
11. a
12. c
13. b
14. c
15. d

Unit 13

Part A

1. d
2. a
3. a
4. b
5. d
6. c
7. a
8. d

Part B

9. a
10. a
11. c
12. b
13. d
14. a
15. b

Unit 14

Part A

1. d
2. c
3. a
4. c
5. b
6. c
7. a
8. d

Part B

9. B
10. D
11. C
12. A
13. C
14. B
15. A

Unit 15

Part A

1. f
2. i
3. h
4. c
5. d
6. a
7. b
8. g
9. e

Part B

10. a
11. c
12. a
13. d
14. c
15. d

Cover Art

Sky and Water I, 1938, M.C. ESCHER. National Gallery of Art, Washington, D.C., Cornelius Van S. Roosevelt Collection.

Photographs/Illustrations

- Colin Hay. p. 17
- Bill Mayer. p. 27
- © R. Weldon/Gemological Institute of America. p. 39
- Annie Dodge Wauneka © 1981, LAURA GILPIN, Laura Gilpin Collection, Amon Carter Museum, Fort Worth, Texas. p. 62
- © 1988 J. Messerschmidt/FPG International Corp., New York. p. 72
- *Man and the Stars,* 1974 ANGUS McKIE. p. 113
- *A Tight Fix* (detail), 1861, CURRIER & IVES. The Granger Collection, New York. p. 124
- © 1987 Blaine Harrington III/The Stock Market. p. 133
- Courtesy San Francisco Maritime NHP, Union Lumber Co. Collection. p. 157
- Courtesy Arizona Department of Library, Archives and Public Records. p. 167
- Right: Roentgen 1898. The Bettmann Archive, New York. p. 177
- Left: The Bettmann Archive, New York. p. 177

Personal Vocabulary Log

Use the following pages to keep track of the unfamiliar words you encounter in your reading. Write brief definitions and pronunciations for each word. This will make the words part of your permanent vocabulary.

Personal Vocabulary Log

Personal Vocabulary Log

Personal Vocabulary Log

Personal Vocabulary Log

Personal Vocabulary Log